100 COLLEGES

WHERE

AVERAGE

STUDENTS

CAN EXCEL

Joe anne Adler

ARCO

THOMSON LEARNING

Australia • Canada • Denmark • Japan • Mexico
New Zealand • Philippines • Puerto Rico • Singapore
South Africa • Spain • United Kingdom • United States

[Macmillan]

Contents

Author's Notes

The word *average* has several different meanings. The definition I chose for this book is, "Average: something that represents a midpoint between extremes on a scale of valuation." The "average" student for whom I wrote this book can identify with one of the following criteria: a high school grade point average between 2.0 and 2.9 on a scale of 4; a class rank between the 40th and 60th percentile; an SAT 1 score between 950 and 1050 or comparable ACT composite score.

The colleges and universities profiled in this book recruit, accept, and educate students who fall within these "average" ranges. As you read through the book, you will see that most of these colleges have honors programs, opportunities for international study, internships, and independent study. They also provide an educational environment that emphasizes student success—not by watering down their academic programs but by energizing them with small classes, interactive learning, concerned and committed faculty members, and student participation. They offer a full college experience with residential facilities, campus activities, and support and enhancement programs that complement the learning process.

I wrote this book for all the high school students in the United States who have been characterized by that haunting refrain, "Oh, he (or she) is just an average student." I hope this book will lead you to a college or university where being "average" is just a starting point. Every school profiled in this book believes that an "average" high school performance does not exclude a student from future academic and professional success. Each of these schools is dedicated to providing their students with the opportunity to achieve success!

I'd like to thank several people for their help with this book. Martha Libby, a senior at Salve Regina University, was a terrific intern. Phyllis Walker, a teacher at The Summit School in Winston, North Carolina (and my summer neighbor), spent endless hours proofreading my copy. George Walker, a lawyer, law professor, author, scholar, and Phyllis' husband, kept my spirits high when I was behind schedule and spent much of his free time proofing my copy and entertaining my husband when I was writing. A special thanks goes to my husband Jay for the love, patience, and financial support he has always given me.

100 Colleges

Where

Average Students

Can Excel

Abilene Christian University

Abilene, Texas 79699-6000
(915) 674-2650 or (800) 888-0228

Abilene Christian University was founded in 1906. The school is affiliated with the Church of Christ and is one of the largest private universities in the southwest. The university has achieved a national reputation offering a strong liberal arts and pre-professional education within a Christian environment.

Each year, top companies from throughout the country come to campus to interview and hire students. Abilene Christian graduates have gone on to responsible and successful careers with Fortune 500 companies, international corporations, and national organizations.

Academics

Degrees Offered: Associate, Bachelor's, Master's, Doctoral

Undergraduate Majors: 100+

Student/Faculty Ratio: 17 to 1

Number of Faculty: 250 full and part time

Abilene Christian University emphasizes the individual attention students receive both in and out of class. All courses are taught by professors and not teaching assistants, and the school stresses the dynamic personal relationships established among faculty and students. Students have unique opportunities to work side by side with their professors conducting research, presenting papers at national conferences, and participating in many experiential learning opportunities.

With over 100 majors to choose from, students at Abilene Christian can surely pursue their individual and unique career goals. The university provides a quality education for students of diverse academic backgrounds. Through programs like accelerated degrees, double majors, and an honors program, academically talented students are challenged and enriched. Students who are less prepared for the rigors of academic life can also be successful. Small classes, professors and staff who are available for extra help, and the Learning Enhancement Center provide academic support. Students can work with peer tutors, receive computer assisted help, and participate in college skills workshops.

The campus facilities, which include microprocessor laboratories, business classrooms with Apple Power Macs, and science research labs with the latest in technology, are all dedicated to student use. In addition to two large farms, university students have access to 2,500 acres of land for observation, research, and agricultural and ecology projects. Experiential learning is important at Abilene Christian, and students are encouraged to pursue internships to strengthen their career preparation.

Students and Student Life

3,050 undergraduate students from 52 states and 6 foreign countries
700 full and part-time graduate students
30% are from outside of Texas
10% are students of color
5% are international
55% live on campus

The university sponsors more than 100 clubs and organizations, including an active student government, a student newspaper (*The Optimist*) that has received All-American recognition since 1975, and an AM/FM radio station and VHF TV station that broadcast daily. There are 12 local fraternities and sororities on campus, and approximately 20 percent of the students are members. Other activities include choral groups, concert and jazz bands, marching and pep bands, theater group, opera, symphony orchestra, Campus Service Organization, Mission Outreach, professional clubs, special interest groups, and intramural sports.

Athletics: NCAA Division II
Women's Teams: basketball, cross country, softball, tennis, track & field, volleyball
Men's Teams: basketball, cross country, football, golf, tennis, track & field

Campus and Community

The 200+ acre campus is located in the city of Abilene, Texas. With a population of over 100,000, it offers all the cultural, recreational, and social opportunities of most large cities. In addition, it has been named one of the top All-American cities in the United States. The Abilene Christian University campus is spacious and modern. The renovated science building contains four floors of classrooms, laboratories, and offices, in addition to computer facilities and an observatory. One of the largest buildings on campus is the huge Physical Education Complex, which houses several gymnasiums, an Olympic-size swimming pool, training rooms, racquetball courts, and a state-of-the-art fitness center.

Special facilities that are a part of the Abilene Christian campus are the National Family Life Center and a 400-acre farm, where students majoring in the agricultural fields can conduct research and practice new farming techniques. The university also has access to more than 2,500 acres of land, where agriculture, biology, ecology, and environmental majors can study and observe scientific principles in a natural setting.

Campus housing is spacious and comfortable, and includes both traditional dormitories and apartment-style living arrangements.

Abilene Christian University Academic Offerings

Bachelor's Degrees: Accounting • Advertising • Agribusiness Operations • Agricultural Business • Agricultural & Food Products Processing • Agricultural Science • Agronomy & Crop Science • American Studies • Animal Science • Art • Audiology/Hearing Sciences • Biblical Languages/Literature • Biochemistry • Biology • Business Adm. & Mgt. • Clinical Psychology • Communications • Clothing, Apparel & Textile Studies • Commercial Art & Illustration • Computer Science • Computer Systems Analysis • Computer Science & Computational Mathematics • Counseling Psychology • Criminal Justice • Drama/Theater Arts • Economics • Engineering Physics • English • European Studies • Family & Community Studies • Farm & Ranch Mgt. • Family/Consumer Resource Mgt. • Fashion Design & Illustration • Finance & Banking • Financial Mgt. • Fine Arts • Food & Nutrition • Foreign Languages & Literature • Geology • German Gerontology • Graphic Design • Greek • Home Economics • History • Human Resource Mgt. • Industrial Production Technologies • Information Science & Systems • Interior Design • International Business • Journalism & Mass Communications • Latin-American Studies • Management • Management Information Systems • Manufacturing Technologies • Marketing • Marketing Mgt. & Research • Mathematics • Metal & Jewelry Art • Missionary Studies • Museum Studies • Music • Music—General Performance • Music—Piano & Organ Performance • Voice & Choral/Opera Performance • Nursing • Nutritional Science • Philosophy & Religion • Photography • Physical Science • Physics • Political Science & Government • Portuguese • Psychology • Public Adm. • Public Relations • Radio & TV Broadcasting • Range Science & Mgt. • Sign Language Interpreter • Social Work • Sociology • Spanish • Speech-Language Pathology • Studio Arts • Visual & Performing Arts • Western European Studies • Wildlife & Wetlands Mgt.

Associate Degree: Child Care Nursing (RN)

Teacher Education: Agriculture • Art • Biology • Business • Chemistry • Computer • Drama • Dance • Early Childhood • Emotionally Handicapped • Elementary • English • French • German • Health • Home Economics • Industrial Arts • Journalism • Junior High Ed. • Music • Physical Ed. • Physics • Reading Ed. • Religious Ed. • Social Science • Social Studies • Speech-Communication/Theater • Trade & Industrial Ed.

Admissions Statement

To be considered for admission, students should be in the upper 75 percent of their high school graduating class, have a minimum GPA of 2.0, complete 4 units in English, 2 in social science, 2 in science, 2 in a foreign language, and have a minimum ACT score of 19 or SAT 1 of 850.

Adams State College

Alamosa, Colorado 81102
(719) 589-7712 or (800) 824-6494

A quality education with a personal touch describes the Adams State College experience. The 90-acre campus, located in Alamosa, Colorado, provides an ideal environment for intellectual, physical, and emotional growth. The core curriculum establishes a well-rounded academic base, while the 56 liberal arts and professionally oriented majors provide the specialized tools necessary for a successful career.

The 2,500 men and women who attend the college have access to the invigorating and challenging opportunities of the outdoors, like hiking and climbing the Old Navajo Trail or rafting on the Rio Grande River. The 40 different college-sponsored clubs and activities provide opportunities for leadership, volunteerism, and collaborative learning. Adams State College is surrounded by natural environments that beckon to be studied and investigated. The college takes advantage of these opportunities to provide an education that goes far beyond the limits of the campus.

Academics

Degrees Offered: Associate, Bachelor's, Master's

Undergraduate Majors: 50+

Student/Faculty Ratio: 20 to 1

Number of Faculty: 140

The academic atmosphere at Adams State is supportive, challenging, and competitive. It is a place where students can learn by doing, where the professors teach in an interactive fashion, and where technology is not a new-fangled device, but a usable, important instrument. Although the college is small, the academic opportunities within the four undergraduate divisions reflect more of a university setting.

The School of Arts and Letters focuses on providing a strong academic background, which, as the foundation for the individual development, prepares students for many different career opportunities.

The School of Business places a heavy emphasis on practical experience and integrates internships into all of its degree programs. Opportunities for students to make professional connections in the business community are facilitated through the school's sponsorship of two national professional business fraternities, the Toastmaster's Chapter and the Small Business Assistance Center.

The School of Education and Behavioral Sciences is one of only 500 in the country accredited by the National Council for the Accreditation of Teacher Education (N.C.A.T.E.). Teacher certification is offered in elementary, middle, and secondary education. The school also offers majors in exercise physiology and leisure science, sociology, and psychology.

The School of Science, Mathematics, and Technology offers more than 14 programs. It also offers a pre-engineering program that allows students to spend two years at ASC then transfer to Colorado University, Colorado State University, or Colorado School of Mines to finish their engineering degree. Graduates of the ASC School of Science, Mathematics, and Technology have pursued graduate degrees at schools like the University of California—Berkeley, the University of Northern Arizona, the University of Texas, and the University of Wisconsin.

Students and Student Life

2,500 students from 35 states and 5 foreign countries
20% are from out-of-state
33% are students of color
1% are international
980 live on campus

The student population at Adams State College is both ethnically and geographically diverse. This multi-cultural influence adds energy and character to campus life. One student commented, "The campus is an active place. There's always something going on either in the residence halls or at the college center. The students here are active participants in college life. There are parties, dances, cultural events, and lots of outdoor activities."

With over 40 clubs and activities to choose from, including Rodeo Club, FASF radio station, theater productions, award-winning literary publications, and the Outdoor Program, the students at ASC find that getting involved in activities is easy and fun.

Athletics: NCAA Division II Rocky Mountain Athletic Conference
Men's and Women's Teams: basketball, cross country, track & field

Women's Teams: softball, volleyball
Men's Teams: football, golf, wrestling

Campus and Community

The Adams State campus is a pleasant, inviting place. Located in the San Luis Valley surrounded by the Sangre de Cristo and San Juan mountain ranges, the scenic beauty is everywhere. The campus is comprised of 90 acres and is walking distance from the town of Alamosa, Colorado. There is a close relationship between the town (population 9,000) and the college. Students can easily walk to shopping, movie theaters, and local restaurants, in addition to finding internships and work experiences in town.

On campus, students have an environment that is both aesthetically appealing and functional. The residential facilities include housing for both undergraduate and graduate students. The seven residence halls offer a variety of accommodations, including hall dorms, suite arrangements, and campus apartments. Students can choose single, double, or quad accommodations.

The popular college center is the hub of campus. It houses numerous student government offices, bookstore, cafeteria, and an assortment of other recreational and administrative facilities. Plachy Hall is the center of recreational activities and includes an indoor swimming pool, basketball courts, weight room, and tennis and handball courts.

The surrounding areas are packed with exciting things to see and do. There is skiing in the mountains, only about 45 minutes away. The Great Sand Dunes National Monument is about a half-hour drive. River rafting, swimming, and fishing are close by, along with hiking, camping, and picnicking. The college is in an area of year-round recreational opportunities and students at Adams State College seek out and enjoy all the possibilities!

Adams State College Academic Offerings

School of Arts and Sciences: Art • English • Hispanic/Southwest Studies • History/Government • Music • Spanish • Speech / Theater • Selected Studies

School of Business: Accounting • Advertising • Business Computer Systems • Business Ed. • Economics • Finance • General Business • Management • Marketing • Office Mgt. • Small Business

School of Education and Behavioral Sciences: Elementary and Secondary Teacher Certification • Exercise Physiology and Leisure Science • Psychology • Sociology

School of Science, Mathematics, and Technology: Biology • Chemistry • Geology • Mathematics • Medical Technology • Physics

Admissions Statement

To be considered for unconditional admission to Adams State College a student should have a 2.5 or higher grade point average, rank in the upper two-thirds of his/her graduating class, and have average or above average ACT or SAT scores. Some students who do not meet these requirements may be considered on an individual basis for conditional admission to the college.

American International College

Springfield, Massachusetts 01109-3189
(413) 747-6201 or (800) 242-3143

American International College is an urban institution with a practical, career-oriented focus. Located in the city of Springfield, the college presents a realistic environment for students to learn and develop. The student body is socially, economically, and culturally diverse. Students are drawn to the college by its strong reputation and professional record. For over 100 years AIC has provided academic opportunities that involve students in their own learning process and assist them in becoming mature adults.

The college has the academic offerings, quality faculty, and experiential learning opportunities necessary for an outstanding education; more importantly, it provides the guidance, personal involvement, support, and encouragement necessary to release the potential that students have within themselves.

Academics

Degrees Offered: Associate, Bachelor's, Master's

Undergraduate Majors: 35+

Student/Faculty Ratio: 16 to 1

Number of Faculty: 120 full and part time

The academic programs at American International College are dedicated to helping students reach their full potential as students and as people. In order to do this, the college has intentionally designed the classroom environment to be small, interactive, and discussion-oriented. Professors work with their students instead of lecturing to them. They are involved in the advising process and often develop a mentoring relationship with their students.

At the heart of every degree program at AIC is a small but important core of required courses that provide the general skills and knowledge people in the 21st century must possess to be considered well educated. This core curriculum includes three courses in English, two courses in laboratory science, two courses in humanities, and four courses in social sciences, all as part of a basic liberal arts education. From there students choose a major from one of the four schools within the college.

The School of Arts and Sciences offers 17 majors and many pre-professional programs.

The 12 majors found in the School of Business combine business knowledge and management skills gained in the classroom with practical experience gained through professional internships. Because of the strong reputation the college has among business and community leaders in the state, AIC students can choose from a variety of internship sites with nationally known companies right in the Springfield metropolitan area.

The School of Psychology and Education focuses on the exploration and understanding of the complexities of human behavior and human development. Most of the majors within this school require an extensive field-based component and AIC has set up sites at local schools, agencies, hospitals, and mental health facilities.

The Nursing division at AIC has an outstanding success rate for students passing the national exam for licensure as registered nurses—100 percent find jobs when they finish school. This solid foundation in nursing skills, a comprehensive liberal arts education, and an intensive clinical component are all part of AIC's formula for success.

Students and Student Life

1,350 students from 27 states and 24 foreign countries
41% are from out-of-state
20% are students of color
7% are international
70% live on campus

AIC attracts a diverse group of students, and that makes the College an interesting and active environment in which to live. When the college originally started in 1885 it was founded to educate the growing number of immigrants to the United States. Since then the college has changed and developed into a comprehensive institution, but it has maintained an international perspective.

With over 700 residential students you can be sure there are a variety of college activities going on weekdays, nights and weekends! In fact, the student government sponsors more than 35 different college organizations. AIC has its own radio station, WAIC, that broadcasts daily. The Garret Players, the campus drama association, performs throughout the school year and provides acting, directing, and stage production opportunities for students.

There are about 10 professional clubs related to career fields, and many special interest clubs. P.R.I.D.E., an African American cultural, educational, and social organization, is active on campus, in addition to eight fraternities and ten sororities. Campus life at AIC also includes special lectures, art exhibits, musical programs, plays, movies, comedy nights, and, of course, sports.

Athletics: NCAA Division II College Athletic Conference and the Northeast 10 Conference
Women's Teams: basketball, soccer, softball, tennis, volleyball
Men's Teams: baseball, basketball, football, golf, hockey, lacrosse, soccer, tennis, wrestling

Campus and Community

The 58-acre campus is located in the heart of Massachusetts' second largest city, Springfield. The Academic Campus consists of 16 acres of land and houses 14 major academic facilities, a residence hall for women, and two coed dormitories. Several of the outstanding academic facilities include the Sprague Cultural Arts Center and Griswold Theater for the Performing Arts. The building is devoted to visual and literary arts and accommodates classrooms, conference and seminar facilities, a 500-seat theater with a proscenium stage, flying space, and professional acoustics. The Berkshire Ballet Company is in residence at the College.

The Curtis Blake Child Development Center serves as a diagnostic center for children with learning disabilities and is an integral part of the School of Psychology and Education. The center provides unique opportunities for practicum work and internships for psychology and education majors. Breck Hall is one of two science buildings and provides modern classrooms and laboratories for science, mathematics, and nursing. The Edgewood Gardens Campus includes 37 acres of land and houses three residence halls, a 2,400-seat gymnasium, football stadium, and athletic and recreational fields. A shuttle service runs between the Academic Campus and the Gardens Campus throughout the day and evening.

Springfield is a large metropolitan city and offers a host of cultural, educational, and social opportunities. The Basketball Hall of Fame, symphony orchestra, repertory theater, and Civic Center are just a few. The campus is less than two miles from the downtown area, which gives students easy access to city life.

American International College Academic Offerings

School of Arts and Sciences: Biochemistry • Biology • Chemistry • Communications • Economics • English • History • Liberal Studies • Mathematics

• Medical Technology • Occupational Therapy • Philosophy • Physical Therapy • Political Science • Public Adm. • Sociology • Spanish

School of Business Administration: Accounting • Business Ed. • Business Studies • Economics • Finance • General Business • Hospitality Mgt. • International Business • Management • Management Information Systems • Marketing • Personnel Adm. • Public Adm.

School of Psychology and Education: Criminal Justice • Early Childhood Ed. • Elementary Ed. • Psychology • Secondary Ed. • Special Ed.

Division of Nursing: Bachelor of Science in Nursing

Admissions Statement

The Admissions Committee selects students on the basis of their secondary school achievement record, qualities of initiative and motivation as indicated by character references and academic recommendations, SAT 1 or ACT results, and co-curricular involvement in both school and community.

Ashland University

Ashland, Ohio 44805-3702
(419) 289-5054 or (800) 882-1548

For more than 115 years, students have come to Ashland University to pursue a quality education. Founded in 1878 as Ashland College, the focus, then as now, is on providing a balanced educational experience centered on the individual student. The degree programs offered at the university combine liberal arts and sciences with professional course offerings. Students have 80 majors to choose from and can pursue an associate, bachelor's, master's, or doctoral degree. With an average class size of 20 and a student / faculty ratio of 16 to 1, students are treated as individuals, not numbers, and the university assists each student to reach his or her educational goal.

Academics

Degrees Offered: Associate, Bachelor's, Master's
Undergraduate Majors: 80

Student/Faculty Ratio: 16 to 1

Number of Faculty: 195 full time

Ashland University is composed of five undergraduate schools: the School of Arts and Humanities, the School of Nursing, the School of Business Administration and Economics, the School of Education and Related Professions, and the School of Sciences. The degree programs at the University are designed to prepare students for future careers and enable them to succeed in today's complex society.

The core curriculum creates the educational foundation for future learning. It is comprehensive and includes up to 54 credits in courses like English, speech, religion, humanities, science, social science, and interdisciplinary courses.

The academic services offered at the university are designed to heighten student achievement. Independent study is available for students who want to broaden their knowledge in a chosen field and conduct an individual research project. A four-year Honors Program provides an alternative academic experience for gifted students. The Writing Center and the Writing Improvement Lab sponsor programs that help students improve their writing skills regardless of their achievement level, and the Study Strategies Program assists students in mastering difficult subject material and developing proficient study skills.

Students and Student Life

2,500 students from 32 states and 25 foreign countries
10% are from out-of-state
9% are students of color
2% are international
1,800 live on campus

The warmth and friendliness of Ashland University is evident the moment you arrive on campus. Students say hi to each other as they walk across campus and it is not unusual to see faculty members walking and conversing with students. The university's strong academic reputation and caring environment attract men and women from all over the country and the world.

Campus life at Ashland includes some special features not usually found at other universities. Because the majority of students live on campus, the class schedule, cafeteria, student services, and student activities coincide with their schedule. The Food Court (the university dining commons) is open daily from 7:00 a.m. to 7:00 p.m., and for brunch and dinner on Saturday and Sunday. There is a 50-foot-long soup and salad bar, fresh baked pizza, gourmet hot entrees, and à la cart selections. No long lines, no set serving times, and definitely no institutional food.

All of the campus activities at Ashland contribute in some way to a student's personal, social, intellectual, cultural, and spiritual development. The 16 professional clubs (like the American Marketing Association, Psychology Club, and Council for Exceptional Children) integrate classroom theory into real-world application. The eight national sororities and one fraternity that have campus chapters link the Ashland students with their Greek sisters and brothers throughout the country. The 12 para-professional and campus service organizations develop leadership and cooperative skills in students. The 11 performance groups let students share their musical, theatrical, or vocal talent with fellow students. The three religious organizations provide spiritual development within the individual and foster acceptance of diversity. And that's only a sampling of the 96 clubs and organizations sponsored by the University.

Ashland students are also interested in making a difference in today's world. More than 600 students participate in volunteer and community service activities every semester, through ongoing service programs with local agencies; special projects with senior citizens, homeless individuals and families in need; and concentrated assistance trips over semester breaks.

Athletics: NCAA Division II Midwest Intercollegiate Football Conference
Women's Teams: basketball, cross country, track, soccer, softball, swimming, tennis, track, volleyball
Men's Teams: baseball, basketball, cross country, football, golf, track, soccer, swimming, tennis, wrestling

Campus and Community

Ashland University has a beautiful 98-acre campus. The 35 academic and residential buildings reflect the 115 year history of the institution. The entrance to the university from College Avenue leads to Founders Hall, one of the oldest buildings on campus. Situated next to it is the nine-story contemporary library and media center. The campus is spacious and has a traditional design with a large grass quad in the center of main campus.

The academic facilities include the Home Management House, a practicum environment for students in the home economics department; the Gill Center for Business and Economics, a research and information hub for economic and business information; and the huge Physical Education and Community Center, which contains three basketball courts, a 25-yard swimming pool, a sauna, training rooms, and a gymnasium that can seat 3,000 spectators. The campus also includes seven residential halls and fraternity houses.

The town of Ashland is located in north-central Ohio, midway between Cleveland and Columbus. Ashland is a fairly big town, with shopping areas, restaurants, movies, and entertainment. For big-city excitement, students can be in Cleveland in just about an hour.

Ashland University Academic Offerings

School of Arts and Humanities: American Studies • Art • Art Ed. • Broadcast Sales & Station Mgt. • Christian School Ed. • Commercial Art • Communications Arts • Communication Ed. • Comprehensive Theater • Creative Writing • English • English Ed. • Fine Art • Foreign Language Ed. • French • General Theater • Journalism • Music (applied or academic studies) • Music Ed. • Philosophy • Professional Video • Programming, Production & Performance • Public Communication • Radio/TV • Religion • Spanish • Speech • Speech Ed. • Sports Communication • Theater • Theater Ed.

School of Business Administration and Economics: Accounting • Business Mgt. • Business Mgt. with health specialization • Computer Information Systems • Economics • Finance • Hospitality Adm. • Marketing • Office Adm. • School Business Manager • School Treasurer

School of Education and Related Professions: Adapted Physical Ed. • Athletic Training • Child and Family Studies • Dietetics • Education of the Handicapped • Elementary Ed. • Family and Consumer Sciences • Fashion Merchandising • Foods/Nutrition in Business • Health Ed. • Home Economics Ed. • K-12 Specialist • K-Primary Ed. • Middle Grades Ed. • Physical Ed. • Pre-Kindergarten • Recreation • Recreation Therapy • Sports Science • Special Ed. • Teacher Ed.

School of Sciences: Biology • Biology Ed. • Biology/Environmental Science • Chemistry • Chemistry Ed. • Chemistry/Environmental Science • Chemistry/Geology • Comprehensive Science Ed. • Comprehensive Social Studies Ed. • Criminal Justice • Computer Science • Criminal Justice & Sociology • Earth Science Ed. • Geology • Geology/Environmental Science • History • History Ed. • History/Political Science • International Studies • Mathematics • Mathematics Ed. • Math/Physics/Computer Science • Physics • Physics Ed. • Political Science • Political Science Ed. • Psychology • Social Work • Sociology • Toxicology

Admissions Statement

To be considered for admission, the applicant must be a graduate of an accredited high school and have a record indicating a likelihood of success at Ashland University. The quality of the academic record is shown by an applicant's grades, class standing, schedule of courses taken, and results of the SAT 1 or ACT. The university is very interested in the applicant's personal traits and record as a school citizen and will accept recommendations of the school counselor or principal as to ability, motivation, and character.

Assumption College

Worcester, Massachusetts 01615-0005
(508) 767-7285

Assumption College is a midsize Catholic college located in Worcester, Massachusetts. It was founded in 1904 by the Augustinians of the Assumption, a religious order for men. Over the past 90 years, the college has developed into a well-recognized institution offering bachelor's and master's degrees in over 30 areas of study. Because Assumption College is a member of the Worcester Consortium of Study, Assumption students can participate in the cultural, social, and educational endeavors provided by the 20 colleges and organizations that are consortium members, as well as in Assumption's own academic offerings. As you can see, an Assumption College education stretches beyond the campus and offers students the opportunity to discover and become part of the Worcester community.

Academics

Degrees Offered: Bachelor's, Master's

Undergraduate Majors: 20+

Student/Faculty Ratio: 17 to 1

Number of Faculty: 214 full and part time

The curriculum at Assumption College incorporates three elements: a general education curriculum, a major program, and an elective program. The general education curriculum is designed to introduce students to aspects of their intellectual, cultural, and spiritual heritage, and yet allow them flexibility to choose the courses they take within each subject area.

Major programs at Assumption College are offered in 25 academic areas. They range from traditional majors like biology and psychology to more specialized offerings like international business and social and rehabilitation services. Students at Assumption College have a number of opportunities to expand their original degree program through study abroad, internships, and consortium certificate programs.

The college encourages qualified students to pursue a semester or year abroad as an integral part of their undergraduate education. In the past five years, students from Assumption College have studied in Rome, Florence, Dublin, Cork, Galway, Paris, Avigon, Madrid, Valencia, London, Oxford, Athens, Sydney, Salzberg, and Prague.

Another opportunity students can pursue is the internship. They can develop and design their own work experience or choose one already in existence. At Assumption, the internship includes a reflective journal, readings in the field, and a research paper. In recent years students have held internships with state representatives, in museums and archival work, in radio and television, with newspapers, in public relations, in labor management, and in the health fields.

The last component of the Assumption curriculum is the elective program. Students have between 14 and 20 course electives that make up any one degree program. They can use electives to strengthen their major or minor area of study or investigate new subjects that interest them. Assumption offers two study opportunities in which elective credits can be used.

The Developing Countries Studies Program includes courses that focus on the anthropology, economics, geography, history, and politics of Africa, Asia, and Latin America, and upper division interdisciplinary seminars that address current problems facing these countries. The aim of the program is to give students a background and exposure to developing countries.

The Native American Studies Program focuses on the American Indians and their non-western culture, which has been an integral part of American history. The program includes two interdisciplinary courses, guest lectures, and seminars.

Students and Student Life

1,800 students from 25 states and 15 foreign countries
40% are from out-of-state
9% are students of color
2% are international
80% live on campus

Part of the educational mission of Assumption College is to educate not only a student's mind but the whole person, so the college places emphasis on extracurricular activities and views them as instrumental in developing character, leadership, and spirituality within students. The college has a strong student government and a large and ever-growing number of student organizations.

One of the most popular and active organizations at the college is Campus Ministry. Membership is not limited to Catholic students, but is open to the whole college community. Campus Ministry at Assumption introduces students to the opportunities of service to others and has developed numerous local and international programs where students render assistance. In the past, Assumption students have participated in service programs during semester break in New York City, Mexico, Philadelphia, and Appalachia.

In all, Assumption College sponsors 40 student-centered clubs and activities. Publications include the *Provocateur* newspaper, the *Heights* yearbook, and the *Phoenix* creative arts magazine. There are professional societies, special interest groups, and activity clubs in addition to weekly co-curricular cultural activities that include lectures by visiting professors, art exhibits, recitals, and plays. Of course, the college has an extensive recreational and athletic program.

Athletics: NCAA Division II, members of the New England Conference, and the Northeast-10 Conference
Women's Teams: basketball, crew, cross country, field hockey, soccer, softball, tennis, volleyball
Men's Teams: baseball, basketball, crew, cross country, football, golf, hockey, lacrosse, soccer, tennis

Campus and Community

The 150-acre campus located in Worcester, Massachusetts, houses 20 academic buildings and three residential complexes. The campus is spacious and designed so that all the major academic buildings are in one area. The facilities are contemporary and built with students in mind. Science and nursing laboratories are modern and housed in the Kennedy Science Building. The DiPasquale Building contains the Media Center and a professionally outfitted color-TV studio with special effects and a graphic generator.

Behind the academic area and adjacent to the residential area is the new Plourde Center and most of the athletic fields. The Center, which was built in 1992, houses most of the recreational activities on campus. It includes racquetball courts, an aerobic room, a field house, a six-lane swimming pool, a suspended three-lane track, a fitness area, and a weight-training room.

The residential complexes are versatile and offer students many different living arrangements. The Hill Residences include traditional dormitory accommodations, apartments, and townhouse-style residences. The Salisbury and Wachusset Residence Halls offer suite and apartment accommodations, and the Dion, Moquin, Authier and Westwood provide six-person apartments and townhouse arrangements. In all, more than 1,400 students live on campus.

Assumption College Academic Offerings

Accounting • Biology • Biology with biotechnology concentration • Chemistry • Classics • Computer Science • Economics • Economics with business concentration • English • Foreign Affairs • Foreign Languages • French • History • International Business • Management • Marketing • Mathematics • Philosophy • Politics • Psychology • Social and Rehabilitation Services • Sociology • Spanish • Teacher Ed • Theology.

Admissions Statement

All applicants for admission must be graduates of an accredited high school and have completed four years of English, two years of mathematics and foreign language, one year of history and science, and five additional academic units, and have acceptable scores on the SAT 1. The Admissions Committee is more interested in the quality of work, general promise, and seriousness of purpose of the student than in specific number of secondary school units.

Belmont Abbey College

Belmont, North Carolina 28012-9987
(704) 825-6665 or (800) 523-2355

As a Catholic educational institution, Belmont Abbey College provides an environment rich in opportunities for moral, spiritual, and academic growth. A unique core curriculum centered around the theme of community and guided by the "Great Books," strong liberal arts and preprofessional majors, and a dedicated community of teachers are all part of a Belmont Abbey education. Add to this opportunities to study abroad, develop internships, and take courses at 12 local colleges and you have a small college that offers some big possibilities! For well over 100 years, Belmont Abbey College has been the educational choice for students throughout the Southeast.

Academics

Degrees Offered: Bachelor's, Master's

Undergraduate Majors: 19

Student/Faculty Ratio: 15 to 1

Number of Faculty: 88 full and part time

The liberal arts curriculum at the college is influenced by the school's Benedictine heritage. Through academic subjects, students are exposed to many of the world's major problems so that they can develop a responsible social consciousness. The core curriculum at Belmont Abbey College reflects more than 100 years of commitment to liberal education and uses the "Great Books" as a context for investigation. Courses within the core emphasize Christian values while developing knowledge of other civilizations, modern technology, influential literature, natural and physical science, art and music of western and nonwestern cultures, and global economics and government. The core is built into the four-year curriculum and complements all majors offered at the college.

Lectures are minimal, active, and interdisciplinary; small group studies dominate the learning process. Freshmen begin with a year-long experience that includes seven prescribed courses and activities that bring faculty and students together for seminars, research , debate, lab projects, discussions, and writing assignments. Once students choose an academic area of concentration, they undertake a full exploration of the subject and are encouraged to participate in an internship experience, take courses at one of the 12 neighboring insitiutions that are members of the Charlotte Area Education Consortium, or even study abroad for a semester. In their senior year, students culminate their study with a comprehensive examination, thesis, project, or other major department requirement that demonstrates their knowledge within the field.

As you can see, education at Belmont Abbey is a broad process that includes active participation by students and faculty alike.

Students and Student Life

1,000 students from 29 states and 17 foreign countries
10% are students of color
4% are international
600 live on campus

Belmont Abbey is a community of individuals living and learning together. Extracurricular activities are viewed as an important aspect of college life, and add to the richness of an Abbey education. More than 30 clubs and organizations make campus life active. There is a large intramural sports program and 80 percent of the students take part. Fraternities and sororities are present on campus along with service organizations, religious clubs, and honor societies. The college has a weekly student newspaper, *Abbey Voice*; its own radio station, WABY; and a literary magazine. The Abbey Players provide opportunities for aspiring thespians, and numerous academic clubs bring students together for lectures, fund-raising activities, and practical work experience.

Athletics: NCAA Division II
Women's Teams: basketball, cross country, soccer, softball, tennis, volleyball
Men's Teams: baseball, basketball, cross country, golf, soccer, tennis

Campus and Community

The 650-acre campus is located in Belmont, North Carolina. The campus is a blend of historic buildings and new structures. The newest building is the Student Commons, whose unique structure has won awards from the American Institute of Architects and the Institute of Business Design. The Abbey Church, built in neo-Gothic style in the late 1800s, appears in the National Register of Historic Places. Other buildings on campus include four residence halls that provide suite-style living arrangements for approximately 600 students; the Gaston Science Building, which houses most of the laboratory facilities; and the Taylor Library. Recreational facilities include an outstanding gymnasium, Olympic-sized pool, soccer, softball and baseball fields, and tennis courts.

The city of Charlotte is about 15 minutes from the college. There, students can attend the NBA Hornets games and the NFL Panthers games. The Blumenthal Performing Arts Center, Mint Museum, and Discovery Place sponsor cultural events. Charlotte has many wonderful restaurants, a great shopping area, and an international airport. Students at Belmont Abbey College can also easily visit more than 12 area colleges and universities.

Belmont Abbey College Academic Offerings

Accounting • Biology • Economics • Elementary Ed. • English • Health Care Mgt. • History • Information Systems • Management and Entrepreneurial Studies • Medical Technology • Middle Grades Ed. • Philosophy/Theology • Political Science • Psychology • Secondary Ed. • Sociology • Special Ed. • Sports Mgt. • Therapeutic Recreation

Admissions Statement

A candidate for admission to Belmont Abbey College must be a graduate of an approved high school with a minimum of 16 academic units in the following distribution: four units of English, two units of social studies, two units of science, two units of foreign language, three units of mathematics, and three units of electives. Members of the Admissions Committee give careful consideration to a number of factors: academic records, class standing, scores on standardized tests, teacher/counselor recommendations, extracurricular activities, and, in some cases, a written statement of the applicant's objectives.

Bemidji State University

Bemidji, Minnesota 56601-2699
(218) 755-2040 or (800) 652-9747

The campus of Bemidji State University is framed by lakes, glacial rivers, and natural forests, but that's not the only dynamic characteristic of this university. As a member of the Minnesota State College and University System, Bemidji has been educating men and women who have contributed scientifically, socially, and culturally to society for more than 75 years. The university has an educational environment where more than 5,000 students live and learn among the beauty and friendliness of this campus. Students can choose both liberal arts and career-oriented programs at this strong liberal arts university, which offers more than 50 majors.

Located in northern Minnesota's fabled forest and lake country, the university is an ideal place to study and enjoy all the opportunities of the great outdoors.

Academics

Degrees Offered: Associate, Bachelor's, Master's

Undergraduate Majors: 35+

Student/Faculty Ratio: 20 to 1

Number of Faculty: 200 full time

Business, criminal justice, English, geography, Indian studies, medical technology, physics, social work, and technical illustration are just a small sampling of the programs offered at Bemidji State University. The scope and depth of the curriculum are impressive and provide many alternatives for students to choose from. By combining a major and minor area of study students can prepare for almost any career. With minors like anthropology, art history, chemical dependency, Ojibwe (a Native American language and culture), and space studies, the university provides opportunities for students to learn more than what is usually studied in college.

Bemidji State's traditional curriculum, which prepares students for graduate study and careers in business, health science, and teaching, is also strong, diverse, and relevant. Students interested in biology can prepare for careers in aquatic biology, cellular molecular biology, naturalist biology, or teaching biology. Students who want to work in environmental fields can focus their study on ecosystems, environmental chemistry, policy and planning, toxicology, or geohydrology. In the area of foreign languages, Bemidji offers courses in French, German, Spanish, Japanese, Ojibwe, and Russian.

The university supports its broad course offerings with many enhancing educational opportunities. The C.V. Hobson Forest, located 11 miles from campus, serves as an outdoor laboratory where students can observe and research important issues in environmental studies. Lake Bemidji serves as the university's freshwater laboratory for studies in aquatic biology. Students can do research aboard the university's specially equipped laboratory barges. The university has established a Common Market Program that enables Bemidji students to attend another Minnesota state university for one quarter, or three different institutions for a total of three quarters.

Pluralism and cultural diversity are an important part of an education. Bemidji State University has developed seven study abroad programs that can be integrated into almost any major. For example, the Sinosummer Program is held each summer at Liaoning University in northeast China; the Eurospring Program takes place each spring at Oxford University in England; and Akita is an actual branch campus of the Minnesota State University system located in Japan. Students can spend up to one year at this campus. The Petaling Jaya Community College Program matches Bemidji students with host Malaysian families near Kuala Lumpur, Malaysia, where they are exposed to Chinese, Malay, and Indian cultures while attending classes at Petaling Jaya. Semester programs are also available at Vaxjo University in Sweden and Kieve State University in Ukraine.

Students and Student Life

5,000 students from 45 states and 30 foreign countries
12% are from out-of-state
10% are students of color
6% are international
2,000 live on campus

Campus life at Bemidji has many opportunities for self-fulfillment. The student government sponsors about 50 campus organizations in addition to weekly events like movies, coffee houses, concerts, athletic events, and lectures.

Performance-based activities include theater productions in the Black Box Theater or main stage area of the Bangsberg Fine Arts Center. The center offers a variety of stage productions almost every month, for which students can audition for speaking parts or develop their lighting, set design, and production skills. A weekly student newspaper, literary magazine, yearbook, and radio and television stations provide multiple opportunities for career related activities or recreational interests. There are several religious clubs on campus where students' spiritual development can grow and where they can come together with other students in social and volunteer activities.

The university is committed to cultural diversity and provides activities and clubs where diversity is celebrated and enjoyed. The university also provides a residential area designated for cross-cultural living experiences. Here students have a special opportunity to promote multicultural understanding and participate in cultural experiences every day.

The university campus has six residence halls and an on-campus apartment complex that can accommodate about 2,000 students. Each hall has its own environment: some are small, with about 150 students, while others are large high-rises that house 500 students. There are smoke-free floors, upper-class floors, quiet floors, and handicapped accessible floors.

Athletics: NCAA Division II
Women's Teams: basketball, softball, tennis, track & field, volleyball
Men's Teams: baseball, basketball, football, golf, ice hockey, track & field

Campus and Community

The 83-acre campus houses 25 academic and residential buildings in an environment that reflects the natural beauty of the area. The lakefront campus is an ideal setting for students to study and learn. The waterfront area that covers almost the entire eastern side of campus is used for classes and laboratory activities in aquatic biology and for recreational activities like boating, sailing, and aquatic sports.

The contemporary classroom buildings, interspersed among the campus greens and trees, provide the latest in technology yet blend harmoniously with the rugged setting. While the campus is spacious, students have access to all major buildings via all-season skywalks and underground passages, so inclement weather doesn't usually interfere with daily activities.

The facilities on campus are used by students and members of the Bemidji community. The North Central Minnesota Historical Center, located in the university library, is the central location for historical documents and papers pertaining to the development of the seven counties that make up the north-central area of the state. The Bangsberg Fine Arts Center hosts many community concerts, in addition to plays, recitals, and programs staged by the students. The Clark Library has an information resource base where students and area residents can access library holdings throughout the state.

The university's Physical Education Complex and Recreation/Fitness Center is one of the largest buildings on campus and provides space for a host of indoor athletic activities. It has a large swimming pool and indoor track, and courts for racquetball, handball, basketball, volleyball, and tennis.

The Bemidji community is home to approximately 30,000 people. Students can easily get to the major areas of the city for shopping, part-time employment, or social activities. They also have access to more than 400 lakes, glacial rivers, forests, and the Chippewa National Forest.

Bemidji State University Academic Offerings

Accounting • Applied Psychology • Aquatic Biology •Art • Biology • Business Adm. • Chemistry • Computer Information Systems • Computer Science • Criminal Justice • Economics • English • Environmental Studies • Geography • German • Health • History • Humanities • Indian Studies • Industrial Technology • Mass Communication • Mathematics • Medical Technology • Music • Nursing • Philosophy • Physics • Political Science • Psychology • Social Studies • Social Work • Sociology • Spanish • Sports Mgt. • Technical Illustration/ Graphic Design • Theater

Admissions Statement

Admission is granted to students who rank in the upper half of their graduating class or who score 21 or above on the ACT and have successfully completed the following high school course requirements: four years of English; three years of mathematics, science, and social studies; and three years of elective credit in any two courses including foreign language, world cultures, or the arts.

Benedictine College

Atchison, Kansas 66002-1499
(913) 367-5340 or (800) 467-5340

Since its founding in 1858, Benedictine College has provided students with the environment, curriculum, campus resources, and personal attention necessary to become successful men and women. Small classes and interactive learning are the norm at this college. Faculty are available to support and challenge students both in and out of class. With over 30 liberal arts and career-oriented majors, opportunities to study abroad, internships, and independent study, students have many of the benefits of a larger college and all the advantages of a small Catholic college.

Academics

Degrees Offered: Associate, Bachelor's, Master's
Undergraduate Majors: 30+
Student / Faculty Ratio: 12 to 1

Average Class Size: 30

Number of Faculty: 85 full and part time

The academic curriculum at Benedictine College is a blend of a strong liberal arts core curriculum, concentrated courses in specific academic majors, elective areas of study, and the integration of practical experience. The college prepares students for careers or further study in graduate school and is committed to student success.

Benedictine offers academic programs that meet the needs of its students. An honors program is available for academically talented students and a comprehensive student support program is in place for students who experience difficulties. Students can integrate internships into most degree programs and can design their own majors. The college offers traditional majors like biology, mathematics, and sociology, as well as majors not usually offered at most schools, like classics and astronomy. In fact, Benedictine College is one of only 50 colleges in the country to offer a major in astronomy!

Although the college is small, it has established itself solidly within the educational community and can offer its students interesting academic opportunities. Benedictine is a member of the Kansas City Regional Council for Higher Education, and students can take courses at 15 other colleges and universities within the council. The school has established cooperative programs with other colleges in order to expand student career options. Students at Benedictine College can participate in a program in engineering with either Kansas State University or the University of Missouri-Columbia. The college has developed a similar program with Washington University for students who want to major in occupational therapy.

Students and Student Life

832 students from 35 states and 7 foreign countries
45% are from in-state
10% are students of color
5% are international
525 live on campus in five residential halls

Benedictine College has an active campus life in which students participate in a variety of clubs and organizations. With over 500 students living on campus, something is always going on, from guest speakers to musical performances, dances, theater productions, and community service projects. The college sponsors a student newspaper, magazine, and yearbook, and special-interest clubs like the Afro-American Student Union, Knights of Columbus, Young Democrats, and Young Republicans. The large intramural sports program provides competition and fun for even the novice competitor.

Athletics: NAIA
Women's Teams: basketball, golf, soccer, softball, tennis, track & field, volleyball
Men's Teams: baseball, basketball, football, golf, soccer, tennis, track & field

Campus and Community

Atchison is a small town approximately 45 miles from Kansas City. The 225-acre campus provides many opportunities and facilities for college students. The five on-campus residence halls provide comfortable housing for more than 500 students. Classroom and laboratory facilities are equipped to meet the needs of undergraduate students. Students have access to Kansas City, a major metropolitan city within an hour's drive from campus. Kansas City is a cultural center for the Midwest and has several fine theaters, museums, a concert hall, and business and shopping districts.

Benedictine College Academic Offerings

Associate Degrees: Accounting • Business Adm. • Health Care Mgt. • Information Science & Systems
Bachelor's Degrees: Accounting • Astronomy • Biology • Business Adm. • Chemistry • Classics • Computer & Information Science • Dramatic Arts • Economics • Elementary Ed. • English • English Ed. • Foreign Language Ed. • French • Health Care Adm. • Health Ed. • History • Humanities • Journalism • Junior High Ed. • Latin • Management • Marketing • Mathematics • Mathematics Ed. • Music • Music Ed. • Philosophy • Physical Ed. • Physics • Political Science • Psychology • Religion • Science Ed. • Social Science Ed. • Social Sciences • Social Work • Sociology • Spanish • Special Ed. • Speech & Communication • Youth Ministry

Admissions Statement

In order to be considered for admission, students should be graduates of an accredited high school and should have a minimum GPA of 2.0 in a college prep program, rank in the upper half of their class, and receive acceptable scores on the SAT 1 or ACT.

Black Hills State University

Spearfish, South Dakota 57799
(605) 642-6343 or (800) 255-2478

Black Hills State University is a four-year liberal arts institution tucked into the scenic Black Hills of South Dakota. It is located in Spearfish, a city of about 8,000. The 123-acre campus is surrounded by the natural beauty of the Black Hills. The university combines a rigorous academic program with the personal attention that only a small school can give. The mission of the college is to help students think, reason, evaluate, and integrate personal experiences with collective human experience. The university accomplishes this through classes that are interactive, challenging, and student centered, and campus activities that develop leadership, cooperation, and self-confidence.

Academics

Degrees Offered: Associate, Bachelor's, Master's

Undergraduate Majors: 35+

Student / Faculty Ratio: 24 to 1

Number of Faculty: 100 full time

Average Class Size: 25

There are four undergraduate colleges that make up Black Hills State University. Each combines a liberal arts philosophy with state-of-the-art technology to provide an education that will take students well beyond the 21st century.

The College of Applied Science and Technology's curriculum is designed to develop skills in mathematical, scientific, health-related, and technical subjects and prepare students for a career or continued studies on the graduate level.

The College of Arts and Humanities offers majors in liberal arts subjects that can be taken independently or combined with teacher certification. Artistically creative majors, such as music and art, are designed to unite theory and performance. Music majors are required to participate in at least one music performance organization each semester, and art majors organize and present an exhibit of their work prior to graduation.

The degree programs within the College of Business and Public Affairs combine classroom theory with integrated practical experience. The Center for Business and Tourism provides experiential learning opportunities and outstanding resource facilities for business, industry, and community organizations in the region.

The Center for Indian Studies provides opportunities for students and others to research and study the language, history, and culture of Indian peoples of North America and South Dakota. The Center promotes an awareness and appreciation of cultural differences, values, customs, beliefs, and ceremonies of Native America.

The curriculum in the College of Education and Human Resources Development prepares classroom teachers, special education personnel, and librarians for employment in school districts throughout the state. Teacher certification is available in pre-school through secondary education, including specialty areas like library media, special education, and middle school/junior high endorsement.

At Black Hills State University the focus is on a student-centered learning environment. Professors at the university are involved in their students' education on campus and concerned with their students' contribution to the community off campus. Many professors are directly involved in finding internships and first-time jobs for their students. Each year the university offers more than 700 courses so students can easily enroll in classes that satisfy both degree requirements and their academic curiosity.

Students and Student Life

2,800 students from 39 states and 12 foreign countries
30% are from out-of-state
6% are students of color
1% are international
25% live on campus

A congenial feeling of affirmation and acceptance of diversity on campus comes through in the events and organizations sponsored by the university. Each year Black Hills University celebrates events like Women's History Month, Native American Awareness Month, and Black History Month, in addition to activities like Homecoming, Big 100 Week, and Swarm Days.

The Student Activities Committee and Senate promote more than 60 different clubs and activities on campus. Some popular activities include student concerts, plays, and choral presentations; a large, active intramural program; and the Collegiate Outdoor Leadership Program, which places students in leadership positions within the community. The five residence halls can accommodate 600 students, and there are also university apartments available for married students, single parents, and students over the age of 21.

Athletics: NAIA Division II in the SDIC Conference
Women's Teams: basketball, cross country, track, volleyball
Men's Teams: basketball, cross country, football, track

Campus and Community

Students at Black Hills State University describe the city of Spearfish and the surrounding area as "absolutely the best place for year-round recreational opportunities." Bike paths, hiking trails, boating, fishing, and camping are just minutes from campus. The city of Spearfish sponsors cultural and recreational events throughout the year. Students can easily get into town to shop, eat out, or meet friends.

The Black Hills campus is situated on over 100 acres of land. There are 12 major buildings on campus in addition to the Lyle Hare Stadium, practice fields, and tennis courts. A popular place for students is the Donald E. Young Sports and Fitness Center. It is one of the largest publicly owned buildings in the state and houses an indoor track, aquatic center with two pools, a wellness center, and a gymnasium.

Black Hills State University is located in the northern Black Hills of South Dakota, about an hour from Rapid City.

Black Hills State University Academic Offerings

Accounting • Art • Biology • Business Adm. • Chemistry • Communication Arts • Elementary Ed. • English • Environmental Physical Science • History • Human Resource Mgt. • Human Services • Marketing • Mass Communication • Mathematics • Middle School Ed. • Music • Office Adm. • Outdoor Ed. • Physical Ed. • Political Science • Psychology • Science • Secondary Ed. • Social Science • Sociology • Spanish • Speech • Special Ed. • Technology • Theater • Tourism • Travel Industry Mgt. • Wellness Mgt.

Admissions Statement

Students applying for admission to the University must have completed the following courses with a grade of "C" or better: four years of English; three years of mathematics, laboratory sciences, and social sciences; one-half year of computer science and fine arts. In addition to meeting these core requirements students must also meet one of the following three requirements: minimum GPA of 2.6, or minimum ACT of 18, or class rank in the top 60 percent of the graduating class.

Bradford College

Bradford, Massachusetts 01835
(508) 372-7161 or (800) 336-6448

Bradford College, founded in 1803, was one of the earliest New England co-educational academies. Even then it was ahead of its time. Today, as it approaches its bicentennial anniversary, it has remained an innovative educational institution. In 1983 it again stepped to the forefront with the establishment of the Bradford Plan for a Practical Liberal Arts Education, a unique program that combines the liberal arts with hands-on career preparation.

Bradford is recognized for its historic traditions that continue to enhance the focus of education. Bradford's five comprehensive majors prepare students with the breadth and depth necessary to be knowledgeable in the 21st century. The 24 practical minors provide specific marketable skills. Students who graduate from Bradford are not only educated but also experienced, technologically sophisticated, and globally influenced.

Academics

Degrees Offered: Bachelor of Arts

Undergraduate Majors: Five comprehensive majors with more than 30 concentrations

Student/Faculty Ratio: 12 to 1

Average Class Size: 15

The Bradford Plan is a comprehensive, structured curriculum that ties liberal arts and practical education together in courses, independent projects, internships, service learning, study abroad, and seminars. The plan includes interdisciplinary courses that satisfy the general education requirements all students must meet. Many of these courses are team-taught and provide a cross-discipline view of age-old problems and contemporary issues. During the first two years at Bradford, students develop a portfolio demonstrating their progress toward college-wide learning and development goals. By junior year they select a comprehensive major and practical minor and participate in a semester long internship. The Bradford Plan culminates with a senior project that demonstrates the skills and knowledge acquired during the undergraduate years.

Students at Bradford College can integrate one of several off-campus learning experiences into this program. These include the National Theater Institute, where students pursue a semester of intense study at the Eugene O'Neil Theater Center in Waterford, Connecticut; the Washington Center, where juniors and seniors spend a semester in Washington, D.C. as interns in government offices, national service organizations, or the arts; and the Sea Education Association, which provides semester-long deep-water oceanographic studies in Woods Hole, Cape Cod, and on a sailing vessel.

Bradford uses an individualized advising system in which a faculty member and student work together to choose the courses and curriculum which best meet the student's personal and academic goals. A rigorous honors program is available for bright students seeking the intellectual challenge of small discussion groups focusing on sophisticated themes and ideas. A full-service academic resource center supports the development of all students. Learning specialists, trained peer tutors, faculty, and other staff, working with special computer software packages, videos, faculty-prepared materials, and self-assessment tools, are available to assist students throughout their four years in college.

Although Bradford may be a small college, students do not have to forego opportunities that may be available at larger institutions. Bradford has established several links to major academic programs throughout the United States. Bradford's ties with the Sea Education Association allow students to enroll in a semester-at-sea with other college students from around the country. Students can also take courses at MIT and the New England Aquarium through the Massachusetts Bay Consortium. Through a recent affiliation with the Newburyport Theater Company, Bradford students can participate in this professional theater company's productions.

Opportunities to study abroad are plentiful. Bradford College is affiliated with the Central College International Studies program, the Council on International Education Exchange, the School for International Training, the American Institute of Foreign Studies, and Boston University's International Internship Program.

Students and Student Life

600 students from 28 states and 30 foreign countries
20% are students of color
12% are international
75% live on campus in four residence halls

Bradford is not just a college, it's a community where students are encouraged, supported, challenged, and engaged in all types of learning activities. Co-curricular clubs and organizations are an important aspect of a Bradford education, and community service is one activity in which most students participate. Every club and organization on campus participates in at least one service project during the school year. The Office of Community Service Learning is another avenue for volunteer activities in the community. Bradford's motto, *"Surgo Ut Prosim,"* (I rise to serve) is taken seriously.

Students at Bradford are very much a part of the governance of the college. The Student Senate serves as a decision-making body with full powers of recommendation to the faculty, administration, and board of trustees. It appoints student members to serve on all major college committees. The college has a student-run radio station, newspaper and literary magazine, a theater production company, a dance company, and the Bradford-Pentucker Chorale.

Women's Athletic Teams: basketball, cross country, field hockey, soccer, softball, volleyball,
Men's Teams: basketball, cross country, soccer, volleyball,

Campus and Community

The 70-acre campus includes a lovely pond, winding paths, and acres of scenic landscape, and houses 12 attractive and functional buildings. Most buildings are traditional redbrick, yet all of them have their own unique quality. Denworth Hall contains a dance studio, the 700-seat Kemper Theater, and adjoining theater workshop. The Dorothy Bell Study Center houses the Hemingway Library, the Carlson art wing (with five studios, workshops, darkroom, and lecture rooms), the Laura Knott gallery, and music facilities that include an electronic music studio, rehearsal room, and 225-seat auditorium.

Residential housing is offered in traditional dorm rooms and suite-style living in Academy Hall and Tupelo East and West Halls. Apartment-style housing is also available. The campus is located 35 miles north of Boston, and a frequent commuter train gives students ample access to internships in Boston, and of course to over 100,000 other college students!

Bradford College Academic Offerings

Creative Arts, with concentrations in graphic design; performing arts in dance, music, or theater; and visual arts in studio art or art history • Humanities, with concentrations in American studies, communication studies in video production or media issues, creative writing, European studies, French, history, literature, philosophy, professional writing, romance studies, and Spanish • Human Studies, with concentrations in human studies, international studies, politics, psychology, sociology, and social policy & human services • Management, with concentrations in accounting & finance, administration & management, international studies, and marketing • Natural Science & Math, with concentrations in biology, environmental science, marine science, natural science & mathematics, and mathematics

Admissions Statement

Candidates for admission to Bradford College are selected on the basis of ability and achievement, character, desire for an interdisciplinary and personal approach to a liberal arts education, extracurricular activities and interests, and a sound academic program featuring college preparatory courses.

Bryant College

Smithfield, Rhode Island 02917-1285
(401) 232-6100 or (800) 622-7001

Since 1863, when the school was founded, Bryant College has prepared students "not just for their first job, but for careers in a wide range of fields from advertising to law." The 10 academic areas of study offered blend business and liberal arts to provide a foundation for almost any career. The college has a great deal to offer students: a technologically enhanced modern campus; accomplished, capable faculty; an educational environment that integrates collaborative learning, internships, discussion, and technology; and an active community of teachers and learners.

Academics

Degrees Offered: Associate, Bachelor's, Master's

Undergraduate Majors: 10 with more than 20 concentrations

Student/Faculty Ratio: 18 to 1

Average Class Size: 30

A Bryant education prepares students not only for a career, but for a lifetime. Bryant does this by focusing on the intellectual and professional development of students, preparing them for leadership positions and equipping them with universal skills that can be transferred to all career positions. One example of Bryant's lifetime preparation is the comprehensive Learning for Leadership Program, which develops leadership skills and provides students with opportunities to use these skills in academic and social activities while they contribute to the community. This program consists of a two-semester sequence that includes a leadership course followed by a mentorship with a professional from a public or private organization. This very successful program gives students valuable life and career experience in addition to a sense of accomplishment.

Another way Bryant broadens its students' education is through experiential learning. The college has developed a formal internship program that combines significant work with directed study. This is not a program in which students go out and find a job related to their major; rather it is a well-defined and supervised work experience that is correlated with a directed study component, so students can interface with professionals and faculty to discuss and analyze the experience.

The college also builds computer proficiency training into every degree program allowing students to begin their career with proficiency in computer skills, word processing, and spreadsheets—necessary components for any career.

Students and Student Life

2,250 students from 31 states and 49 foreign countries
6% are students of color
2% are international
80% live on campus

Bryant College offers an active college environment with over 90 percent of the student body participating in at least one (if not more) of the 60 school sponsored clubs. On weekends an average of 75 percent of the residential students remain on campus. This is no suitcase campus!

At Bryant, students can expand their social consciousness by becoming involved in organizations like the Hunger Coalition, Big Sister, Students for Social Awareness, or the Environment Club. Students can write for the student newspaper or work at the campus radio station. The 10 professional organizations, including the Entrepreneurship Club and Pre-Law Society, bring together students who share similar career goals and give them opportunities to network with professionals and attend regional conferences.

Other campus organizations include 14 fraternities and sororities, an International Student Organization, Multicultural Student Union, religious organizations like the Newsman Club and Hillel, and an active Student Senate.

Athletics: NCAA Division II Northeast-10 Conference ECAC
Women's Teams: basketball, cross country, soccer, softball, tennis, track, volleyball
Men's Teams: baseball, basketball, cross country, golf, soccer, tennis, track

Campus and Community

The 387-acre campus is modern, spacious, and designed with students in mind. Most of the major structures are built around a large pond in the center of campus. All classrooms and laboratories and most of the faculty offices are housed in the unique Unistructure, an impressive modern glass structure with a wonderful glass-domed rotunda.

The Koffler Technology Center houses more than 200 microcomputers and work stations, as well as advanced computer and actuarial labs. The Hodson Memorial Library is recognized as one of the region's most extensive and comprehensive business libraries. Its resources include a computerized reference system; online electronic data bases including LEXIS, NEXIS, and DIALOG; and worldwide expanded research capabilities. The campus has a Learning Center, activities center, and residence facilities that provide traditional dorm-style housing, suite arrangements, and campus apartments.

Bryant College Academic Offerings

Accounting • Applied Actuarial Mathematics • Communications • Computer Information Systems • Economics • English • Finance • History • International Studies • Management • Marketing • Five-year BS/MBA

Admissions Statement

The Admissions Committee considers each candidate individually and bases its acceptance decision on a number of factors including depth and quality of scholastic achievement demonstrated by the applicant; the results of standardized tests; and the scores of the SAT 1 or ACT. The committee also places importance on recommendations from the high school guidance department concerning character traits and personal qualifications not shown in the academic record.

Canisius College

Buffalo, New York 14208-1098
(716) 888-2200 or (800) 843-1517

Canisius College is one of 28 prestigious Jesuit colleges and universities in the United States. Located in Buffalo, New York the college offers a blend of academic, social, and spiritual growth opportunities incorporated into every student's education. Over the past 126 years the school has established a reputation for being one of the outstanding colleges in the Northeast. This is evident when you look at some of the 32,000 alumni who have graduated from Canisius: two U.S. Congressmen, a mayor, president of a large medical complex, CEO of a large bank, financial officer for a national specialty retail clothing store, and 20 percent of all physicians, attorneys, dentists, and accountants in Western New York!

Academics

Degrees Offered: Associate, Bachelor's, Master's
Undergraduate Majors: 30
Student/Faculty Ratio: 17 to 1 (most classes usually do not exceed 30 students)
Number of Faculty: 375 full and part time

Canisius College is made up of three divisions: the Colleges of Arts and Sciences, the Richard J. Wehle School of Business, and the School of Education and Human Services. Together they offer over 40 academic majors that accommodate students' individual academic and career goals while educating the whole person. The college has made a substantial effort to provide top-of-the-line facilities and instruction in all programs, and this futuristic planning can be seen throughout the three divisions.

The College of Arts and Sciences is home base for the 54-credit core curriculum that focuses on humanistic studies through literature, physical and social sciences, oral and written communication, philosophy and religious studies. This division also offers more than 25 majors. Many of them have incorporated modern technology into the curriculum so graduates can lead the way in the job market. Canisius College is one of only a few colleges that integrates electronic imaging, video disk, and CD-ROM multimedia technology into the art history major.

The new molecular biology lab used by undergraduate students replicates facilities and technology presently being used in graduate schools and biotechnology laboratories. The college is one of a few educational institutions in the country that possesses the *Ibycus* computer, which accesses most of ancient Greek, Latin, and scripture literature.

The Wehle School of Business, accredited by the prestigious American Assembly of Collegiate Schools of Business, offers specialized programs in human resource management, entrepreneurship, a certificate in international business, a joint program in fashion merchandising with the Fashion Institute of Technology in New York City, and a five year BA/MBA program.

In the School of Education and Human Services, all programs include extensive field-based experiences and are accredited by the National Council for the Accreditation of Teacher Education.

Students and Student Life

3,300 undergraduate students from 25 states and 40 foreign countries
12% are students of color

8% are international
1,000 live on campus

Canisius College sponsors 90 clubs and organizations, including special interest organizations, professional clubs, intramural sports, campus newspaper and radio station, campus ministry, national fraternities and sororities, and several community service organizations. You name it, and Canisius College probably sponsors it!

Campus life centers around four specific places: the residence halls where more than 35 percent of all students live; the Palisano Pavilion, home of the Upper Deck and Harriet's Lounge, a great place to hang out; the Student Center, headquarters for most of the clubs and organizations on campus; and the Koessler Athletic Center, where students can pump up, jog it off, or take part in a pickup game.

Athletics: NCAA Division I. Football is Division 1 AA.
Women's Teams: basketball, cross country, soccer, softball, swimming, synchronized swimming, tennis, track, volleyball
Men's Teams: baseball, basketball, cross country, football, golf, ice hockey, lacrosse, soccer, swimming, tennis, track
Coed: rifle

Campus and Community

The 25-acre urban campus is located in Buffalo, New York. The campus was originally established in 1870 with a single building. Today more than 36 buildings make up the college. The older academic structures have all been renovated and the college is presently completing renovation of existing dorms and constructing new townhouses for resident students. Most of the academic buildings are connected via underground walkways to residence halls, so that during inclement weather students do not have to brave the elements to get to class.

The new sports complex and adjoining athletic center have top notch facilities for classes, recreation, and sports. The downtown and business areas of Buffalo are easily accessed via the metro rail system that stops right by the college. Buffalo metropolitan area has a population of over 1.4 million. It has major museums, a philharmonic orchestra, professional sports, theaters, and just about anything else a student might be interested in. In addition, there are six other colleges in the city and several more within a half hour's drive.

Canisius College Academic Offerings

College of Arts and Sciences: Art History • Biochemistry • Biology • Chemistry • Classics • Communication Studies • Computer Science • Economics • English • Fine Arts • French • German • History • Humanities • International Relations •

Mathematics • Medical Technology • Military Science • Modern Languages •
Music • Philosophy • Physics • Political Science • Psychology • Religious
Studies • Social Science • Sociology and Anthropology • Spanish • Studio Art •
Urban Studies
Wehle School of Business: Accounting • Computer Information Systems •
Economics • Finance • Hotel Mgt. • Management • Marketing
School of Education and Human Services: Elementary/Early secondary (grades
N-9): English, French, German, mathematics, science, social studies, Spanish •
Physical education (K-12) • Secondary education (grades 7-12): biology,
business, chemistry, English, French, German, mathematics, physics, social
studies, Spanish

Admissions Statement

Men and women of ability and achievement are welcome in all divisions of Canisius
College. Their acceptance as students is judged by the Committee on Admissions
and is based on aptitude, achievement, and character alone.

Castleton State College

Castleton, Vermont 05735
(802) 468-5611

Castleton State College is one of the oldest institutions of higher learning in the
country. Just four years after the Revolutionary War, the Republic of Vermont char-
tered the school and empowered it to educate teachers for the public schools. Two
centuries later, the college is still educating teachers—along with musicians, jour-
nalists, corrections officers, business managers, and many other professionals.

The college is very much a part of the intellectual, creative, and scientific growth
of Vermont and New England. It has developed programs in areas like exercise science and children's literature; it has made Internet access available to students in the
Calvin Coolidge Library; and it has an Honors Hall where bright students live and
engage in projects designed to enrich their collegiate experience. As the largest state
college in Vermont, Castleton's mission is to "help students develop the knowledge,
competence, and character necessary for contribution, leadership, and success in a
complex and increasingly global society." And from all accounts it is succeeding.

Academics

Degrees Offered: Associate, Bachelor's, Master's

Undergraduate Majors: 25+

Student/Faculty Ratio: 17 to 1

Number of Faculty: 175 full and part time

The Castleton curriculum is diverse, challenging, and rooted in a strong liberal arts core. Students can choose a major from 14 departments and more than 25 programs. The core curriculum includes 46 credits and incorporates courses in writing, speaking, computers, foreign cultures, history, literature and the arts, mathematics, natural sciences, philosophical / psychological analysis, and social analysis.

Two interesting majors at Castleton State are psychology and geology. The psychology department offers an honors program for bright students who work individually with a faculty member in a rigorous academic curriculum and perform original research. Not many colleges offer a geology major, although it is one field in which numerous career opportunities are available. The Castleton geology program incorporates classroom theory and experiential learning, including geological surveys taken in other parts of the country.

The small classroom environment allows students of all abilities to thrive. The college has developed an honors program for selected students majoring in English, history, psychology, and sociology and several programs have been introduced into the curriculum to broaden academic experiences. Study abroad is available through the International Student Exchange Program administered by Georgetown University, or through Experiments in International Living. Students can study in 17 countries, including places like Ghana, Greece, Nepal, Sri Lanka, and Tanzania.

Individualized educational experiences can easily be incorporated in any degree program. The Cooperative Education Program at Castleton is flexible, so students can choose how much and what type of cooperative experience they want. They can take a full semester's work in the co-op program or integrate several part-time experiences into their degree program. Another special offering is Independent Study, which gives students the opportunity to work individually with a faculty member in a subject area or on a project. Students may also participate in internships and/or practica within their major. While some majors, like education and nursing, require on-the-job placement, all students are strongly advised to participate in some type of off campus learning experience.

Castleton provides services for students who want to succeed in college. Through Success Through Educational Programs (STEP), students with different educational backgrounds can receive academic counseling, tutorial services, and learning disabilities services. The STEP center is located in Babcock Hall and is open seven days a week. "It is both a teaching and a learning center," comments one student. "Students who really know and understand the material in a specific course act as tutors for kids who may be having some difficulty. There's no negative stigma attached to going to the STEP Center, because here at Castleton the center is just one more way we can help ourselves become better students."

Students and Student Life

> 1,700 students from 24 states and 3 foreign countries
> 45% are from out-of-state
> 4% are students of color
> 1% are international
> 700 live on campus in 6 residence halls

One student characterized her fellow students this way: "The kids here come from places like New York, New Jersey, and a lot from New England, but they're not all alike. We've got students with green hair, kids that are computer geeks, guys that roller blade around campus, and even some girls with puffy hair. We've got kids that watch the soaps every day and kids that work out every day. We've got kids from New York City who wanted to go to school in ski country and kids from upstate Vermont who think Rutland is a big city. It's a great place to be because the college works really hard at getting everyone to know one another and to work together."

A popular activity on campus is sports and the college offers a full range of intramural, club, and intercollegiate teams. Club sports include exciting things like freestyle skiing, orienteering, rock climbing, rugby, and snow boarding! The Glenbrook Gymnasium and the SHAPE facilities provide two gymnasiums, a six-lane pool, racquetball courts, and a physical fitness center. And Vermont provides miles of walking trails, mountains to climb, ski slopes to traverse, and rivers and lakes to navigate!

But don't get the wrong idea: While sports and outdoor activities are very popular, the college sponsors more than 20 other types of clubs and activities. Each semester, approximately 25 different cultural events are brought to campus including plays, concerts, lecture series, and dance troupes. There is a literary club, film committee, student newspaper, and a student-run radio station. New clubs are always being started and the Student Association makes every attempt to provide social events and programs for all students.

> **Athletics:** Mayflower Conference, the NAIA, the Eastern College Athletic Conference, and the NCAA Division III
> **Women's Teams:** basketball, cross country, lacrosse, softball, soccer, tennis
> **Men's Teams:** baseball, basketball, cross country, lacrosse, soccer, tennis

Campus and Community

Castleton State is located just 12 miles from Rutland, the second largest city in Vermont. Here students can shop at the new mall, catch the latest movie, or enjoy dinner out. There is a bus that runs frequently between the campus and the city, so students who do not have a car still have access to off-campus activities. Middlebury College is about 15 minutes north, and Green Mountain College is even closer. So there is no isolation from other college students.

The Castleton campus comprises about 130 acres and houses 22 academic and residential buildings. It is walking distance from the village of Castleton, and adjoins the Pond Hill Ranch, a 2,000-acre equestrian facility with over 70 miles of riding trails. The college is only a few minutes away from Pico Ski Area and Lake Bomoseen, a popular recreational area.

Residential facilities on campus include six halls that provide both corridor-style residences and suite-style accommodations. About 700 students live on campus, and students can choose floors that provide special options including a wellness floor, a substance-free floor, a no-smoking floor, and all-male or all-female floors.

Castleton State College Academic Offerings

Art • Business Adm. • Communication • Computer Information Systems • Criminal Justice • Education • History • Literature • Mathematics • Music • Natural Sciences • Physical Ed. • Psychology • Social Work • Sociology • Spanish • Theater Arts

Admissions Statement

The college requires that all candidates for admission be graduates of accredited high schools or have satisfied high school requirements through the GED or special official arrangements. Each applicant is evaluated individually and preference will be given to those candidates who, in the judgment of college officials, present the greatest potential for successful collegiate performance.

Catawba College

Salisbury, North Carolina 28144-2488
(704) 637-4444 or (800) CATAWBA

Catawba College, founded in 1851, is affiliated with the United Church of Christ. Its goal is to provide " . . . an education rich in personal attention that blends the knowledge and competencies of liberal studies with career preparation." Catawba College accomplishes this goal through the faculty's involvement in all aspects of student life, a large academic curriculum with more than 40 majors, and a full-time co-curricular program that encourages students to develop leadership skills, have fun, and make lifelong friendships.

Academics

Degrees Offered: Bachelor's, Master's

Undergraduate Majors: 40

Student/Faculty Ratio: 14 to 1

Number of Faculty: 85

As early as the first year, students are guided toward their academic and personal goals. The Freshman Studies program " . . . is designed to assist students in making the sometimes difficult transition to college." It is a year-long program that focuses on works from Western and Eastern civilizations. The readings are explored through lectures, writing assignments in a companion composition program, and discussion in small groups led by Master Learners. The discussion groups meet twice weekly throughout the year and also give attention to the personal and intellectual growth needed for success in college.

Throughout the four years at Catawba, students receive individual attention and opportunities to maximize their potential. These include incorporating a minor area of study, completing a double major, and developing an independent study project. The honors program, internships, and pass/fail grading are other options. Teacher certification is available in early childhood, elementary, and secondary education, and in nine specific subject areas. Study abroad is available in England.

Catawba College offers over 40 major fields of study; pre-professional programs in law, medicine, dentistry, optometry, and veterinary medicine; and the option for custom-designed majors. Cooperative programs are available with area universities in forestry and environmental studies, medical technology, physician assistant training, and deaf education.

Catawba makes special accommodations for students who are learning disabled. These accommodations include permitting audio taping in class, doubling the usual time for full-period tests and exams, and providing a distraction-free environment during full-period tests and exams.

Students and Student Life

1,000 students from 27 states and 4 foreign countries
50% are from out-of-state
10% are students of color

1% are international
650 live on campus

At Catawba College, a full social life is supported by the 24 organizations including student government; a newspaper, literary magazine, and yearbook; many music and theater groups; and eight honor societies. The college also brings big name performers to campus at least twice a month. Sports and outdoor activities are popular on campus. Over one third of the students participate in intercollegiate sports, and more than a quarter of the students are involved in intramural sports on club and dormitory teams.

Athletics: NCAA Division II
Women's Teams: basketball, cross country, field hockey, soccer, softball, tennis, volleyball
Men's Teams: baseball, football, golf

Campus and Community

The 210-acre campus is spacious and comfortable. Many of the 24 buildings on campus were part of a significant renewal and modernization project that was recently completed. Dormitory and administrative buildings were remodeled and the Charles A. Cannon Student Center and Ralph W. Ketner Hall for Business and Teacher Education were built. The eight residence halls (which accommodate more than 65 percent of the students) are located throughout the campus. Four halls are for men and four are for women. Students can choose traditional dorm-style housing or suite-style arrangements. The athletic facilities include the Johnson Tennis Complex, Shuford Football Stadium, Newman Basketball Park, and Frock Athletic Complex.

Catawba College is located in Salisbury, North Carolina, a city of 25,000. It is within 50 miles of Charlotte, Greensboro, and Winston-Salem. These cities and their colleges and universities provide many social, cultural, and educational opportunities for Catawba students.

Catawba College Academic Offerings

Accounting • American Politics • Arts Adm. • Biology • Business Adm. • Chemistry • Chemistry Ed. • Church Music • Communication Arts • Computer Information Systems • Computer Science • Elementary Ed. • English • Forestry/ Environmental Studies • French • History • International Business • International Relations • Mathematics • Medical Technology • Middle School Ed. • Music • Music Ed. • Music Industry • Musical Theatre • Physical Ed. • Physician Assistant • Political Science • Premedical Science • Psychological Services

• Psychology • Recreation • Religion/Philosophy • Sociology • Spanish • Special Ed. • Sports Medicine • Theatre Arts • Therapeutic Recreation

Admissions Statement

The Admissions Committee examines four specific academic criteria, in addition to other qualities in order to predict an applicant's probability of success. These include the student's academic course selection, his or her grade point average, the student's scores on the SAT or ACT, and the students rank in class. Graduation from secondary school is recommended; GED is accepted; 16 units and the following program of study are required: four units of English; two units of mathematics; two units of laboratory science; two units of social studies; and six units of electives (of which two units must be academic).

Cazenovia College

Cazenovia, New York 13035
(315) 655-8005 or (800) 654-3210

Since its founding in 1824, Cazenovia College has recognized and supported students' individuality within the learning process. At Cazenovia, a student is able to learn by those methods that he or she is best able to comprehend. Because of its small size and residential characteristic, students can develop mentoring relationships with their professors, get to know the deans and other administrators, and have an opportunity for personal and intellectual growth free from the pressures sometimes found in large institutions.

Courses, programs, and degrees aim to help students reach their potential, accomplish their goals, and get the best and fastest start possible on their life after college. With a choice of associate or bachelor's degrees in 20 areas, students can find just the right program to fit their career aspirations.

Academics

Degrees Offered: Associate, Bachelor's

Undergraduate Majors: 26 associate and four bachelor's degree majors with more than 17 areas of specialization

Number of Faculty: 110 full and part time

The curriculum at Cazenovia focuses on educating the whole person and the college has established a variety of courses, learning opportunities, internships, and mentoring opportunities where this can take place. Each year the college offers more than 400 different courses, 100 internships, and travel opportunities to places like England, Switzerland, Ireland, or Australia. The competency-based curriculum enables students to gain skills and understanding in their field of interest, and acquire a basis for becoming life long learners.

The Center for Teaching and Learning, a professionally staffed tutorial facility, offers a variety of excellent practical services to assist students in achieving their academic and professional goals. The center provides professional and peer tutoring, group study sessions, basic skills building, and test-taking workshops. It's an important part of the college and is open days, evenings, and weekends. One student commented, "The center is not just there for kids who are having a problem in a subject . . . it's there for all of us. I go over and participate in some of the group study sessions. It's the kind of resource center that has something for everyone from the A-student to the C-student!"

Bright students who come to Cazenovia have the opportunity to participate in the honors program. This flexible, intellectually challenging program allows students three options: Students can attend scheduled honors courses that are held in many subject areas, register for selective honors seminars, or earn honors credit in most regular courses by completing additional work beyond the scope of the course. The variety of class delivery systems enables honors students to excel in learning environments that suit their individual needs. This is a consistent mission of the college.

Students and Student Life

900 students from 10 states and 3 foreign countries
14% are from out-of-state
20% are students of color
1% are international
85% live on campus

Campus life is very much a part of a Cazenovian education. The Campus Activities Board and the Student Council (both student elected groups) oversee a full scope of activities, clubs, and events that shape residential life. There are more than 20 social organizations and many career related clubs. The Cazenovia College Theatre is consistently booked with student events like the annual fashion show, which celebrates the creations designed by students in the Fashion Studies program, and theatrical plays and shows directed by and starring Cazenovia students. It also provides stage area for plays, concerts, and films.

Athletics: Provisional member of the NCAA Division III
Men's and Women's Teams: basketball, crew, soccer, and tennis. The national award-winning equestrian team includes both men and women riders.
Women's Teams: softball, volleyball
Men's Teams: baseball, golf

Campus and Community

The 20-acre campus is located in the picturesque village of Cazenovia, New York. The Village is in the Finger Lake district of central New York, and Cazenovia Lake is less than a mile from campus.

The 24 buildings on campus are located around a central quadrangle. The five residence halls accommodate over 800 students and provide both single-sex and coed housing. Each academic building is equipped with the facilities and technology necessary to support specific career majors. The Gertrude T. Chapman Art Center has classrooms, ceramic and painting studios, and a professional gallery where students and visiting artists exhibit their work. The Witherill Information Resources Center/ Library has an online interlibrary loan network and shelves more than 56,000 volumes. Eckel Hall houses science laboratories, a photo laboratory, and fashion design studios.

In addition, the college maintains a 20-acre farm with modern equine facilities. The South Campus, located about two blocks from the main quad, houses the major facilities for the illustration, graphic design, and interior environmental design majors.

The village of Cazenovia is within walking distance from the campus. It is also 19 miles from Syracuse, a major city and college town.

Cazenovia College Academic Offerings

Associate Degrees: Accounting • Advertising/Graphic Design • Business Mgt. • Child Studies, with specialization in day-care service, early childhood ed., special ed assistant • Commercial Illustration • Equine Studies • Fashion Studies • Human Services, with specialization in community mental health, social services for children & youth, social services for the elderly • Individual Studies • Liberal Arts • Studio Art
Bachelor's Degrees: Bachelor of Fine Arts in Interior Environmental Design, Visual Communications (advertising/graphic design, commercial illustration) • Bachelor of Arts in Liberal Studies: fine & performing arts, interdisciplinary social science, literature & culture, science & society • Bachelor of Science in Liberal & Professional Studies: fine & performing arts, human services,

interdisciplinary social sciences, literature and culture, science & society •
Bachelor of Professional Studies: business mgt., equine business mgt.

Admissions Statement

Cazenovia College seeks students whose high school records, SAT 1 or ACT scores, and official recommendations indicate the ability to handle college-level work. Students who have an average of "C" or better are encouraged to apply. But more than that, we are also looking for the student who has certain qualities of character known to promise success in college, outside as well as inside the classroom: maturity, motivation, initiative, imagination, ambition, and self-reliance. Individuals with these qualifications contribute to the overall quality of student life, creating a stimulating environment beneficial to all.

Central Methodist College

Fayette, Missouri 65248-1198
(816) 248-3391

For more than 140 years, Central Methodist College has been preparing men and women for promising futures. This small, church-related college combines a strong liberal arts and pre-professional curriculum, Christian values, and interactive learning experiences to provide each student with the education and skills necessary to succeed in the very competitive 21st century. Opportunities like interim semesters abroad, cooperative degree programs in medical technology, engineering, physical therapy, and law, and strong internship programs are all part of the curriculum at Central Methodist College.

The 52-acre campus, designated a National Historic District, is located in the small town of Fayette, Missouri, midway between St. Louis and Kansas City. It is an active campus where students live and learn in an environment characterized by enriching activities, challenging academics, dedicated faculty, and personalized attention.

Academics

Degrees Offered: Associate, Bachelor's
Undergraduate Majors: 30+

Student/Faculty Ratio: 12 to 1

Number of Faculty: 82 full and part time

Central Methodist College offers associate and bachelor's degree programs in more than 30 areas. While many of the majors are career oriented, the bachelor's degree curriculum includes a structured, 62-credit general education requirement in addition to opportunities for internships, study-abroad programs, and interdisciplinary studies. Part of the general education requirements includes the Mission Core, a planned program of courses and experiences that cross all disciplines and focus heavily on values, physical and mental well being, writing skills, and critical thinking.

The curriculum at Central Methodist is broad enough to meet the needs of a diverse student population. For both honor students and average students, the college provides interesting and enriching courses that are appropriate, challenging, and relevant. Students who rank in the top 10 percent of their class are invited to participate in honors colloquiums, and seniors enrolled in the program may elect to write a thesis. Students who need additional help with their courses can receive assistance in reading, writing, math, and general study skills at the Student Development Center.

Central Methodist College has incorporated several opportunities into its academic offerings. Students who want to create their own major may elect the Interdiscipline Studies major, in which they (in conjunction with appropriate department heads) can develop a plan of study that will achieve their goals and fulfill all the college requirements for a degree. The Interim Janaway program lets students participate in off-campus cultural and learning experiences during winter break. In the past, CMC has offered Janaway courses like Arts in New York City, German Culture/Arts, Greek Odyssey, and Literary Britain.

Students and Student Life

1,000 students from 14 states and 6 foreign countries

11% are from out-of-state

9% are students of color

2% are international

600 live on campus

At Central Methodist College, the faculty and administration realize that some of a students' most important learning experiences happen outside the classroom. Because of this philosophy, the college emphasizes student involvement in campus and community activities; more than 40 college sponsored clubs and activities are established.

The Student Government Association includes all students of the college and consists of an Executive-Legislative Branch and a Judicial Branch. SGA plays an active role in the college experience. Another component of student life on campus are the six fraternities and five sororities; more than 50 percent of the students are members of the Greek system.

To complement performance-based majors in communication, music, and theater, the college supports a large number of performance groups like concert band, a cappella choir, jazz band, KCKM-AM, and KCMC-TV (campus radio and television stations), a weekly student newspaper, and more than 15 honor societies related to academic areas of interest.

Being a Christian college, CMC takes a special interest in supporting its students' religious activities. Students at CMC come from various religious backgrounds and have established chapters of the Newman Center, the United Methodist Student Organization, the Baptist Student Union, and the Fellowship for Christian Athletes, along with several other religious organizations.

Athletics: NAIA and the Heart of America Athletic Conference
Women's Teams: basketball, cross country, golf, soccer, softball, tennis, track, volleyball
Men's Teams: baseball, basketball, cross country, football, golf, soccer, tennis, track

Campus and Community

The 52-acre campus is home to more than 30 buildings, including the beautiful and historic Brannock Hall, the Swinney Conservatory of Music, the Smiley Library (which includes online database capabilities), and the Morrison Observatory (with three refractor telescopes). The Little Theater includes a 190-seat auditorium, dressing rooms, and scene shop and is one of the finest small-college theaters in the area. The physical education and fitness areas are located in the Phillips Recreation Center at the Puckett Field House. The college has seven residence halls that accommodate over 500 students. Residence halls include campus apartments and dormitory-style housing.

Central Methodist College is located in the small town of Fayette, Missouri (pop. 2,888). Students can easily walk into town to see a movie, eat out, or shop. Fayette is surrounded by rural beauty but is only 30 minutes from Columbia, the capital of Missouri and home to several large universities, museums, and cultural opportunities. Students at CMC have the best of both worlds: a beautiful, park-like campus with the security and safety of the suburbs, and accessibility to the city of Columbia.

Central Methodist College Academic Offerings

Accounting • Athletic Training • Biology • Business Adm. • Business Mgt. • Chemistry • Communication and Theater Arts • Computer Science • Criminal

Justice • Economics • Elementary Ed. • Foreign Languages • History • Interdisciplinary Studies • Mathematics • Music • Music Performance • Nursing • Philosophy • Physical Ed. • Physics • Political Science • Psychology • Public Service • Recreational Adm. • Religion • Secondary Ed. • Sociology • Teacher Certification

Admissions Statement

Applicants are selected on the basis of academic preparation, aptitude for college study, character, and motivation. Students accepted for admission to Central Methodist College usually have completed a college preparatory program with at least a 2.0 cumulative GPA on a 4.0 scale. A suggested preparatory program of high school courses would include four units of English, three units of mathematics, and two units of science, foreign language, social studies, and humanities.

Chadron State College

Chadron, Nebraska 69337
(308) 432-6221

Chadron State College is nestled between a national forest and a park. The college has a friendly and inviting small-town environment, yet offers many big-time opportunities that will expand any student's horizons. Academically, the college offers 56 undergraduate degree programs; sponsors faculty-led study-abroad programs in Belgium, Japan, London, and Mexico; and provides a flexible yet challenging Cooperative Education/Internship Program.

Located less than an hour from the Black Hills of South Dakota, the campus has recreational activities that can challenge your limits and stretch your imagination. The 67 college clubs and activities provide leadership opportunities and alternative ways for students to learn. For more than 80 years, this Nebraska state college has provided outstanding educational opportunities to students from all over the Midwest.

Academics

Degrees Offered: Bachelor's, Master's
Undergraduate Majors: 25+
Student/Faculty Ratio: 18 to 1

An honors program, strong core curriculum, Student Success Services, and dedicated faculty are all characteristics of the Chadron State education. Although it is a state college, classes are relatively small: the student/faculty ratio reflects the individual attention students get in the classroom.

Chadron provides the academic environment that meets the needs of both honors students and average students. The Honors Program at Chadron is unique. It is conducted entirely by small seminars and organized around a "Great Books" format. Students can apply for admission into the highly competitive program in their first year or later semesters. For students who need additional assistance with college-level courses, Chadron has created Student Success Services, which provides tutorial assistance, a variety of college level courses that help students maximize their potential, and individual and small-group evening study and help sessions.

At the heart of all degree programs at Chadron State is the core curriculum. It is composed of 47 credits in general studies courses that include the arts, humanities, communication, composition, ethics, and global studies. With this intellectual background students can then choose from over 25 major and 75 minor areas to develop an academic program that is right for them.

Three popular majors at Chadron State are education, justice studies, and business. In every area, Chadron has emphasized the quality of its academic programs and has received national recognition for many of its departments. The physical education teacher preparation program is only one of 70 in the nation to be accredited by the National Association of Sports and Physical Education. The justice studies program at Chadron allows students to choose a criminal justice or legal studies concentration, and the business major includes concentrations in unique areas like agri-business, office management, and real estate in addition to the usual management, marketing, accounting, and economics areas.

Students and Student Life

2,600 undergraduates from 36 states and 13 foreign countries
21% are from out-of-state
5% are students of color
1% are international
35% live on campus

Approximately 2,600 undergraduate and 700 graduate students attend classes on the Chadron State College campus. The majority of these students come from Nebraska, Wyoming, South Dakota, Colorado, and other Midwestern states.

The university offers campus-wide activities directed toward the interest of the students. Some of the more popular activities center around physical endeavors like intramural sports, mountain biking, Rodeo Club, and hiking, and performing arts like theater, jazz band, and choral groups. Although located in a rural area, there is a lot to do on campus. The Student Senate and Campus Activity Board schedule cultural, recreational, and social events. One recent graduate commented, "There was always something going on on campus. We had popular country music performers, the Omaha Symphony Orchestra, and major theater performances, in addition to the usual dances, singers, and entertainers that appear regularly on campus." In all, the college sponsors more than 60 clubs and activities.

Athletics: Rocky Mountain Athletic Conference, NCAA Division II
Women's Teams: basketball, golf, track & field, volleyball,
Men's Teams: basketball, football, track & field, wrestling

Campus and Community

The 281-acre campus of Chadron State College is located within walking distance from town. Chadron, although not a booming metropolis, has its share of restaurants, clubs, and activities. The college is located in the northwest corner of the state, in an area noted for its scenic beauty and pioneer history. The Nebraska National Forest is about five miles from campus and the Pine Ridge National Recreation Area is only a short distance away.

The picturesque campus houses 25 academic and residential buildings amid tall pine-clad buttes. The Reta E. King Library is centrally located on campus and is connected via computer to all the academic and residential halls. Students can access the Net or search the library reference books right from their dorm room. The Physical Activity Center is another popular place on campus. It has a six-lane indoor track; five racquetball courts; athletic facilities for basketball, volleyball, and tennis; a gymnastics room, and wrestling facilities.

There are a variety of residential accommodations on campus, including an 11-story high-rise dorm, several halls with suite accommodations, and apartment housing. There is also a special Honors Hall where academically talented students can choose to live.

Chadron State College Academic Offerings

Art • Aviation • Biology • Business Adm. • Chemistry • Clinical Laboratory Science • Education • Educational Media • Elementary Ed. • English • Health and Physical Ed. • History • Human Ecology • Human Services • Industrial Technology • Interdisciplinary Studies • Justice Studies • Mathematics • Music • Natural Science • Physics • Psychology • Range Mgt. • Recreation • Social Science • Social Work • Speech Communication • Theater

Admissions Statement

All students seeking admission for enrollment in a degree-granting program should be a graduate of an accredited high school, complete a college preparatory program, and take the ACT or SAT exam.

Chowan College

Murfreesboro, North Carolina 27855-9902
(919) 398-4101 or (800) 488-4101

Chowan College is the second oldest of North Carolina's seven Baptist colleges. Since its establishment in 1848 the college has expanded its academic programs and established itself as a noted Christian college. Chowan meets the diverse academic needs of its students by offering both associate and bachelor's degrees, allowing students to incorporate a minor concentration into their degree program, and providing a strong liberal arts foundation. It provides an educational environment that is comfortable, yet enriching and challenging, where all students can develop socially, spiritually, and intellectually. Small classes, taught by faculty members who are invested in their students' success, make Chowan a special place.

Academics

Degrees Offered: Associate, Bachelor's

Undergraduate Majors: 12

Student/Faculty Ratio: 12 to 1

Number of Faculty: 67

Chowan College has developed majors that combine liberal arts and career-oriented subjects. For almost 60 years the college offered associate degrees exclusively. When it decided to establish bachelor's degree programs, it carefully built upon its success and reputation by developing only those programs that would reflect the high academic quality for which the college is noted. Although Chowan expanded its curriculum, it did not lose its student-centered focus, nor its commitment to providing a quality education.

Each bachelor's degree program includes 54 credits in general education courses that are chosen from traditional course offerings like English, social sciences, laboratory sciences, speech, mathematics, and computer science, and comprehensive knowledge in a major field. Most degree programs center around prescribed courses that are universally recognized as important elements within the major and include an upper division independent study or internship.

Students and Student Life

> 647 students from 26 states and 13 foreign countries
> 58% are from out-of-state
> 25% are students of color
> 80% live on campus in 6 residence halls

The college provides a family-like atmosphere where students take pride in their accomplishments and learn from one another. Co-curricular activities are looked upon as another way of learning and developing socially. With more than 40 clubs and organizations, students have a lot to choose from, including student government, newspaper, literary magazine, yearbook, and Baptist Student Union.

Athletics: NCAA Division III
Women's Teams: basketball, cheerleading, soccer, softball, tennis, volleyball
Men's Teams: basketball, cheerleading, football, golf, soccer, tennis

Campus and Community

Chowan is located in Murfreesboro, North Carolina (population 6,000) and is 60 miles from Norfolk. The beaches of Virginia and North Carolina are within easy reach. The 289-acre campus is a combination of woodlands and park-like surroundings.

The beautiful Lake Vann borders the campus, and the more than 20 major buildings reflect the evolution of the college including a beautiful antebellum mansion, contemporary classroom buildings, and six residence halls. The Helms Center provides a variety of recreation and sports facilities including a gymnasium, Olympic-size pool, and several basketball and racquetball courts. The Camp Science building has updated laboratory facilities and a large computer lab, and the Graphics Center is equipped with the latest in imaging technology.

Chowan College Academic Offerings

Associate Degrees: Accounting • Business Adm. • Computer Information Systems • Liberal Arts • Merchandise Mgt. • Music • Music Business • Printing Production & Imaging Technology • Social Studies

Bachelor's Degrees: Applied Science • Art Ed. • Business Adm. • Education • Graphic Design • History • History/Social Studies Ed. • Liberal Studies • Mathematics • Music/Music Ed. • Physical Ed./Sports Mgt. • Physical Ed./ Sports Science • Printing Production & Imaging Technology • Religion • Science • Science Ed. • Studio Art

Admissions Statement

Admission requirements include graduation from secondary school or GED and 19 units including four in English, three in mathematics, two in science, one in science lab, two in social studies, and one in history. Students must have a minimum SAT score of 800, rank in the top half of their class, and have a minimum GPA of 2.0.

Colby-Sawyer College

New London, New Hampshire 03257-4648
(603) 526-3700 or (800) 272-1015

The learning environment at Colby-Sawyer College provides individualized attention, faculty mentors, small classes, and a picturesque, safe New England campus. The social environment is enlivened by an active student body; a host of clubs, activities, and organizations; and splendid opportunities to grow and develop personally.

Colby-Sawyer is the kind of college where students begin to realize and actualize their potential. Through the assistance of an involved, accessible, and learned faculty, students are guided toward their educational goals. No large lecture halls here, just small, interactive classes where every student's comments and opinions are heard and discussed. Internships are strongly encouraged and students can expand their educational base through opportunities to study abroad or classes at other colleges in New Hampshire or Washington, D.C. Colby-Sawyer has developed a living, learning community where students can discover who they are and where they're going and prepare for a career.

Academics

Degrees Offered: Associate; Bachelor of Arts, Fine Arts, Science

Undergraduate Majors: 13

Student/Faculty Ratio: 14 to 1

Number of Faculty: 70

Average Class Size: 18

If you think that this small New Hampshire college is miles away from the real world, read on. Colby-Sawyer College has placed recent interns with top-rated corporations and organizations like American Express, Amnesty International, the Buffalo Bisons, Conde Nast Publications, NBC News, and Walt Disney World. The modern graphic-design studio has a graphic darkroom, CD-ROM, video camera, and scanners (both black-and-white and color). Its computer lab houses full-color Macintosh computers with capabilities for page layout, digital imaging, and the creation of dimensional art. Seniors have served internships at graphic-design firms throughout the country because of their training on this equipment.

Colby-Sawyer students have participated in student-exchange programs at the Franklin College in Lugano, Switzerland, and the college has a network of more than 11,000 alumni across the country. It may be a small college and it may be in New Hampshire, but it definitely will prepare you for the real world!

The curriculum at Colby-Sawyer College is designed to prepare students for careers or for further study in graduate school. While courses in each specific major are concentrated and focused, the general education curriculum is designed to broaden students' education. The college has developed a 41-credit liberal arts immersion through which students develop proficiency in writing, mathematics, and computing skills.

The courses that make up the liberal arts core cross content areas and give the student an interdisciplinary look at the fundamental ways knowledge is constructed, collected, and used in decision making. Courses in creative expression, judgment and belief, and the process of discovery are woven into the exploration of the fine arts, humanities, natural sciences, and social sciences, providing a solid academic base. Graduates are competent, well-educated professionals.

The college works just as hard to prepare students for careers as it does to provide a top-notch education. The Harrington Center for Career Development has a four-year sequence of events and programs that teaches students to clarify interests, abilities, values and goals, plan courses and career-related experiences, explore internships and other work-related opportunities, develop a resume, research possible employers, and participate in on-campus and off-campus job fairs and interviews. The college also has a program in which students work closely with their advisors to design a major that matches their own personal and career goals and interests.

Students and Student Life

700 students from 27 states and 6 foreign countries
4% are students of color
4% are international
600 live on campus in 10 residence halls

The center of campus activity generates from the residence halls where almost all Colby-Sawyer students live. With such a significant population of resident students, the college has activities going on days, nights, and weekends. A sampling of some of the special interest clubs, associations, and volunteer opportunities include Key Association, Choices (an alcohol- and drug-awareness program), Dance Club, Environmental Action Committee, Film Society, Outing Club, and much more.

The student newspaper *The Courier* and the radio station keep students up-to-date on campus-wide activities and news. Volunteer programs are offered through the Adopt-A-Grandparent program, Habitat for Humanity, and Special Olympics. Professional organizations like the Student Nurses Association and the Art Student's League bring professional speakers and programs to campus.

The gorgeous campus and the beautiful surroundings encourage any and all recreational activities. There's skiing, mountain climbing, horseback riding, tennis, boating, and many other outdoor activities right in the area.

Athletics: NCAA Division III. Men's and women's alpine skiing is Division I
Women's Teams: alpine ski racing, basketball, lacrosse, riding, soccer, tennis, track & field, volleyball
Men's Teams: alpine ski racing, baseball, basketball, riding, soccer, tennis, track & field

Campus and Community

The 80-acre campus is located on the crest of a hill in New London, New Hampshire, the heart of the Dartmouth–Lake Sunapee region. Old Academy, the oldest building on campus, was built in 1838. It was the original home of Colby Academy and now serves as a meeting place for college social functions. In contrast, Rooke Hall, completed in 1994, is a modern residence facility which provides apartment-style living for over 100 upperclass students. The campus blends both architectural venues well and surrounds all the buildings with the beauty of the New Hampshire countryside.

There is a large Health and Sports Center with classrooms, offices, and laboratories for the Sports Science department. The Sawyer Fine and Performing Arts Center is the place for theatrical performances, art studios, and the modern graphic design studio. The Reichhold Science Center offers students exceptional laboratory and classroom areas and has space for students to conduct individual research and experimentation. In all, there are 15 academic buildings and 10 residence halls. Students can reside in traditional-style halls, apartment-style accommodations, or a small house that accommodates eight students. The campus is a total living/learning center with outstanding facilities and accommodations.

The Dartmouth–Lake Sunapee region is home to some of the finest outdoor recreational sites in the state. Students can visit or attend social events at several other colleges and universities in the area: Dartmouth College, the University of New Hampshire, New England College, and New Hampshire College are all less than an hour's drive.

Colby-Sawyer College Academic Offerings

Art • Biology • Business Adm. • Child Development • Communication Studies • English • Graphic Design • Nursing • Psychology • Sports Science, with specializations in athletic training, exercise science, sports management • Teacher Certification: art ed. (K-12), biology secondary ed., early childhood ed. (K-3), English secondary ed., social studies secondary ed.

Admissions Statement

Admission to Colby-Sawyer College is based upon a careful review of all credentials presented by the candidate. The quality of an applicant's secondary school achievement, especially during the last two years, is the primary factor in the selection process. The Admissions Office also places emphasis on the required essay, counselor and teacher recommendations, extracurricular activities, and the results of standardized testing.

The College of Santa Fe

Santa Fe, New Mexico 87505
(505) 473-6133 or (800) 456-2637

The College of Santa Fe is a very unique school. It is the largest private college in the state of New Mexico and has a history spanning more than 100 years. It is a place where students can discover themselves, their talents, beliefs, and values. The college is located in the artistically and historically rich city of Santa Fe, New Mexico (7,000 feet above sea level), and its curriculum presents the liberal arts as lively, enriching, and relevant life subjects. The 60 professors who teach at the college are interesting and educated, and their small, friendly classes stimulate discussion and make students participate actively in the learning process. All of this on a serene, expansive campus where students can be themselves and yet reach beyond their limits.

Academics

Degrees Offered: Associate, Bachelor's, Master's

Undergraduate Majors: 40+

Student/Faculty Ratio: 14 to 1

Number of Faculty: 60 full and part time

The curriculum at the College of Santa Fe focuses on developing students who can challenge new ideas, learn to think for themselves, and expand their base of knowledge. A liberal arts education is the core of every program, because no matter what career students choose, they will have to think logically, analyze problems, make ethical choices, and communicate clearly.

But the liberal arts at CSF is not about reading Shakespeare, memorizing the scientific symbols for water and helium, or knowing all the Civil War battles in numerical order. It is about discovering the relationships among subject areas; charting the progress of man in terms of his social, ethical, political, and mechanical achievements; and hearing the fugue within a musical composition. Courses like science and sense, thinking about the universe, prophets and poets of the Old Testament, and science fiction are all included in the 45-credit liberal arts core.

Even the design of course majors is different at CSF. The college offers eight specific academic areas, and students have several major options within an area. The eight academic areas are art, business, education, humanities, moving image arts, performing arts, science and mathematics, and social science. Students who are interested in exploring a more unique program may work with their advisor and other faculty members to design an independent major.

The emphasis in every academic area is on a student-centered education. Classes are small with less than 25 students in most courses. The student/faculty ratio is small, and a major component of almost every course is class participation. The college has several unique and intensive opportunities for students to "practice" their major. The New York Arts program is one example. Selected students are placed with studio artists or in internships/apprenticeships with various museums, galleries, or art organizations, giving them an intimate and realistic view of the world of the established professional artist in New York City.

The London Semester, designed by the Performing Arts Department, places selected students in London for intensive theater study with leading actors, directors, and playwrights of the British stage. Through the integration of experiential learning and the liberal arts in all academic areas, the College of Santa Fe has created a dynamic curriculum and delivery system in which students learn by doing.

Students and Student Life

700 students from 42 states and 8 foreign countries
60% are from out-of-state
34% are students of color
3% are international
350 live on campus

The College of Santa Fe has a culturally rich student body and attracts students from many different heritages including Native Americans, Hispanics, African Americans, and Asian Americans. Campus activities tend to focus on professional and departmental clubs, recreational sports, and cultural programs. The college does not sponsor any intercollegiate teams, but does have a large, active outdoor recreational program that includes rafting in the Rio Grande, skiing the Sangre de Cristo mountains, or hiking among the ruins of Bandelier National Monument.

Most students are involved in outdoor recreation. The Santa Fe area has activities for every season like horseback riding, biking trails, downhill skiing, snow boarding, hot-air ballooning, and just about any other outdoor activity. The Driscoll Fitness Center provides all the latest in fitness and recreational sports including racquetball and squash courts, a gymnasium, aerobic and weight rooms, and a walking track. The Shellaberger Tennis Center is one of the finest outdoor tennis facilities in the city.

Students at the college are very active in projects related to their field of study. Since all the majors offered at the college are labor intensive and span several disciplines, campus activities center on things like play rehearsal, dance practice, film editing, and preparing for one of the many art openings held at the campus gallery. There is a strong student government at the college, and members of the Associated Student Government sit on most college committees, attend all Board of Trustee meetings, and coordinate most of the student activities on campus.

Campus and Community

The College of Santa Fe is situated on a 98-acre campus in an urban area about 15 minutes by car from the historic Plaza, the center of Santa Fe. The city of Santa Fe is a mecca for the arts and has 200 art galleries, seven museums, 12 formal music festivals, and a multicultural center reflecting the influences of Indian, Hispanic, Anglo, and other ethnic groups. More than 60,000 people live in Santa Fe, and the city supports a host of restaurants, boutiques, fine arts events, and entertainment. It is, in all respects, a world-class tourist destination.

The campus is composed of 40 architecturally appealing buildings that capture the spacious feeling of the southwest and incorporate all the sophisticated modern technology necessary for the 21st century. The Fogelson Library houses online databases and Internet connections as well as print and microform materials. It also holds the Southwest Room (a unique local history collection), the John Lloyd radio collection (consisting of over 7,000 radio programs from the 1930s, '40s and '50s), and the Institute of American Indian Art Resource Center.

The Greer Garson Theater Center is one of the finest collegiate theaters in the country. It has a 500-seat theater, the 100-seat Weckesser Studio Theater, classrooms, dance studio, practice rooms, and costume and scene shop. The Garson Communications Center is home to the Moving Image Arts department and has classrooms, editing facilities, a multimedia computer lab, two student production studios, and two professional sound stages. It is also one of the finest and most innovative facilities for cinema studies on any college campus in the world, and has been used for the filming of Billy Crystal's *City Slickers*, Willem Dafoe's *White Sands*, and Kevin Costner's *Wyatt Earp*.

The three residence halls—La Salle, Martin Luther King, and St. Michael's— provide several different types of student accommodations. They are conveniently located in the quad area of campus where students can sit out on the lawn and soak up the sun or just enjoy the beautiful scenery.

College of Santa Fe Academic Offerings

Art: Art History • Art Therapy • Moving Image Arts: A comprehensive program that integrates cinema studies with film and video production • Studio Art: painting, drawing, photography, sculpture, print making

Business: Accounting Applications • Arts & Entertainment Mgt. • Computer Application Design • Environmental Mgt. • International Business and Mgt. • Organizational Mgt.

Education: Elementary or Secondary Education

Humanities: Creative Writing • English • Humanities • Religious Studies • Southwest American Studies • Technical Communication

Performing Arts: Acting • Contemporary Music • Design/Theater Technology • Music Theater • Performance • Production • Theater Mgt.

Science and Mathematics: Biology • Chemistry • Computer Science • Environmental Science • Mathematics • Pre-dental • Pre-med • Pre-veterinary

Social Science: Applied Psychology • Human Services • Organizational Psychology • Pastoral Studies • Political Science • Psychology

Admissions Statement

The college welcomes applications from high school seniors who have maintained a GPA of at least 2.5. Letters of recommendation, an essay, and a campus interview may be required of those with less than a 2.5.

Curry College

Milton, Massachusetts 02186-9984
(617) 333-2210 or (800) 669-0686

Curry College is a small residential institution located in the Boston suburb of Milton, Massachusetts. The college has a national reputation for providing an educational environment that helps students reach their full potential as learners and as successful citizens. Students are provided with every opportunity to succeed, from the small class size and student-centered living/learning residence halls, to the dedicated faculty who take a personal interest in students' lives. Experiential learning is an important part of the curriculum and the college's close proximity to Boston provides a wealth of opportunities. Because Curry is a small, student-centered college, the men and women who come here receive a personalized education that includes the resources, experiences, and academic programs that are right for them.

Academics

Degrees Offered: Bachelor's, Master's

Undergraduate Majors: 16

Student/Faculty Ratio: 12 to 1

Number of Faculty: 210 full and part time

Curry College offers bachelor of science and bachelor of arts degrees in 16 major and 23 minor areas in addition to graduate programs in education. The curriculum combines a central liberal arts core that is the basis for all majors and includes an international or multicultural component. The college has developed strong, career-focused majors and has committed outstanding facilities and resources to its undergraduate programs. These include an experiential education program in which students earn up to 30 credits, extensive academic support services, and a comprehensive Essential Skills Center that provides tutoring, workshops, and guidance in all academic areas.

The business-management curriculum, a popular major, offers a broad liberal education while teaching skills in planning, organizing, individual and group motivation, and effective decision making. The major provides seven areas of specialization, and students are encouraged to participate in a field experience. In recent years, Curry students have interned at Smith Barney, Reebok International, McDonalds Corporation, and The Limited.

The four-year baccalaureate nursing program at Curry College prepares men and women for professional practice at hospitals, schools, community and health agency settings. The program is accredited by the National League for Nursing. It accommodates both first-year students and students with prior preparation including licensed practical nurses and registered nurses. Clinical rotations through metropolitan hospitals, schools, mental health and community agencies provide Curry students with the latest nursing techniques and methodology. Sites include Beth Israel Hospital, Brigham & Women's Hospital, Children's Hospital, and Mass General Hospital.

No matter what major students choose, they will receive the knowledge, skills, and experience they need to succeed.

Students and Student Life

1,200 undergraduate students from 27 states and 23 foreign countries
6% are students of color
4% are international
60% live on campus

With Boston so close (seven miles) you might think that students would not be interested in campus activities, but at Curry it is not like that. The students are filled with energy and ideas. The Programming Board organizes coffeehouses, concerts, dances, films, fine arts, lectures, and many recreational activities in addition to sponsoring about 30 college clubs. There are religious organizations (including Hillel and the Newman Club), performance clubs, a growing international student organization, and eight professional associations.

The college has a student newspaper, *The Currier Times,* and magazine, *The Curry Art Journal.* WMLN 91.5 FM, the college's own award-winning radio station, broadcasts the latest news, sports, political coverage, and music daily. It has been cited for programming excellence by the Massachusetts Associated Press six years in a row. Sports facilities include basketball and volleyball courts; football, baseball, softball, and lacrosse fields; and 12 outdoor tennis courts. Almost all of the students participate in intramural sports, and the more competitive athletes play one of 11 intercollegiate sports.

Athletics: The Curry Colonels are members of the NCAA Division III.
Women's Teams: basketball, soccer, softball, tennis
Men's Teams: baseball, basketball, football, ice hockey, lacrosse, soccer, tennis

Campus and Community

I can't imagine a more ideal situation than a beautiful, 120-acre New England campus only seven miles from Boston, one of the top cities in the world! The campus is accentuated by rolling hills, shaded tree knolls, and flower beds. The redbrick buildings blend in nicely with the landscape.

The Curry campus is divided into north campus and south campus; each has both academic and residential buildings. The north campus houses the Levin Memorial Library, the Hafer Academic building, an outdoor pool, tennis courts, and several residence buildings. The south campus includes the Kennedy Academic Building, the Alumni Recreation Center, Drapkin Student Center, and additional residence halls. North and south campus are traversed by a 5,000-meter cross country and fitness trail.

All the buildings are well kept and the campus is spotless. Science labs are modern and classrooms are refreshingly bright and airy. The seven residence halls provide a variety of living accommodations and offer a community environment. Boston is accessible via the "T," and the college provides a shuttle-bus service to the station. Boston is a haven for over 100,000 college students, a mecca for the arts, and a financial hub. And it's all at Curry College's doorstep!

Curry College Academic Offerings

Biology • Business Mgt. • Chemistry • Communications • Criminal Justice • Education: preschool, elementary, moderate special needs • English • Environmental Studies • Health Ed. • Nursing • Philosophy • Physics • Politics and History • Psychology • Religion • Sociology • Visual Arts

Admissions Statement

Freshman students are selected on the basis of a combination of the following criteria: secondary school record, standardized test scores on the SAT 1 or ACT, recommendation of the secondary school, and the college readiness of the candidate.

Daemen College

Amherst, New York 14226-3592
(716) 839-8225 or (800) 462-7652

Located in a quiet suburb of Buffalo, Daemen College has all the characteristics that make college the experience of a lifetime. The curriculum focuses on career-oriented majors and includes opportunities for co-operative placements and internships. The small class environment allows students to question and discuss the issues. The lively campus environment encourages involvement and creates an atmosphere of friendship, energy, and enrichment. Buffalo, the second largest city in New York, is only a few minutes away and offers a wealth of cultural and educational benefits that include the Albright-Knox Art Gallery, Studio Arena Theater, the Philharmonic Orchestra, and at least 10 other colleges and universities!

Academics

Degrees Offered: Bachelor's, Master's

Undergraduate Majors: 40+

Student/Faculty Ratio: 15 to 1

Number of Faculty: 150 full and part time

Every academic programs at Daemen College possesses four significant characteristics that shape the education students receive: a comprehensive course selection in each major, a logical and systematic progression of courses that link together and build on knowledge, a junior-year program that introduces students to the relevant reading material and analytical studies that exist within the major field, and a senior seminar taught with an interdisciplinary focus that relates the student's major to other components of the curriculum. Through this four-year process, Daemen students acquire an extensive background in their major, a liberal education that will strengthen and broaden the scope of their major field, and they participate in learning experiences that define and develop career skills.

At Daemen, major areas of concentration are chosen from one of four academic divisions within the college. They include the Business and Commerce Division, the Fine and Performing Arts Division, the Humanities and Social Science Division, and the Natural and Health Science Division.

The Business and Commerce Division curriculum is built around a rigorous core of professional courses that provide a foundation for all areas of business and develop skills necessary to succeed. Emphasis is placed upon ethics, computer literacy, analytical and research skills, and theoretical knowledge.

The Fine and Performing Arts curriculum provides a solid background in basic art disciplines in addition to studio concentrations in painting, printmaking, sculpture, graphic design, and drawing/illustration. With 10 professional art studios available for student use and one of the largest bronze-casting foundries of any college in the country, the fine-arts facilities at Daemen are outstanding.

All the majors in the Humanities and Social Science Division offer a broad intellectual foundation that enables students to become life-long learners. While many of these majors are not intended to provide preparation for a specific career, students can complete a minor in areas like communications, public relations, business, or take courses in technical skills like computers or graphic design. In this way students develop an educational portfolio that will provide excellent career preparation in a number of fields.

The curriculum in the division of Natural and Health Sciences combines a strong academic foundation in the sciences with practical knowledge through internships, research, or clinical experiences.

As you can see, the focus at Daemen College is on preparing students for careers, and the college does a very good job!

Students and Student Life

1,200 students from 16 states and 7 foreign countries
Less than 10% are from out-of-state
10% are students of color
3% are international
550 live on campus

While a majority of the 1,800 students at Daemen College come from New York and surrounding states, they bring with them a spectrum of different cultures, educational backgrounds, and talents. One third of the students attend college on a part-time basis. Many of these students are over 25. The 1,200 traditional age students are equally divided between commuting and residential students and in general the ratio of women to men is about 2:1.

The college sponsors over 22 clubs that include national and local sororities and fraternities, professional clubs, honor societies, student government, cheerleading, and athletics. Close to 600 students live in campus housing consisting of conventional dorm-style residences and campus apartments.

Because the college is located in close proximity to Buffalo many students view the city as an extension of the campus. The city, which is minutes from campus, has dance clubs, coffee houses, movies, plays, lectures, museums, professional sports teams, and opportunities for part-time employment, co-ops, and internships. Between the activities, clubs, and organizations sponsored by the college and the enormous amount of events and activities that take place in and around Buffalo, students at Daemen might have a difficult time deciding what to do with their out-of-class time!

Athletics: NAIA
Women's Teams: basketball, soccer
Men's Teams: basketball, soccer

Campus and Community

Daemen College's 39-acre campus is located in Amherst, New York. Since the College was founded in the late 1940s the campus has a rather contemporary look. One of the newest buildings on campus is Schenck Hall; it is equipped with state-of-the-art laboratory facilities. Classrooms and academic areas throughout the campus are modern and equipped with technology for the 21st century. The Marian Library houses over 135,000 volumes in four floors of open stacks. The campus apartments consist of 19 modern, two-story buildings and provide a nice alternative to dorm living. The campus provides spacious grass areas and presents a colorful picture throughout the four seasons. It is a comfortable environment with a serene atmosphere and terrific access to Buffalo!

Daemen College Academic Offerings

Accounting • Art • Art Ed. • Biology • Business • Business Ed. • Chemistry • Communications/Public Relations • Drawing/Illustration • Early Childhood • Economics • Elementary Ed. • English • Environmental Studies • French • Graphic Design • Health Systems Mgt. • History and Government • Human Services • Humanities • International Business • Management • Marketing • Mathematics • Medical Technology • Natural Sciences • Nursing • Painting/Sculpture • Physical Therapy • Physician Assistant • Printmaking • Psychology • Religious Studies • Social Work • Spanish • Special Ed. • Sports Mgt. • Transportation • Transportation & International Business • Transportation & Travel Mgt. • Travel & Tourism

Admissions Statement

The Committee on Admissions places particular emphasis on evaluating the secondary school record, and results of the SAT 1 or ACT. Our students have a median high school average of 86 and combined SAT scores of 1100.

Dakota State University

Madison, South Dakota 57404-1799
(605) 256-5139 or (800) 952-3230

What makes Dakota State University stand out among other small state universities is its nationally recognized curriculum, which fully integrates computer theory, practice, and application into strong traditional academic programs. Computer science and systems technology are part of every major offered at the university. With over 500 fully networked PCs on campus, a student/computer ratio of 6 to 1, and access to the university computer network from every dorm room, students at Dakota State University are on the leading edge of information technology. Combine this with internships and co-op education experiences led by leaders in business and industry and you have the reason why so many Dakota State graduates are sought after by employers throughout the Midwest.

Academics

Degrees Offered: Associate, Bachelor's

Undergraduate Majors: 30+

Student/Faculty Ratio: 16 to 1

Number of Faculty: 68 full and part time

At Dakota State, students can choose from over 50 areas of study that lead to an associate or bachelor's degree. The majority of the programs offered at DSU are career oriented, but each one is well grounded in the liberal arts. Approximately 43 credits are taken in general education requirements and distributed in subjects like computer literacy, health, humanities, fine arts, language, science, and social sciences.

A common educational experience shared by most students is an internship or co-op program. More than 80 percent of all students at the university complete one of these experiential learning activities, where they gain professional experience and evaluate their talents and skills within their chosen field. In the past, Dakota students have been placed at internship sites with the U.S. Department of Agriculture, Citibank, and South Dakota Information Processing Services, in addition to public and private schools throughout the area and many of the finest hospitals in the state.

All students at DSU are taught by professors, not teaching assistants. Academic achievers can be invited into the university scholars program and can take honors courses during their freshman and sophomore years, honors seminars during their junior year, and may complete a senior thesis prior to graduation.

Students who need additional assistance with college-level courses can receive tutorial assistance from the Academic Resource Center or enroll in one of several academic skills courses in reading, study skills, and mathematics. In addition, most professors are available after class for questions and to advise students. Students who live on campus can also participate in the Residence Tutor program, which provides approximately 12 hours of tutoring per week in each dormitory. At Dakota State, learning is not limited to the classroom.

Students and Student Life

1,500 students from 32 states and 17 foreign countries
20% are from out-of-state
4% are students of color
1% are international
600 live on campus

Future writers, artists, teachers, entrepreneurs, and scientists are all part of the student body and the 40+ college activities reflect the vast interests, cultural backgrounds, and career ambitions of the 1,500 men and women enrolled at the university. There are more than 10 student organizations associated with academic disciplines like the business club, computer club, and literary club. Theatrical opportunities are available through student productions staged in the Arena Theater and the Dakota Prairie Playhouse and range from major stage productions to one act plays. The university also sponsors a concert band, jazz band, choir, and other instrumental and singing groups. Aspiring DJ's have their own campus radio station where they can play their favorite music, and literary students can write for the college newspaper, yearbook, or theater group.

DSU offers a variety of recreational, club, and intercollegiate sports. The school also sponsors club sports for men in weightlifting, soccer, and rodeo, and for women in rodeo and cheerleading. Well over 30 percent of the students participate in intercollegiate or club sports, and almost all students participate in the university's intramural sports program.

The Dakota Student Association Senate is another integral part of the university. The Senate is the voice of the students and representatives from the senate sit on all major committees involved in institutional governance. In addition, the Student Association Senate is a member of the South Dakota Federation of Student Governing Bodies, which provides an avenue for student communication with the Board of Regents and the public.

Athletics: South Dakota-Iowa Conference of the NAIA
Women's Teams: basketball, cross country, golf, softball, tennis, track, volleyball
Men's Teams: baseball, basketball, cross country, football, golf, tennis, track

Campus and Community

The 22-acre campus is located in Madison, South Dakota, a community of 6,500 people. The campus is compact and has 17 buildings. Computer technology is installed in all the academic buildings and students can access the college's computer network right from their dorm rooms. Several computer facilities are open 24 hours a day. The Karl E. Mundt Library has more than 200 online data bases and a direct online catalogue networking to 37 state-run library systems throughout the Midwest.

The four residence halls accommodate over 600 students and offer a variety of living arrangements, including suite-style rooms, coed halls, and single-sex halls. They are strategically located so that residential students have easy access to every area of campus. The Body Shop, a state-of-the-art wellness center, is a popular place on campus. Here students can work out in comfort. The athletic facilities include the Fieldhouse and Trojan Field, located two blocks from the main campus.

The town of Madison is less than an hour's drive from Sioux Falls, the state's largest city. Surrounding the Madison area are two glacial lakes and one of South Dakota's largest state parks. Students have easy access to all the great recreational opportunities in the area, including water-skiing, sailing, fishing, hunting, cross-country skiing, and snowmobiling.

Dakota State University Academic Offerings

College of Business and Information Systems: Accounting • Business Ed. • Computer Ed. • Computer Information Systems • Computer Science • Finance • Health Information Adm. • Information Systems • Management • Marketing • Materials Mgt. • Office Adm.

College of Education: Co-op Elementary/Early Childhood Certification • Elementary Ed. • Elementary Ed. and Special Learning & Behavioral Problems • Second Wind Certification

College of Liberal Arts: English Ed. • English for Information Systems • Fine Arts Adm. • Fine Arts Ed. (music or art focus) • Fitness/Wellness Mgt. • Health & Physical Ed.

College of Natural Sciences: Biology Ed. • Biology for Information Systems • Chemistry Ed. • Chemistry for Information Systems • Mathematics Ed. • Mathematics for Information Systems • Physics Ed. • Physics for Information Systems • Respiratory Care

Admissions Statement

For admission to baccalaureate degree programs, high school graduates must complete a college preparatory course requirement with an average grade of C (2.0), *or* demonstrate appropriate competencies in discipline areas where course requirements have not been met *and* rank in the top 60 percent of their high school graduating class, *or* obtain an ACT composite score of 18 or above, *or* obtain a high school GPA of at least 2.6.

Davis & Elkins College

Elkins, West Virginia 26241-3996
(304) 636-5850 or (800) 624-3157

Davis & Elkins College, founded in 1904, is a private liberal-arts institution affiliated with the Presbyterian Church USA. The college offers majors and programs "that will expand students' knowledge, prepare them for effective citizenship and creative leadership, and assist them to find meaningful life work." Through small interactive classes, a faculty of outstanding teachers who remain active in the forefront of their academic fields, and an educational environment that is supportive and academically challenging, students at Davis & Elkins receive an outstanding education.

The college is located on a gorgeous campus that provides top-rate academic and residential facilities where students can live and learn. A full schedule of campus activities and over 40 clubs provide opportunities to develop leadership skills; socialize with students, faculty, and area professionals; and develop lifelong friendships. The accent is on students, and the entire campus and college community are dedicated to their success.

Academics

Degrees Offered: Associate, Bachelor's
Undergraduate Majors: 33
Student/Faculty Ratio: 12 to 1
Number of Faculty: 55 full time

Davis & Elkins College is "founded on traditions and focused on success". The comprehensive liberal arts and sciences integrated into all majors gives students the insight and understanding necessary for a lifetime of creative thinking, while the career-oriented programs such as human services, accounting, and nursing give students professional skills and entree to the job market. As part of the general education core, students explore literature and the fine arts; develop an understanding of other cultures; gain insight into the major events in history, religion, and philosophy; and acquire experience in the natural and social sciences.

When students choose a major they begin an inclusive study of a particular field, from its basic foundation to its present existence and form. Throughout their education at Davis & Elkins, students are guided by faculty who are experts in their field and who bring real-word exposure to their students. The curriculum at the college is rigorous and exciting, and includes programs to assist students and enhance their academic progress.

The Academic Resource Center (ARC) located in Albert Hall is the center of support programs on campus. The professional staff works with students to strengthen their abilities and skills. Peer and professional tutoring is available, along with a computer laboratory and software programs in skills areas. Davis & Elkins also offers Head Start for College, an intensive month-long summer program designed for identified learning-disabled students. Courses include foundations of mathematics, writing, reading, and study skills.

While most students take four years to attain a bachelor's degree, Davis & Elkins has established an accelerated program in which bright students can earn their degree in three years. The degree program is planned so that students carry at least 17 to 18 credits each semester and complete nine semester hours during two full summer semesters. The Honors Programs is another way bright students can embellish their education. Students in the total Honors Program take a minimum of 21 honors credits throughout their degree program and complete a senior thesis and oral presentation. Students can also choose to enroll in a minimum of 12 credits of selected honors courses that interest them.

Other specific learning opportunities offered at Davis & Elkins include The Augusta Heritage Arts Workshop that takes place each summer. Students from all over the world come to the Davis & Elkins campus to participate in more than 100 classes in traditional folk music, dance, crafts, and folklore. Seniors majoring in science or mathematics can spend one semester at the Argonne National Laboratory working with scientists on research projects and attending advanced classes. The college also sponsors an extensive study abroad program and the Washington Semester Program.

Students and Student Life

900 students from 30 states and 12 foreign countries
8% are students of color
3% are international
50% live on campus in four residential halls

At Davis & Elkins College, students can participate in one or several of the 50 college clubs and activities. A full complement of individual and group sports and recreational activities is offered through the campus's intramural programs. The Boiler House Theater provides aspiring actors and actresses a place to practice their craft.

Literary students can write for the *Senator* (weekly newspaper), *Senatus* (yearbook), or *Aurora* (literary magazine). There is a campus radio station (WCDE-FM); academic and career-related organizations that sponsor activities, speakers, and programs; and seven sororities and fraternities with chapters on campus. Students can even join the West Virginia Highlanders Bagpipe Band or take piping and drumming lessons!

Athletics: NCAA Division II West Virginia Intercollegiate Athletic Conference (field hockey Div. I)
Women's Teams: basketball, cross country, field hockey, softball, tennis
Men's Teams: baseball, basketball, cross country, golf, soccer, tennis

Campus and Community

The 170-acre campus is located in Randolph County, West Virginia, the heart of a booming recreational area. The campus, surrounded by the tranquillity of mountains, exhilarating fresh air, and lush, green trees, reflects the beauty and serenity of the adjacent Monongahela National Forest.

The 20 major buildings on campus include Victorian mansions, traditional Georgian college halls, modern science facilities, and a state-of-the-art library. Graceland Hall and Halliehurst Hall are designated National Landmarks and are included on the National Register of Historic Places. In contrast, the campus also houses the fabulous Booth Library, constructed in 1992. Other facilities include the Student Center at Jennings Randolph Hall, the Boiler House Theater, the Eshleman Science Center, and the Kelly Observatory, which houses the campus telescope. There is also the 30-acre Robert E. Urban Nature Study Area, which is used as an outdoor teaching resource and preserve.

Davis & Elkins College Academic Offerings

Associate Degrees: Accounting • Business Administration • Computer Science-Business • Fashion Merchandising • Health-Care Mgt. • Nursing • Office Administration • Psychology & Human Services • Real Estate • Word Processing

Bachelor's Degrees: Accounting • Art • Biology • Biology & Environmental Science • Business Adm. • Chemistry • Communications • Computer Science • Economics • Education • Engineering • English • Environmental Science • Fashion Merchandising • Foreign Language • Forestry • Health • History • Hospitality Mgt. • Management • Marketing • Mathematics • Medical Technology • Music • Nursing • Physical Ed. • Political Science • Psychology & Human Services • Recreational Mgt. & Tourism • Religion & Philosophy • Sociology • Theater Arts

Admissions Statement

Students accepted for admission to Davis & Elkins College should be high school graduates who have completed a solid college prep program and who meet two of the following requirements:

1. Have an overall GPA of 2.0 or above (on a 4.0 scale),
2. Rank in the top 50 percent of their class,

    OR

3. Have a minimum ACT composite of 19 or SAT 1 combined score of 920.

Delta State University

Cleveland, Mississippi 38733-0001
(601) 846-4040 or (800) 468-6378

Delta State was created in 1925 as a regional teacher-training school. Over the past 70 years, the school has grown into a comprehensive university enrolling over 4,000 students in liberal arts and professional degree programs. Today this midsized university is located in the heart of the Mississippi Delta in the city of Cleveland. The area draws thousands of tourists each year, who come to enjoy the favorable climate and natural beauty. The students at Delta State have a great setting in which to study and mature. The more than 40 undergraduate majors offered at the school provide a stimulating educational environment, and the 100 clubs and organizations on campus afford opportunities for leadership, community service, and personal enjoyment.

Academics

Degrees Offered: Bachelor's, Master's, Specialist, Doctoral

Undergraduate Majors: 40+

Student/Faculty Ratio: 16 to 1

Number of Faculty: 270

Delta State University offers majors ranging from accounting and audiology to special education and speech pathology and almost everything in between. It is a teaching and research institution that emphasizes the liberal arts and professional studies. The 14 baccalaureate degrees provide 44 major areas of concentration in the arts and sciences, business, education, and nursing. With over 3,000 undergraduate students, it is large enough to offer a wide range of high-quality programs and small enough to provide a friendly environment, limited-enrolled classes, and opportunities for significant student-faculty interaction.

All the undergraduate programs at the university are organized into four divisions: the School of Arts and Sciences, the School of Business, the School of Education, and the School of Nursing. Common to all schools is a 44-credit general education requirement that encompasses courses in English, mathematics, fine arts, social sciences, speech, and laboratory sciences.

While each school offers different areas of study, they all provide an education that has been recognized for its quality and achievements. Graduates of the School of Business have some of the highest pass rates in the Southeast on the Certified Public Accounting Examination. The percentage of Delta State students accepted for medical, dental, and other health-science schools is far above the nation's average.

The Commercial Aviation program, accredited by the Federal Aviation Administration, is the only program of its kind in the state. The Music and Art departments have received national and international awards, and have achieved a reputations for excellence in the fine arts. Education majors at Delta State rank at or near the top in the state in scores achieved on the National Teacher Examination.

Students and Student Life

3,700 students from 29 states and 9 foreign countries
Less than 10% are from out of state
25% are students of color
2% are international
600 live on campus

The campus of Delta State University is a hub of activity because the university firmly supports the notion that the college experience should involve more than classroom learning. Through the student government, the school sponsors more than 100 different clubs and organizations. These include religious organizations like the Baptist Student Union, Canterbury Club (Episcopal), Wesley Foundation (Methodist), and Newman Club (Catholic); special interest clubs like Young Democrats, College Republicans, Outback and Kayak Club; and academic organizations like American Chemical Society, Psychology Club, and Financier's Club. The university also has a large and active Greek system. Over 25 percent of students are members of the six fraternities or six sororities.

Students interested in literary and performance-based activities have a wide choice. The university has three student-run publications including _The Delta Statement_ (the weekly student newspaper), a large theater organization called Delta Playhouse, and more than six different musical groups that encompass vocal and instrumental, classical, jazz, and contemporary styles. Renaissance, a contemporary vocal and instrumental group, tours Mississippi and the southern region annually. All of these extracurricular activities foster personal growth, leadership qualities, and social interaction among students. These activities, combined with the solid academic preparation offered at the university, provide students with the total Delta State experience.

> **Athletics:** NCAA Division II, Gulf South Conference, and the new South Intercollegiate Swim League
> **Women's Teams:** basketball, cross country, diving, fast-pitch softball, swimming, tennis
> **Men's Teams:** baseball, basketball, diving, football, golf, swimming, tennis

Campus and Community

The 274-acre campus has 44 academic and residential buildings, including an extraordinary commercial aviation flight-instruction center, the Sillers Coliseum (a unique round facility for basketball and other arena events), and the Wiley Planetarium. Other resources include Jobe Hall, with its experimental theater and 300-seat auditorium. Jobe Hall's complete stage area includes a counter-weight system, orchestra pit, make-up and dressing areas, and a fully equipped shop for scenery construction. The Wright Art Center contains sculpture, painting, drawing, and photography studios and shops; a large lecture hall; and exhibition areas for artwork. The Wyatt Gymnasium houses the division of Health, Physical Education, and Recreation.

The 14 residence halls include single-sex halls, freshman-only buildings, and 76 apartment units. All the rooms are comfortable and designed to meet the needs of students. Each building has a spacious lobby where students can enjoy socializing with friends while watching a favorite TV show or video. Individual rooms have phone and cable TV hookups.

Located in the city of Cleveland, in the heart of the Mississippi Delta, cultural resources are plentiful at Delta State. The Delta is the birthplace of the blues, and an annual blues festival attracts music fans from around the country. The numerous lavish ante-bellum mansions provide fascinating historical adventures, and the southern cuisine adds a delectable flavor to daily life. Other local activities include tennis, golf, hunting, and fishing. The Delta State campus is centrally located midway between Memphis, Tennessee and Jackson, Mississippi.

Delta State University Academic Offerings

> **Bachelor of Arts:** Art, with teacher certification option • English, with concentrations in oral communication or written communication • Foreign Language,

with teacher certification in French, German, or Spanish • History • Music • Political Science • Psychology • Social Work

Bachelor of Business Administration: Accounting • Computer Information Systems, with options in programmer/analyst or software specialist • Finance • General Business • Insurance and Real Estate • Management • Marketing • Office Administration

Bachelor of Commercial Aviation: Airway Science • Aviation Mgt. • Flight Operations

Bachelor of Fine Arts: Art, with emphasis in crafts, graphic design, interior design, painting, photography, sculpture

Bachelor of Music Education: Music Education, with concentration in instrumental music education, choral music/general music, vocal, keyboard

Bachelor of Science: Audiology and Speech Pathology • Biology • Chemistry, with options in ACS certified standard, teacher certification, health • Criminal Justice, with concentration in corrections or law enforcement • Environmental Science • Family and Consumer Sciences, with concentrations in child development, consumer relations, family financial planning, home economics education • Fashion Merchandising • Mathematics • Medical Technology • Nursing • Social Work

Bachelor of Science in Education: Biology • Business • Elementary • English • Health, Physical Education & Recreation • Mathematics • Social Science • Special Education, with options in mild/moderate handicapped or severely/profoundly handicapped

Bachelor of Science in General Studies: Audiology & Speech Pathology • Health, Physical Education & Recreation, with concentrations in sports information, sports management • History • Social Science, with concentrations in economics, geography, philosophy, political science, sociology

Delaware Valley College

Doylestown, Pennsylvania 118901-2697
(215) 345-1500 or (800) 2-DEL-VAL

The key to success in today's competitive job market is valuable work experience. At Delaware Valley College, internships and practicums are built into each major program so that students receive extensive practical work in their area of study. Many of these work opportunities are located on the 550-acre campus, which houses the Henry Schmieder Arboretum, a livestock farm, over 60 acres of horticulture crop plantings, a 49 stall horse barn, and 400 acres of agricultural research land.

Students can also take the commuter train that stops on campus into Philadelphia for internships or research opportunities. As one student commented, "My education here at Delaware Valley extends far beyond the campus, and my professors have introduced me to so many new things. I may be studying business, but I also like the shows at the Fels Planetarium, enjoy classic films, and visit the Philadelphia Museum of Art. I didn't even know about these places before I came to school here."

Academics

Degrees Offered: Associate, Bachelor's, Master's

Undergraduate Majors: 35+

Student/Faculty Ratio: 16 to 1

Number of Faculty: 106 full and part time

The 20 associate and bachelor's degree programs at Delaware Valley College center around a strong career education in agriculture, business, science, education, and the liberal arts. The curriculum integrates experiential learning, the liberal arts, and professional studies. The liberal arts core is comprised of 48 credits taken over the four-year period. It includes courses in speech, science, world cultures, mathematics, computer applications, and a cultural enrichment program.

Professional studies, the heart of every major, make up almost 70 percent of every degree program. Students usually begin taking courses in their major during their first year at the college. The course work in professional studies provides the necessary knowledge, skills, and experience in the technology of the subject field. It is correlated with a 24-week work experience which includes actual job training. This type of curriculum ensures that graduates of Delaware Valley are technically competent; skilled in the use of language, mathematics, and computers; and also have a broad appreciation for the liberal arts.

The college provides educational opportunities that engage students in active learning. The teaching methods used most often include demonstration, discussion, and group projects. As one student commented, "Here at Delaware Valley we learn by doing. Our classrooms are not lecture halls. They're more like demonstration areas where our professors work with us."

The facilities on campus are truly extraordinary. Delaware Valley College is one of only a few private colleges in the country to offer a comprehensive degree in agriculture, and it supports this major and all majors with outstanding technology, facilities, and professional instructors. Students work directly with the superintendent of livestock, crop production manager, and the superintendent of greenhouses at the campus facilities as part of their course work. The college provides an honors program for academically talented students and academic support services for academically challenged students.

Students and Student Life

1,300 students from 19 states and 3 foreign countries
32% are from out-of-state
4% are students of color
1% are international
800 live on campus

All students seem to share a strong work ethic and a desire to have fun. The 40 college clubs and organizations provide an opportunity for students to do both. The College sponsors a large number of clubs that are affiliated with a specific academic major or special interest within a major, like Future Farmers of America, Equine Club, and the Horticulture Society. These and other clubs promote leadership skills, establish friendships, and broaden students' exposure to real-world opportunities.

But not all clubs reflect students' career interests. The campus radio station, band, *Ram Pages* (newspaper), and TAG (Theater Arts Group) give students an avenue to show off their communication and performance skills. The three religious clubs on campus include the Newman Club, Christian Fellowship, and Hillel. The college is a member of the National Intramural Sports Association and offers a large intramural athletic program where students compete in touch football, volleyball, floor hockey, bowling softball, and a host of other activities.

Athletics: NCAA Division III and the Middle Atlantic States Collegiate Conference
Women's Teams: basketball, cross country, field hockey, soccer, softball, track & field, volleyball
Men's Teams: baseball, basketball, cross country, football, golf, soccer, track & field, wrestling

Campus and Community

Delaware Valley College is an exciting, active campus located in central Bucks County, Pennsylvania, about 30 miles north of Philadelphia and 70 miles south of New York City. The campus is situated in the gently rolling countryside of Pennsylvania, which is rich in historic tradition. The buildings on campus feature neo-Georgian architecture and are situated around a central green. The five residence halls accommodate over 800 students and offer a variety of living arrangements.

From a distance Delaware Valley College looks like many of the other beautiful colleges in the area, but once you set foot on campus you realize that there are more than just classrooms, residence halls, and a library! A major part of the campus is occupied by special facilities that support the educational growth of the students and provide actual career laboratories where students work. There is a large greenhouse complex that features five climatized areas, a large landscape design studio, and an arboretum that holds membership in the American Association of Botanical Gardens and Arboreta. Behind the campus railroad station is the Equestrian Center, the Dairy Science and Animal Biotechnology Center, and over 400 acres of farmland.

Students at Delaware Valley College live and study in a beautiful rural landscape and still have full access to big-city excitement. The commuter train stops right on campus and then continues on to the heart of Philadelphia.

Delaware Valley College Academic Offerings

Agriculture and Environmental Studies: Agribusiness • Agronomy and Environmental Science • Animal Science • Contracting & Management • Crops Production • Dairy Science • Equibusiness • Equine Science(*) • Floriculture • Food Science • Food Science and Management • Food Science • Food Service Mgt. • Horticulture • Landscape • Large Animal Science • Marketing and Management • Ornamental Horticulture & Environmental Design • Plant Science and Biotechnology • Production and Marketing • Small Animal Science • Soil and Environmental Science • Supply and Service • Sustainable Agriculture • Turfgrass Mgt.

Business and Computer Information Systems: Accounting • Business Adm. • Computer Information Systems Mgt. • Criminal Justice Adm. • Management • Management Information Systems • Marketing

Arts and Science: Animal Biology • Biology • Chemistry • English • Environmental Biology • Mathematics • Microbiology • Plant Biology • Secondary Education

(*) Two-year Associate degree

Admissions Statement

Each student's academic background, motivation, and ambitions are carefully considered to determine his or her potential for success at Delaware Valley College. Candidates for admission to the freshman class must be graduates of an approved secondary school or have earned the GED. Criteria used when making an admission decision are the transcript of academic work, rank in class, the SAT 1 or ACT, letters of recommendation, and a personal interview.

Dickinson State University

Dickinson, North Dakota 58601-4896
(701) 227-2175 or (800) 279-4295

Located just minutes away from the beautiful Badlands of North Dakota, Dickinson State University serves as a cultural, social, recreational, and intellectual center for the 90,000 residents of the West River region. Offering associate and bachelor's degree programs to over 1,600 students, the university recognizes the individuality of each student and provides a wide spectrum of educational opportunities. Small classes, dedicated faculty, and a large selection of course offerings are a few reasons why students like it here. The college was established in 1918 to train teachers, and the past 75 years have brought many changes to the campus. It now has university status, offers degrees in more than 25 areas, and consistently sends its men's and women's athletic teams to the regional competitions.

Academics

Degrees Offered: Associate, Bachelor's

Undergraduate Majors: 28+

Student/Faculty Ratio: 15 to 1

Number of Faculty: 100 full and part time

The foundation for every four-year degree program offered at the university is 39 semester hours of general education courses. The purpose of the general education curriculum is "to help students develop breadth of view and judgment in order to be more intellectually, socially, and culturally responsive as citizens, consumers, and leaders." Students fulfill this requirement by taking courses in five areas including communication, scientific inquiry, expressions of civilization, understanding civilizations, and individual health and recreation. Some course options within the general education curriculum include photography, theater experience, creative writing, concert band, and physical geography. These offerings expand the curriculum beyond the typical theoretical courses.

More than three quarters of all the classes offered on campus have fewer than 30 students, so the classes are interactive and student centered. The Stoxen Library has an automated online library system and students have access to educational and research institutions all over the country. In addition, all student dorm rooms have access to the main academic computer, e-mail, and the Internet.

The Student Support Services, located in May Hall, offers services for students of every academic background. Peer tutoring is available in all academic areas. Tutors are selected by their instructors, and trained in tutoring methods by professional staff. They earn academic credit while helping other students in a particular course. The Student Support Services also provides computerized career-planning programs and Graduate Admissions Test preparation. Several specialized courses are also offered for credit by the professional staff in addition to other educational services.

Students and Student Life

1,500 students from 22 states and 3 foreign countries
23% are from out-of-state
5% are students of color
2% are international
450 live on campus

Dickinson State University is the only four-year educational institution in the area. It attracts students from North Dakota, Montana, Wyoming, South Dakota, Minnesota, and Canada. Approximately 1,000 members of the student body are college age, and almost half of them live on campus. In addition, 500 adult students attend the uni-versity.

Student government is the official voice of the students and is made up of the Senate, the Campus Activity Board, and the Campus Program Committee. The Student Government funds and monitors all clubs and activities, and Senate members sit on almost every campus committee.

In all there are about 50 different clubs and organizations at Dickinson State. Two of the most popular activities are recreation and sports, which the university supports through its outstanding indoor and outdoor facilities. The Rodeo Club has an outdoor and state of the art indoor arena where the Blue Hawk Cowboys and Cowgirls practice and perform. Scott Gymnasium, renovated in 1995, provides ample space for all types of floor sports like basketball, volleyball, and wrestling.

Athletics: NAIA Division II, North Dakota Athletic Conference
Women's Teams: basketball, cross country, golf, rodeo, softball, tennis, track & field, volleyball
Men's Teams: baseball, basketball, cross country, football, golf, rodeo, tennis, track & field, wrestling

Campus and Community

The 100-acre campus is located in Dickinson, North Dakota, a small rural town with a population of about 16,000 people. The campus has over 20 buildings, including three residence halls and four apartment buildings. Students can choose single-sex or coed dorms and upperclass students can live in the campus apartments. Most of the academic buildings were constructed in the 1960s and 1970s and all have been up-dated periodically.

The university is located in Dickinson, which provides students access to shops, theaters, and restaurants. There are a lot of things to do in the area. The Theodore Roosevelt National Park and the historic town of Medora are located just 30 miles from campus. The Badlands offer miles of outdoor space to hike, camp, and ride horses and the Dakota Dinosaur Museum highlights the archaeological finds in the area. If you like horses, farming, and cattle ranching, you've come to the right spot. Dickinson is the rodeo capital of North Dakota.

Dickinson State University Academic Offerings

Accounting • Agriculture • Art • Biology • Business Adm. • Chemistry Computer Science • Elementary Ed. • English • French • German • History • Mathematics • Music • Nursing • Physical Ed. • Political Science • Psychology • Science • Secondary Ed. • Social Science • Social Work • Sociology • Speech • Theater • University Studies

Emporia State University

Emporia, Kansas 66801-5087
(316) 341-5465

Founded in 1863, Emporia State University was one of the first universities in Kansas. Over the past 100 years, the university has continued to be an innovator in the field of education. It is the only state educational institution in Kansas that has its own laboratory school (Butcher Children's School) where education majors can develop their skills. It has a large and growing international student body: More than 250 students from 65 different countries provide a global presence on the campus. It is the home of the Kansas Business Hall of Fame, where top entrepreneurs through-out the state are honored. It is also the institution where more than 40 percent of the school counselors and one fourth of the school administrators in Kansas earned their degree. Located in east-central Kansas, this midsize state university has made a name for itself throughout the Midwest.

Academics

Degrees Offered: Bachelor's, Master's, Doctoral

Undergraduate Majors: 55+

Number of Faculty: 300 full and part time

Emporia State University is a comprehensive institution that offers degree programs in areas as traditional as history and as modern as computer information systems. The three schools that make up the university are the School of Business, the College of Liberal Arts and Sciences, and the Teachers College. The university has also established the Center for Great Plains Studies, making ESU one of the few universities in the United States with extensive academic programs, public service activities, and research projects that center around the Great Plains of North America.

Emporia State classes are taught in a variety of learning environments, from small seminar courses to large lecture classes. There are over 270 full-time professors who teach and do research at the university, and it is not uncommon for some courses to use teaching assistants as part of the instructional mode.

Emporia State attracts students from many different educational backgrounds, and provides several educational services to meet their academic needs. The Reading Laboratory, staffed by a faculty member and graduate assistants, offers individualized instruction that focuses on improving reading comprehension, vocabulary, reading rate, time management, and study skills. The Mathematics Laboratory offers tutoring to all students experiencing difficulty in math classes.

At the Writing Center, students of all levels are able to get individual advice and tutoring in essay writing, including selecting and narrowing a topic, organizing and developing ideas, and editing the final copy. The center is staffed by specially trained graduate students and peer tutors. The university offers several prep courses in both math and English. To meet the needs of academically talented students, the university has a challenging honors program that includes honors level courses, interdisciplinary seminars, and opportunities to work one-on-one with faculty members.

Students and Student Life

4,500 students from 46 states and 65 foreign countries
Less than 10% are from out-of-state
10% are students of color
3% are international
1,000 live on campus

Approximately 4,500 undergraduates and 1,550 graduate students attend Emporia State University. The majority are from Kansas and neighboring states. The Associated Student Government sponsors more than 150 student organizations and some type of major happening almost every week. There are seven fraternities and four sororities that have chapters at ESU. The "Greeks" make up about 20 percent of the student body and all are involved in community service and campus activities. Fraternity and sorority houses are located within several blocks of campus and have residential facilities for many of the brother and sisters.

The university has a large recreational program that includes 30 organized intramural sporting events that occur throughout the school year, and a growing number of club sports including bowling, soccer, and rugby.

Residential life offers several options. Many upperclass students live in sorority or fraternity houses or in one of the campus apartments. The university has two large residence halls that house more than 1,100 students in a variety of living accommodations. Since a large number of students live on campus, social activities go on late into the night and on weekends. This is not a campus where students pack up and head home for the weekend.

Athletics: NCAA Division II, Mid-America Intercollegiate Athletic Association
Women's Teams: basketball, cross country, softball, tennis, track & field, volleyball
Men's Teams: baseball, basketball, cross country, football, tennis, track & field

Campus and Community

The Emporia State University campus is composed of over 30 academic, residential, and historic buildings located on over 200 acres of land in the northeast quarter of Kansas. The campus is home to Butcher Children's School, that serves as an elementary school for district children (grades K-4), and a laboratory school for Emporia education majors, the National Teachers Hall of Fame, and the historic One-Room School built in 1873. The academic facilities at the University are expansive and include Taylor Hall, with professional stage and orchestral facilities and seating for 1,200; the Eppink Art Gallery, where faculty and students can exhibit their art work; and the Peterson Planetarium.

The two housing complexes on campus include dormitory rooms and suites located in Twin Towers, residential facilities, and apartment-style living. Together these areas can house approximately 1,000 students. The town of Emporia has a population of 30,000 and provides a number of cultural and recreational facilities. Students have easy access into town and to the three metropolitan areas of the state—Wichita, Topeka, and Kansas City.

Emporia State University Academic Offerings

School of Business: Accounting • Business Adm. • Business Ed. • Computer Information Systems • Distributive Ed. • Economics • Finance • Financial

Planning • International Business Mgt. • Marketing • Office Ed. • Office Systems Mgt.

College of Liberal Arts and Sciences: Art • Biology • Botany • Chemistry • Communications • Computer Science • Dramatic Arts • Earth Science • Engineering • English • Environmental Biology • French • History • Journalism • Mathematics • Medical Technology • Microbial and Cellular Biology • Music • Nursing • Physical Science • Physics • Political Science • Social Science • Social Work Cooperative Program • Sociology • Spanish • Speech Communications • Statistics • Zoology

The Teachers College: Elementary Education, with concentrations in art, bicultural ed., early childhood special ed., health, language arts, mathematics, natural sciences, psychology, social sciences, special ed. • Psychology • Recreation • Rehabilitation Services Ed. • Secondary Education Certification in art, biology, business ed., chemistry, earth science, economics, English, foreign language, health ed., history, mathematics, music, physical ed., physical science, physics, political science/government, psychology, special ed., speech communication, social science, sociology/anthropology, theatre

Admissions Statement

Emporia State University admits all graduates of accredited Kansas high schools who have not had previous college work. Graduates of accredited high schools outside of Kansas who show promise of doing college work successfully will be admitted. The admission decision for an out-of-state student will be based on academic record and test scores.

Endicott College

Beverly, Massachusetts 01915
(508) 921-1000 or (800) 325-1114

Endicott College has made practical work experience a part of every associate and bachelor's degree program it offers. During the first two years of college, Endicott students spend each January working at jobs in their field. During the last two years, students spend an entire semester on an internship assignment. The college's proximity to Boston opens up a world of opportunities not only for internships but also for cultural, social, and entertainment possibilities. On campus, students have comfortable facilities, talented professors, and a community of friends that shape their education.

Academics

Degrees Offered: Associate, Bachelor's

Undergraduate Majors: 29 associate degree majors and 19 bachelor's degree majors

Student/Faculty Ratio: 11 to 1

Number of Faculty: 100 full and part time

There are two very special qualities that are part of an Endicott education: the academic support services and the well-established internship program. Student Support programs at Endicott are open to all students and take many different forms. The Academic Support Center provides one-to-one, group, or workshop programs. Tutoring sessions are available, along with a structured study program in several introductory courses. There are weekly math workshops where students can receive assistance in course work, homework, or general skills.

There is a strong peer-tutor program in place that has been nationally certified on an advanced level by the College of Reading and Learning Association. There are organized study groups led by trained upperclass students. Students are encouraged to participate at whatever level they feel is appropriate, and it is not uncommon to find "B" students participating in study groups so that they can become "A" students!

Endicott was one of the first colleges to believe that students working in their intended career areas could gain practical experience, sharpen their insight, and increase their marketable skills. They have been perfecting the internship program for more than 40 years. At the associate degree level, the Endicott Internship Program consists of a four-week, 140-hour, off-campus work experience completed during the January internship period. Two internships are required for graduation.

Bachelor's degree candidates complete a one-month internship in their junior year and a 12-credit, full-semester internship during their senior year. The senior year internship is coordinated with a senior seminar and regularly supervised by a faculty advisor. Internship sites in recent years have included the Boston Ballet Company, Bermuda Department of Tourism, Copley Plaza Hotel, Neiman-Marcus, Viking Penguin Publishing, Merrill Lynch, and the Smithsonian Institution. This integration of classroom theory and practical work experience has become a cornerstone of an Endicott education.

Students and Student Life

800 students from 25 states and 43 foreign countries
20% are students of color
11% are international
75% live on campus in 11 residential halls

Athletics, professional clubs, social organizations, and performance based activities are all a part of campus life at Endicott College. Students have more than 30 different clubs in which to participate. The student newspaper, photography club, and *Endicott Review*, the campus magazine, provide opportunities for students interested in literary activities, while the sailing club, fitness club, and numerous intramural sports are just a few ways students can channel their energy in sport activities.

Athletics: NCAA Division III and the Eastern College Athletic Conference
Women's Teams: basketball, cross country, fast-pitch softball, field hockey, lacrosse, soccer, tennis, volleyball
Men's Teams: baseball, basketball, fast-pitch softball, lacrosse, soccer, tennis

Campus and Community

The 150-acre campus is located in Beverly, Massachusetts, just 20 miles from Boston. The campus straddles Hale Street. On one side a pond, wooden bridge, and several academic and residential buildings are set off from the street. On the other side, the campus stretches right to the Atlantic Ocean, where the students have their own beach.

The more than 20 buildings on campus include a variety of architectural styles, from one of the oldest structures in the area (Winthrop Hall) to the modern townhouse apartments built in 1988. Like Winthrop Hall, several other campus buildings were originally private residences dating back to the 1920s and '30s. The college has restored all of them, preserving their unique character and charm. Endicott College facilities include the Art Center, which includes studios, classrooms, and exhibit areas; the Student Center, which is the hub of student activities; and the Academic Center, where many classrooms, labs, and several residence halls are located.

Endicott College Academic Offerings

Associate Degrees: Accounting • Advertising • Allied Health • Athletic Training • Business Adm. • Communications • Criminal Justice • Culinary Arts • Early Childhood Ed. • Fashion Design • Fashion Marketing • Graphic Design • Hotel/Restaurant • Interior Design • Liberal Arts • Nursing • Paralegal • Photography • Physical Ed. • Physical Therapist Assistant • Psychology • Radio/TV • Retailing • Sports Mgt.

Bachelor's Degrees: Advertising/Visual Communications • Business Adm. • Communications • Elementary Ed. • Entrepreneurial Studies • Fashion Merchandising/Retailing • Fine Arts • Graphic Design/Visual Communications • Hotel/Restaurant Adm. • Interior Design • Liberal Studies • Nursing • Physical Ed. • Psychology • Psychology/Athletic Training • Psychology/Criminal Justice • Psychology/Public Relations • Retailing • Sports Mgt. • Visual Communications

Admissions Statement

Endicott College demonstrates a commitment to enrolling students from a wide geographic range as well as from all ethnic and racial heritages. When considering candidates for admission the committee looks at the entire individual. In addition to reviewing the application and student essay, the committee concentrates on a student's academic record, recommendations, extracurricular activities and test scores.

Eastern New Mexico University

Portales, New Mexico 88130
(505) 562-2178 or (800) 367-3668

Eastern New Mexico University is a dynamic learning community dedicated to providing quality education through small classes, close student-faculty relationships, and cultural diversity. The university has been designated by the state of New Mexico as the Center for Teaching Excellence. Its 60-year history reflects the university's commitment to the educational, public service, and research needs of the area. Through openness to innovation, scholarly research, and the integration of technology within the curriculum, Eastern New Mexico has made a dynamic impact on the educational system in the state. With more than 40 majors, two campuses, and more than 3,000 full-time undergraduate students, the university has come a long way from its beginnings as a two-year college.

Academics

Degrees Offered: Associate, Bachelor's, Master's
Undergraduate Majors: 40+

Student/Faculty Ratio: 22 to 1

Number of Faculty: 180

Eastern New Mexico is the third-largest university in the state. Each semester more than 250 undergraduate courses are offered. The university is proud of the fact that more than 93 percent of all classes are taught by professors, and that teaching assistants usually teach physical education classes or the laboratory components of courses.

The curriculum at Eastern is designed to prepare students for a lifetime of learning and responsible citizenship. Incorporated into each degree program is approximately 50 credits in general education courses like communications, life science, mathematics, human social behavior, humanities, fine arts, and physical education. One student said, "The general education requirements introduced me to subjects I would not have taken. Now that I'm close to graduating I see how those liberal arts courses broadened my scope of things and let me see beyond my major."

The university provides educational programs for a broad range of students. The Platinum Honors Program is a four-year, 23-credit curriculum that brings together outstanding students and talented faculty in an innovative educational process that combines special courses with intellectual and social events, and culminates in a senior project. The Learning Support area of Student Academic Services provides advising, tutoring, and microcomputer labs. Tutors are trained and certified by the College Reading and Learning Association and provide tutoring at no cost to the student.

Students who want to add an off-campus experience to their university education have two programs to choose from. The National Student Exchange allows eligible sophomores, juniors, and seniors to spend a semester or two at one of 90 colleges throughout the U.S. For a more global experience, the International Educational Exchange enables ENMU students to complete a semester or year of study at selected universities in England, Japan, Canada, and other countries.

Students at Eastern also have access to another off-campus educational facility. Seven miles from campus, the Blackwater Draw National Site provides wonderful opportunities for students interested in museumology, archaeology, and anthropology. Noted archaeologists have dated some of the artifacts found here from the Early Man Period, dating back 12,000 years.

Students and Student Life

3,500 students from 50 states and 22 foreign countries

25% are from out-of-state

28% are students of color

3% are international

1,400 live on campus

Approximately 3,500 undergraduate and 700 graduate students are enrolled at ENMU. The university's residential population is close to 50 percent of the undergraduate students. The variety of dormitory facilities on campus represent almost every type of housing accommodation. There are singles, doubles, suites, apartments, and honors, single-sex, and coed halls. Many of the residence halls are new, and older halls have been renovated in a timely fashion. Student rooms are cable-ready and equipped to access the online advanced computer library, allowing students to search the library acquisitions and do research right from their dorm rooms.

With over 100 organizations on campus, students at ENMU can participate in cultural, religious, educational, or recreational activities all year round. The campus has a safe, friendly environment and is the center of activity seven days a week. Since over 85 percent of the men and women at ENMU are full-time students, Greek life, student government, intramural sports, and professional clubs are popular ways in which students develop leadership skills, grow in self-esteem, and just have fun with their friends.

Athletics: NCAA Division II, Lone Star Conference. Rodeo team competes in the National Intercollegiate Rodeo Association, Southwest Region.
Women's Teams: basketball, riflery, tennis, volleyball
Men's Teams: baseball, basketball, football, riflery

Campus and Community

The 400-acre campus is located in Portales, on the far-eastern side of the state. The city of 12,000 sits in a valley rich in agriculture and ranching. The climate is one of the most favorable in the country: The winters are dry and mild, the summers pleasant with cool nights. The entire region enjoys bright sunshine all year long.

The spacious campus at ENMU is a combination of traditional buildings and modern structures. The 84 collegiate buildings are centered around a large pedestrian mall. Several of the more notable buildings in the main area of the campus include the University Theater Center, which houses a 420-seat proscenium theater and 250-seat experimental theater; the Broadcast Center, which includes three 100,000-watt stations; and the Golden Library, a computer-enhanced library that also serves as a depository for U.S. and New Mexico government documents. The Greyhound Sports Arena, baseball diamond, and track are located across the street, along with the West Campus Apartments.

The area around Portales provides many recreational opportunities for ENMU students. There is skiing about three hours away, boating and swimming areas within an hour and a half, and miles of hiking trails. Albuquerque, Santa Fe, and Taos are within a four-hour drive, and the cities of Lubbock and Amarillo, Texas are two hours away.

Eastern New Mexico University Academic Offerings

Accounting • Agricultural Business • Anthropology • Art • Biology • Business Adm. • Chemistry • Communications • Communicative Disorders • Computer Science • Computer Information Systems • Economics • Education • English • Finance • Geology • History • Home Economics • Human Resource Mgt. • Marketing • Mathematics • Medical Technology • Music • Nursing • Physical Ed. • Physics • Political Science • Psychology • Religion • Social Studies • Sociology • Spanish • Student-Designed Program • Technology • Theater • University Studies • Wildlife and Fishery Science

Admissions Statement

Eastern New Mexico University is committed to the policy of providing educational opportunities to all qualified students. To be considered for admission to the University a student should have a high school GPA of 2.5 or higher OR a score of 21 or above on the ACT (860 or above on the SAT) OR a high school GPA of 2.0 to 2.49 and an ACT score of at least 20 (SAT score of at least 800).

Eastern Oregon State College

LaGrange, Oregon 97850-2899
(541) 962-3393 or (800) 452-8639

Eastern Oregon State College is a small public institution that provides a strong community environment which fosters opportunities for academic and personal growth. Diverse course offerings, quality programs, small classes, and professors who involve their students in the learning process are all part of the education students receive at Eastern Oregon State College.

Founded in 1929, the college has grown significantly from its early beginning as a teacher's college. Today the school offers two associate and 21 bachelor's degree programs and the master's of arts in teacher education. With approximately 2,000 students and a 121-acre campus that is nestled amid the gorgeous Blue Mountains, the college is noted for the fact that it is "large enough to offer diversity and quality, yet small enough to preserve individuality and personal warmth."

Academics

Degrees Offered: Associate, Bachelor's, Master's

Undergraduate Majors: 22

Student/Faculty Ratio: 14 to 1

Number of Faculty: 147

Eastern Oregon State College offers degree programs that incorporate classroom theory and experiential learning. While many of the majors are career oriented, all students receive a solid liberal arts education as part of the core curriculum. The college's general education curriculum is flexible, yet it provides an introduction to many liberal arts areas. Students can take 15 credits in each of four areas: humanities, natural science, social science, and arts, language, and logic. There are over 20 courses in each area from with to choose.

The college has several experiential learning programs in which students can earn credit, gain valuable experience, and become involved in community and state-wide endeavors. Business students can investigate solutions to regional problems by participating in Eastern's Small Business Institute. Nursing students get experience at a nearby 49-bed hospital. Science students research insects and parasites that threaten the region's forests. Education students observe and practice teaching in 32 Oregon school districts. Performing arts students bring cultural events to many Oregon communities.

The college is also committed to promoting the future of native leaders and to this end has established the Native American Program. The primary goal of the program is to recruit, retain, and graduate American Indians and Alaskan Native students. At present there are over 50 Native American students representing tribes from six western states and Canada.

Eastern Oregon is a member of the National Student Exchange, and offers students the opportunity to incorporate a semester or year long study program at one of over 100 colleges and universities throughout the United States. Students who participate in this program are assured of credit transferability and pay tuition similar to the cost of attending their home school.

Students and Student Life

2,000 students from 32 states and 23 foreign countries

33% are in-state

10% are students of color

5% are international

450 live on campus

The college sponsors more than 50 clubs and organizations, and because of the variety of the co-curricular activities, it is easy to find something of interest. KEOL-FM is a student operated radio station where aspiring DJs can try out their format. *Eastern Voice*, the campus newspaper, is operated "quasi-professionally" and staff members gain valuable experience. *Oregon East*, the college literary magazine, has been nationally ranked and recognized as one of the country's high quality small campus magazines.

Performance clubs include concert choir, Grande Ronde Symphony, jazz ensemble, chamber choir, and brass ensemble. The theater department produces five major and three student-directed productions each year and even takes a show on tour. Other student organizations include rodeo club, international relations, cycling club, and many honorary societies and professional organizations.

Athletics: NAIA; Ski Team—National Collegiate Skiing Association; Rodeo—National Intercollegiate Rodeo Association
Women's Teams: basketball, fast-pitch softball, volleyball
Men's Teams: baseball, basketball, football
Coed Teams: cross country, rodeo, skiing, track & field

Campus and Community

The 121-acre campus overlooks the city of LaGrange, Oregon. The 12 academic buildings are a blend of modern and traditional design and are in harmony with the beautiful natural surroundings. The City of LaGrange is located in northeast Oregon. The cultural and recreational activities in the area include the state's oldest continuous symphony orchestra, downhill and cross-country skiing, rafting, hunting, fishing, and camping.

Eastern Oregon State College Academic Offerings

Agricultural Business Mgt. • Agriculture & Resource Economics • Anthropology/Sociology • Art • Biology • Business/Economics • Chemistry • Crop Science • Education (multiple disciplinary studies) • English • Fire Service Adm. • History • Liberal Studies • Mathematics • Music • Nursing • Physical Ed. & Health • Physics • Psychology • Rangeland Resources • Theater Arts

Admissions Statement

In order to be considered for admission, students should be high school graduates who have satisfactorily completed a minimum of 14 units which fulfill the Oregon State System of Higher Education requirements with a GPA of 2.5 or higher, and have acceptable scores on the SAT 1 or ACT.

Ferrum College

Fairfax, Virginia 24088
(703) 365-4290 or (800) 868-9797

Ferrum is not just a college, it's a community of learners, where students, professors, administrators, and staff work together, defining the questions, finding the answers, and testing out the solutions. Because of this community atmosphere Ferrum campus is a lively place where students and faculty live and learn together. More than 90 percent of the enrolled students live on campus, and many of the professors and their families reside in faculty housing.

The gorgeous campus is a great place to spend four years, with its spacious grounds, groomed athletic fields, outstanding Performing Arts Center, and riding stables. Each year as the graduating class leaves campus, they take with them a more than 90-year tradition of excellence, a new definition of who they are, and lifelong friendships among fellow students and college staff.

Academics

Degrees Offered: Bachelor's

Undergraduate Majors: 35+

Student/Faculty Ratio: 14 to 1

Number of Faculty: 98 full and part time

The process of acquiring a bachelor's degree at Ferrum College does not take place by attending class, completing courses, and receiving a diploma at graduation ceremonies. Rather, it is a four-year experience that includes personal development and discovery, active participation, and yes, hard work.

The major focus of freshman-year studies is on achieving proficiency in five academic skill areas. These skills include the ability to write and speak with unity of purpose, to read and think critically, to analyze quantitative information, to gather and evaluate information from libraries and other sources, and to use microcomputers effectively. Freshman courses utilize small classes, interactive teaching methods, and available faculty to help students attain these skills.

Students who experience difficulties have several support programs they can turn to. Professional staff from the Academic Resource Center work with students in small groups and one on one. The Composition Center, staffed by English faculty and student tutors provides assistance in writing strategies, organization, development, style, and mechanics. The Computer Center also staffed by faculty and student assistants, has tutorial help and instruction. Students are never alone in the educational process at Ferrum. Faculty, administrators, staff, and peers are always available to work with each student.

Another aspect of a Ferrum education is that all degree programs include a substantial knowledge and appreciation of the liberal arts. Students complete 55 credits in multidisciplinary courses distributed across the academic divisions. These courses provide the fundamental skills and knowledge that must be developed in anyone who is college educated. This course distribution also establishes the foundation for the curriculum in all majors. Included within the distribution requirements are courses in English, religion and philosophy, physical education, fine arts, mathematics, natural science, literature, and social science.

At Ferrum, students learn by doing, and this element of education usually takes students beyond the confines of a regular class. Most of the majors at the college require either a senior seminar or an internship in which students conduct an intense investigation into some aspect of their major.

Students and Student Life

1,000 from 23 states and 11 foreign countries
15% are from out-of-state
16% are students of color
1% are international
90% live on campus

In all the college sponsors 60 clubs and organizations. There are three major publications students can work on: *The Iron Blade* newspaper, *The Beacon* yearbook, and *Chrysalis*, the literary magazine. Performing arts groups include concert choir, handbell ensemble, jazz combo, classical ensemble, and theater group. There are more than 12 academic and professional organizations, like Students in Free Enterprise and Psi Chi (for Psychology majors). Special interest clubs like the African-American Student Association and Femphasis, a group that highlights women's issues, are also available.

Religious life is another important aspect of college living. While Ferrum is associated with the United Methodist Church, students of all faiths are enrolled. The college sponsors organizations that celebrate Judeo-Christian experiences including Catholic Campus Ministry, Student Christian Fellowship, and Canterbury Club.

Intercollegiate athletics are a winning tradition and a source of pride at Ferrum. Panther football is consistently ranked among the best Division III squads in the nation. In the last six years the baseball team has averaged nearly 30 wins a season. All athletes at Ferrum are students first, and it is not uncommon for male and female athletes to be nominated for Academic All-American and All-Regional honors.

Athletics: Dixie Intercollegiate Athletic Conference of the NCAA Division III
Women's Teams: basketball, soccer, softball, tennis, volleyball
Men's Teams: baseball, basketball, football, golf, soccer, tennis

Campus and Community

Ferrum College is lovely. The majority of the buildings are red brick and joined by walking paths that criss-cross the vast greens that surround the buildings. On nice days there are always students sitting out by the lake studying, chatting, or just enjoying the beauty of the campus.

The 800-acre campus is divided into three areas: The center area forms the academic quad and houses 16 structures that include all the major academic buildings and two residence halls. Located in this area are the Grousbeck Music Center (with a 100-seat recital hall, practice rooms, media center, and faculty teaching labs), the Stanley Library (with over 100,000 volumes in open stacks and a 24 hour quiet study room), Schoofield Hall (with the Sale auditorium and a separate flexible theater), and the recently renovated Garber Hall (with updated science and computer facilities).

To the left of the academic quad is Adams Lake and three residence halls. The large fitness center and some practice fields are also located here. On the right side of the academic quad are the Norton Field house, additional sport fields, and Hillcrest apartments. Students have a large selection of residential accommodations to choose from, including single-sex dorms, coed residences, and apartments.

The college is located in the foothills of the Blue Ridge Mountains in Ferrum, Virginia. The area is noted for its beauty and recreational activities. Smith Mountain Lake, Philpott Lake, and Fairy Stone State Park are close by and offer a variety of activities for students. Roanoke is about 35 miles away, and has all the modern shopping, dining, and cultural facilities of a large city.

Ferrum College Academic Offerings

Accounting • Agriculture(*) • Art • Biology(*) • Business Administration, with emphasis areas in decision support systems, financial management, management, marketing • Chemistry(*) • Computer Science • Criminal Justice • Dramatic and Theater Arts • English(*) • Environmental Science • Fine Arts • French(*) • History(*) • Information Systems • International Business • International Studies • Liberal Arts • Liberal Studies • Mathematical Science • Medical Technology • Outdoor Recreation • Philosophy • Physical Education, with concentration in sports medicine, teaching/coaching • Political Science(*) • Psychology • Recreation and Leisure • Religion • Religion/Philosophy •

Russian(*) • Spanish(*) • Social Studies • Social Work • Teacher Education, with certification in elementary, middle school, or secondary

(*) Teaching endorsements available in these subjects.

Admissions Statement

The Admissions Committee considers the following factors when reviewing an applicant's admission: courses taken in high school, grades in these courses, extracurricular activities, SAT 1 or ACT results, and recommendations.

The University of Findlay

Findlay, Ohio 45840-3653
(419) 424-4540 or (800) 548-0932

A technologically enhanced curriculum, more than 200 experienced faculty members, and outstanding campus facilities help make the University of Findlay one of the fastest-growing private universities in the country. Students come to Findlay from all over the country and all around the world. The friendly, supportive atmosphere only enhances the vibrant academic tone that exists in every class. And it doesn't stop there. Campus activities are designed to bring out the best in each student. Skills like leadership, cooperation, and volunteerism are developed along with personal and social goals, all within an atmosphere of adventure, fun, and friendship. Internships in the city of Findlay bridge the gap between book knowledge and experience, and the welcoming spirit of the people makes students feel at home.

Academics

Degrees Offered: Associate, Bachelor's, Master's

Undergraduate Majors: 100+

Student/Faculty Ratio: 15 to 1

Number of Faculty: 250 full and part time

The University of Findlay is made up of three colleges, the College of Liberal Arts, the College of Professional Studies, and the College of Science. Within the

College of Liberal Arts there are 50 career paths students can take, from art to theater production. The college has a full scale of courses, professional facilities, and top-notch faculty to support each major.

In the College of Professional Studies, classroom theory in business, education, and multicultural studies is paired with learning experiences. These experiences include Business Internships, the Accounting Cooperative Program, the Marketing/Fashion Merchandising Exchange at the Art Institute of Pittsburgh, student teaching, study abroad, and the Students in Free Enterprise Program, a national collegiate activity in which Findlay has won six national championships and 14 regional competitions in the last 20 years.

The College of Science is one of the few schools in the country offering Environmental and Hazardous Materials Management and Nuclear Medical Technology. Both of these programs engage high-tech machinery and special facilities. The university has developed two facilities— the Environmental Resource Training Center and the Nuclear Medicine Institute—where students can gain work-related experiences.

No matter what area students major in, they will graduate from the University of Findlay well prepared for a career, personal success, and productive service to others.

Students and Student Life

3,000 undergraduate and 600 graduate students from 35 states and 23 foreign countries
16% are from out-of-state
7% are students of color
8% are international
850 live on campus

The Campus Program Board, a student-run organization, is responsible for planning more than 60 activities, clubs, and events that take place on and off campus. Each year service clubs like Circle K, religious organizations like the Newman Community, and professional clubs like the Pre-Vet Club provide opportunities for students to develop leadership skills and work together on group and community projects.

Aspiring singers can audition for the Findlay Choir or the University Singers, and musicians can perform with the Jazz Ensemble, Wind Ensemble, or Lima Symphony Orchestra. The university also has four student media clubs: *The Argus* (yearbook), *Pulse* (student newspaper), WLFC-FM radio station, and the *Optimist,* a weekly newspaper written by the university's adult students. There are two national sororities and four national fraternities that have houses near the university. The Findlay campus is also home to more than 200 international students who are enrolled in the Intensive English Language Institute.

Athletics: The Oilers are a member of the NAIA.
Women's Teams: basketball, cross country, golf, soccer, softball, swimming, tennis, track & field, volleyball
Men's Teams: baseball, cross country, football, golf, soccer, swimming, tennis, track, wrestling

Campus and Community

The 140-acre campus is a blend of historic buildings like Old Main (built in 1884), and new structures like the Gardner Fine Arts Pavilion (completed in 1994). The older buildings have all been updated and provide outstanding facilities for students. The Egner Fine Arts Center has a 300-seat theater, practice rooms for music majors, and the college radio station. Other campus facilities include the Newhard Planetarium, located in the Brewer Science Hall, a greenhouse in the Frost Science Center, and an indoor swimming pool in the Croy Physical Education Center. There are six modern residence halls that accommodate 900 students.

The university is located about ten blocks from the center of town. Findlay is a friendly city, with a population of 36,000. The city has plenty of cultural, recreational, and commercial opportunities for the students. It is one of the top-rated small cities in the U.S., and university students feel right at home. The city is large enough to offer all the activities students could want, and still small enough to be a friendly and safe place to live.

The University of Findlay Academic Offerings

Accounting • Art, with emphasis in interior design, industrial design, photography/multimedia, visual communications • Art Ed. • Athletic Training • Bilingual Business Ed. • Biology, with emphasis in agriculture, ecological assessment, education, life science, wildlife management • Business Economics • Business Ed. • Business Mgt. • Business Systems Analysis • Communications, with emphasis in broadcast journalism, music-video production, public relations, radio and television, technical writing • Comprehensive Business Ed. • Comprehensive Communication Ed. • Comprehensive Social Science • Computer Science, with emphasis in business, mathematics, operating systems, professional education, technical writing • Criminal Justice • Drama/Theater • Education • Elementary Ed. • English, with emphasis in creative writing, general writing, linguistics, literature, teaching • English as a Second Language • Equestrian Studies (English & Western) • Equine Business Mgt. • Environmental and Hazardous Materials Management, with emphasis in environmental policy and compliance, health physics, industrial hygiene, science • General Social Science • Health Ed. • History • Human Resource Mgt. • International

Business • Japanese • Marketing • Mathematics • Medical Technology • Nature Interpretation • Nuclear Medicine Technology • Occupational Therapy • Philosophy • Physical Ed. • Physical Therapy • Physician Assistant • Psychology • Recreational Therapy • Religion • Small Business Entrepreneurship • Social Work • Sociology • Spanish • Spanish Business • Speech • Speech Communication Ed. • Theater Performance • Theater Production

Admissions Statement

Students interested in attending the University of Findlay should have earned a high school diploma, and completed four years of English, three years of mathematics, and social science, two years of science, and foreign language. The criteria used as standards for freshman admission include high school grades, class rank, ACT or SAT scores, and other indicators of academic and personal success.

Florida Southern College

Lakeland, Florida 33801-5698
(800) 274-4131

A modern lake-front campus where the sun shines 335 days a year, the camaraderie of 1,600 students, a curriculum that features both graduate and undergraduate degree programs, and a teaching style centered around dialogue, discussion, and debate describe the Florida Southern experience. The 100-acre campus is a terrific setting in which to live and learn. The curriculum, a combination of liberal arts and professional majors, is designed to educate students for the 21st century and includes many opportunities for study abroad, internships, and participation in special programs.

Academics

Degrees Offered: Bachelor's, Master's

Undergraduate Majors: 40

Student/Faculty Ratio: 15 to 1

Number of Faculty: 123 full and part time

Accounting, paralegal studies, citrus and horticulture, physics, and theater arts are just a small sampling of the majors offered at Florida Southern. The College has three major divisions that offer more than 40 areas of study: Humanities, Natural Science, and Social Science. Within these divisions students choose a major and build a degree program.

The majors offered at the college are quite extensive and include specialized areas, like business in ornamental horticulture, criminology, sports management, and more common majors like art, education, and psychology. Students are encouraged to make the most of their education, and are supported by a faculty of experienced teachers and leaders in their fields. Many degree programs include an internship, and students can use the May Option short term to acquire experiential learning or take an intensive study abroad course. Each year the college organizes an intensive five-week program in Gratham, England, where a faculty member and students study and take in the sights on the British Isles.

Florida Southern offers a number of different learning opportunities in other areas in the United States. The United Nations program at Drew University in Madison, New Jersey is available. There is a theater arts "Showmester" in New York City, along with an environmental science "Snowmester" in Arizona, a marine science study in Jamaica, and a Washington Semester at American University in Washington, D.C. There are a lot of ways to gain hands-on experience when you are a student at Florida Southern.

Students and Student Life

1,600 students from 40 states and 38 foreign countries
30% are from out-of-state
8% are students of color
4% are international
85% live on campus in 28 residence halls

Florida Southern College is surrounded by communities that have year round cultural and recreational events, but students really don't have to leave campus to have fun. Lake Hollingsworth, on the south boundary of campus, offers recreational water sports like water-skiing, sailing, and canoeing. The Student Center, with its fully equipped fitness center, is also the center of activity for many of the 40 college clubs and organizations. The college publishes *The Southern* newspaper and a literary magazine called *Cantilevers*. Performing-arts activities include concert chorale, concert band, jazz band, symphonic orchestra, and a theater-arts group called Vagabonds.

Many students at Florida Southern work within the Lakeland community in volunteer programs through Circle K, Students Offering Service, and the 12 national fraternities and sororities that have chapters on campus. While the college is affiliated with the Methodist Church, it welcomes students of all faiths and sponsors denominational groups for Baptists, Catholics, and Jewish students. Water sports are popular activities on the Florida Southern campus. It is one of the few colleges in the country to have a water ski team and water ski club.

Athletics: The Moccasins are a member of the NCAA Division II.
Women's Teams: basketball, cross country, golf, soccer, softball, tennis, volleyball
Men's Teams: baseball, basketball, cross country, golf, soccer, tennis

Campus and Community

The campus, located in Lakeland, Florida, is in the middle of everything. In just 15 minutes students at Florida Southern can be at any one of 24 movie theaters, a dozen night spots and restaurants, six golf courses, a huge shopping mall, and the Lakeland Civic Center. Many of the students (even freshmen) have cars, so it's easy to hop a ride to just about anywhere. If you'd rather stay on campus, you can still have fun. One look around and you could mistake the campus for a beautiful resort. There are 12 exquisite buildings designed by Frank Lloyd Wright, which combine functional structure with the beauty of the natural surroundings.

The recreational facilities include indoor and outdoor basketball courts, jogging trails, tennis and racquetball courts, a game room, swimming pool, and lake. And the academic buildings are the top of the line. The Spivey Fine Arts building, Chatlos Journalism building, and more than ten other academic facilities have the latest in technology and are dedicated to undergraduate student use. The 22 residence halls are all air conditioned and house from two to 60 students. There are 12 men's halls and 17 women's halls. All residence facilities are alcohol- and smoke-free.

Florida Southern College Academic Offerings

Accounting • Biology • Chemistry • Criminology • Economics • English • French • German • History • Mathematics • Natural Science/Environment • Physics • Political Science • Psychology • Sociology • Spanish

Art: Art Communications • Art Education • Studio Art

Business Administration: Business—Citrus • Business—Ornamental Horticulture • Computer Information Systems • Financial Mgt. • Hotel/Resort Mgt. • Human Resource Mgt. • International Business • Marketing Mgt. • Paralegal Studies • Law Office Mgt.

Citrus and Horticulture: Citri-Business • Citrus • Ornamental Horticulture

Mass Communications: Advertising • Broadcast Journalism • Print Journalism • Public Relations

Education: Elementary • Primary • Secondary • Specific Learning Disabilities

Music: Music Education • Music Mgt. • Performance • Sacred Music

Physical Education: Sports Mgt. • Teacher Education

Religion: Christian Ed. • Philosophy

Theater Arts: Performance • Technical

Admissions Statement

To be considered for admissions students should have: a C+ average or better in academic college-prep courses, rank in the upper half of their class, and score 1,000 or better on the SAT or 22 or better on the ACT.

Fort Lewis College

Durango, Colorado 81301-3999
(303) 247-7184

Fort Lewis College is located in Durango, Colorado amid the magnificent beauty of three national parks, dozens of high country lakes, and more than a million acres of the San Juan National Forest. The outstanding scenic beauty of the area is only one of the many characteristics that instill the quest for life-long learning within Fort Lewis College students.

With more than 24 majors in areas like agriculture, Southwest studies, and computer science/information systems, and a strong, active Native American population, the college provides invigorating and exciting academic opportunities in a multi-cultural environment. As one student says, "Fort Lewis is a place where you'll make many new and different friends, experience academic opportunities similar to those at a modern university while attending classes that combine large lecture and smaller class environments, and develop a lasting concern and respect for the outdoors."

Academics

Degrees Offered: Associate, Bachelor's

Undergraduate Majors: 50+

Student/Faculty Ratio: 21 to 1

Number of Faculty: 170 full time

Fort Lewis College is a midsize state college and part of the Colorado State University System. More than 4,300 students are enrolled in the School of Arts and Sciences, School of Business, and School of Education. While it has many of the features of a small private college, like an average class size of 22, a broad-based liberal arts core curriculum, and opportunities for internships and Senior Seminar, it also provides the kind of research opportunities, lecture classes, and cultural diversity usually found at larger universities. Students at Fort Lewis College have the academic advantages of both types of institutions!

The School of Arts and Sciences enrolls almost 2,000 students and offers 22 different major areas of concentration. Almost all of the majors incorporate some type of experiential learning. Anthropology majors can attend a field school in southwest Colorado where they excavate prehistoric Pueblo Indian sites. International Studies majors are encouraged to pursue a semester or year abroad where they can experience a more global education. Theater majors develop their performing, technical, and administrative skills by working with the Fourth Wall Student Productions or the FLC Theater Company.

The School of Business Administration provides a professional education that prepares more than 675 students for the dynamic, globally competitive world of business. As an accredited member of the American Assembly of Collegiate Schools of Business, the business program at Fort Lewis College is rigorous and diverse. Opportunities to earn college credit and practical experience exist through internships at Colorado ski resorts, industrial sites, and international corporations in the U.S., France, England, and other countries.

The School of Education at Fort Lewis College includes the Departments of Teacher Education, Psychology, and Exercise Science. It enrolls more than 500 students. In addition to providing a top-notch teacher-education program, the school has established research internships for its psychology majors at hospitals in California and offers exercise science majors outstanding practical experiences on campus, at regional schools, and at recreational resorts.

The cornerstone of a Fort Lewis College education is the practical experience that goes hand in hand with theoretical knowledge.

Students and Student Life

4,300 students from 46 states and 12 foreign countries
30% are from out-of-state
18% are students of color
2% are international
1,600 live on campus

The cultural diversity of the student body is reflected in the variety of clubs, organizations, and activities that occur on campus. The college sponsors more than

35 major clubs and organizations that are affiliated with academic departments or focus on community service, environmental awareness, or cultural diversity. The college has its own radio station (KDUR), a weekly student newspaper, a large intramural and recreational sports program, and the Center for Service Learning, where students incorporate community service into their classroom studies. The Outdoor Pursuits Program sponsors all types of activities including backpacking trips, cross-country skiing excursions, river-rafting trips, and bicycle tours.

The largest minority on campus is Native American students, who represent almost 12 percent of the student population. For more than 100 years, Fort Lewis College has been influenced by the heritage of southwest Colorado's Anasazi indians and other Native Americans. It is the only college in Colorado to provide tuition scholarships to all qualified American Indians who meet admission requirements.

Sports are a favorite activity for many students at Fort Lewis. There are over 30 intramural programs offered each year, and more than six different club sports.

Athletics: The Fort Lewis Skyhawks are members of the Rocky Mountain Athletic Conference and the NCAA Division II.

Women's Teams: basketball, cross country, soccer, softball, volleyball

Men's Teams: basketball, cross country, football, golf, soccer

Campus and Community

The 350-acre campus is built into the vast Southwest terrain. Almost all of the 43 academic and residential buildings are handicap-accessible, and reflect the modern yet historical character of the region. There are seven residence halls on campus, offering dorm rooms, suites, and apartments. On-campus residence offers a supportive environment in which to live along with easy access to all educational facilities and campus activities.

The campus atmosphere is relaxed, yet visually stimulating. The snow-capped mountains on the horizon provide an excellent vehicle for winter sport activities, while the river valley and mesa in the area are home to deer, wildlife, and ancient Pueblo ruins. Students can easily reach the city of Durango by public transportation and enjoy all the amenities of Western city life. With a population of more than 13,000 people, Durango is the largest community in Southwest Colorado and serves as a hub of commercial activity for the region.

Fort Lewis College Academic Offerings

Accounting • Actuarial Science Prep. • Agricultural Business • Agriculture • Anthropology • Art • Biology • Business Adm. • Chemistry • Communications • Computer Science Information Systems • Economics • Engineering •

Engineering Mgt. • English • Exercise Science • Finance • Forestry • French • General Science • Geography • Geology • German • History • Humanities • Independent Study • International Business • International Studies • Japanese • Journalism • Management • Marketing • Mathematics • Music • Navajo • Operations Mgt. • Philosophy • Physical Science • Physics • Political Science • Psychology • Sociology & Human Services • Southwest Studies • Spanish • Theater • Tourism and Resort Mgt. • Women's Studies

Teacher Licensing: Bilingual Education • Early Childhood • Elementary • English Second Language • K-12 for art, physical education, or music • Middle School • Secondary

Admissions Statement

Students interested in attending Fort Lewis College should be high school graduates who have completed 15 acceptable secondary school units with preference being given to students who have followed a strong college preparatory program.

Franklin Pierce College

Rindge, New Hampshire 03461-9988
(603) 899-4050 or (800) 437-0048

The goal of Franklin Pierce College is "to bring students and truly outstanding teachers together in a way that enables a sharing of both personal and professional insights; to provide campus-wide opportunities for personal and intellectual growth; and to initiate in the student the desire to be of service to society." The college has accomplished this goal through its rich academic offerings, skilled and resourceful faculty, and innovative curriculum.

Academics

Degrees Offered: Bachelor's

Undergraduate Majors: 30

Student/Faculty Ratio: 15 to 1

Number of Faculty: 111 full and part time

Through its individual and community-integrated curriculum, the college has developed a comprehensive core that brings together interdisciplinary study, community service, and professional education in a four-year progressive program. This core curriculum of 42 credits is team-taught and explores the theme of individual and community.

Students complete 17 credits during their freshman year in five specific courses, including "The Individual and Community." This course examines aspects of community life in modern America. Sophomore year students take 13 credits within the core. In addition to a course that focuses on the cultural experiences of the American population and one that examines the 20th century, students take a course entitled "Portfolio Assessment Seminar," in which they reflect in a general way on their own educational experiences and goals, and chart a course for their future academic and personal development. If they haven't already selected a major from the 30 available, this assessment will help them complete the process. Junior year includes three courses that focus on Science and Society, and either Reason and Romanticism or Ancient and Medieval Worlds.

Senior year culminates in a liberal arts seminar that serves as a capstone and vehicle where students apply knowledge and skills gained from their experience with the core curriculum as well as their major field. This core enables students to take an active part in the discovery process and explore the interrelationship of their lives and ideas. It is the heart of a Franklin Pierce education.

Students and Student Life

1,250 students from 27 states and 21 foreign countries
85% are from out-of-state
8% are students of color
5% are international
1,200 live on campus

It's easy to get involved in campus life at Franklin Pierce College. With 35 student organizations, there is an activity or club for just about everyone. The campus sponsors special theme events like Black History Week, Earth Day, and Women's History Month. The large and active publication and media group publishes the *Northern New England Review*, the *Pierce Arrow* newspaper, *The Raven* yearbook, and operates the student radio (WFPR) and TV (WBBG) stations.

Cultural organizations include drama club, the Crimson and Grey Cultural Committee, and a large international student club. Academic clubs in business, English, and law bring students with similar career goals together. Franklin Pierce's student government includes student senate, along with a judicial board and social committee. Students are involved in the planning, and implementation of recreational, social, educational, and cultural activities and share the responsibility for the operation of indoor and outdoor programming on campus.

Athletics: NCAA Division II New England Collegiate Conference
Women's Teams: basketball, soccer, softball, tennis, volleyball
Men's Teams: baseball, basketball, golf, soccer, tennis

Campus and Community

The 1,000-acre campus is located in the small New England town of Rindge, New Hampshire. In addition to fine academic facilities where classrooms and laboratories are modern and well kept, the campus houses a glass-blowing studio, dance studio, the Ravencroft Theater, and a graphic-communication center which enables students to tie in experiential learning with most of the degree programs. The college has a large residential population that live in 11 halls. Granite, Mt. Washington, and New Hampshire halls are reserved for freshmen. Sophomore through seniors can choose coed residence halls, campus apartments, or lakeside cabins.

Recreational facilities include a lake with beach and waterfront area, a 15-kilometer cross-country ski trail and adventure course, a fitness center, and a field-house. Rindge is located about 65 miles from Boston, Massachusetts, and less than a half hour from Keene, New Hampshire.

Franklin Pierce College Academic Offerings

Accounting • Advertising • American Studies • Anthropology/Archaeology • Biology • Business Adm. • Chemistry • Computer Science • Criminal Justice • Dance • Drama • Economic Theory • Elementary/Early Childhood Ed. • English • Environmental Science • Financial Mgt. • Fine Arts • Graphic Communications • History • International Business • Journalism • Management • Marketing • Mass Communications • Mathematics • Music • Political Science • Psychology • Radio Broadcasting • Secondary Education • Social Work & Counseling • Sociology • Sports & Leisure Mgt. • Technical Theater Arts • Television Broadcasting

Admissions Statement

Candidates for admission must be graduates of an accredited secondary school who have completed four units of English, two units of mathematics, two units of science, two units of social studies and six elective units, and have achieved acceptable scores on the SAT 1 or ACT.

Frostburg State University

Frostburg, Maryland 21532-1099
(301) 689-4201

Frostburg State University is a comprehensive public university that offers bachelor's and master's degrees in more than 35 areas of study. The caring community that nurtures academic growth is one of several reasons students are attracted to the school. The beautiful campus, state-of-the-art equipment, more than 300 dedicated full- and part-time faculty, and almost 100 years of tradition are other reasons the university is so popular.

For a university of about 5,000 students, Frostburg State offers academic, athletic, and cultural programs that rival much larger institutions. With more than 75 percent of the classes with enrollments under 27 students and a 17 to 1 student/faculty ratio, students can be assured that they will receive a student-centered education where their opinion is taken seriously and they are appreciated as individuals.

Academics

Degrees Offered: Bachelor of Arts, Science, Fine Arts; Master's

Undergraduate Majors: 35 majors with more than 50 areas of concentration

Student/Faculty Ratio: 17 to 1

Number of Faculty: 300+ full and part time

Frostburg State University serves as a premier educational and cultural center for Western Maryland. The degree programs focus largely on education, business, environmental studies, and the creative and performing arts. The curriculum emphasizes theories, skills, and experiences that are necessary for careers within these fields, and a cross-section of courses in arts, humanities, social sciences, and natural sciences.

The degree program in wildlife and fisheries has received national attention. It provides an extensive professional preparation and meets all educational requirements necessary for certification by the Wildlife Society or American Fisheries Society. The university has designed this program with course options so students can assume scientific research positions with federal agencies in wildlife biology or fisheries biology.

Another major program that is designed to prepare students for professional careers is the five-year Dual-Degree program in engineering that combines a solid liberal arts education at Frostburg State with two years of specialized courses at the University of Maryland. Students can choose to study the following areas in engineering: aerospace, agriculture, chemical, civil, electrical, mechanical, or nuclear. Courses in engineering materials and fire protection are also available.

Students and Student Life

4,600 undergraduate and 700 graduate students from 32 states and 16 foreign countries

15% are from out-of-state

11% are students of color

1% are international

1,700 live on campus in 11 residential halls

Student government, sports, cultural programs and professional development are all available at Frostburg State. A tripartite student government system allows students, faculty, and administrators to work together in deciding many aspects of university life. A Cultural Events Series brings nationally known speakers, performers, and artists to campus. There is also a radio station, a student newspaper, and a literary magazine.

The large intramural sports program provides spirited competition and lots of physical exercise. There are also 10 fraternities and sororities that have chapters on campus. Co-curricular activities number about 100 and include four major theatrical presentations each year by Dramatis Personae; outstanding concerts and recitals by the jazz ensemble, university chorale, and marching band; 14 professional organizations like the American Chemical Society, psychology club, and student education association; more than 15 honorary societies; and nine religious organizations including Baptist Student Union, Catholic Campus Ministry, Hillel, and Latter Day Saints.

Three high-rise residence halls are designed in clusters of suites. Other facilities include traditional single and double rooms and an honors and international residence hall.

Athletics: NCAA Division III ECAC
Women's Teams: basketball, cross country, field hockey, lacrosse, soccer, softball, swimming, tennis, track & field, volleyball
Men's Teams: baseball, basketball, cross country, football, soccer, swimming, tennis, track & field

Campus and Community

On campus, students have access to terrific academic facilities. The 10 classroom buildings have comfortable learning environments that include midsize classrooms, a few large lecture halls and several small seminar style rooms. The Lane University Center includes spacious areas where students can get together, hold dances, and listen to speakers. The Greenhouse restaurant is also located here along with a convenience store, bookstore, and great lounge areas with fireplaces and comfortable seating.

The New Performing Arts Center has the latest in lighting, sound, and rigging systems, and a superlative studio theater, recital hall, and electronic music and piano labs. The 11 residence halls on campus provide modern, comfortable housing for more than 1,700 students. The Physical Education Center has a 3,400 seat arena, three gyms, and a swimming pool. This is a campus that has been designed and built to provide some of the finest educational facilities in the region.

Frostburg State University Academic Offerings

Accounting • Actuarial Science • Art Ed. • Art History • Biology • Business Ed. • Cartography • Chemistry • Computer Science • Dance • Earth Science • Economics • English • Elementary/Early Childhood Ed. • Elementary/Middle School Ed. • Engineering • Environmental Analysis and Planning • Environmental Humanities • Fine Arts • French • General Science • Geography • Graphic Design • Health & Physical Ed. • History • Information Systems • Justice Studies • Mass Communication • Mathematics • Music • Music Ed. • Philosophy • Physics • Political Science • Psychology • Public Relations • Recreation • Social Science • Social Work • Sociology • Spanish • Speech Communication • Theater • Urban Planning • Wildlife/Fisheries Mgt. • Women's Studies • Writing

Admissions Statement

Applicants are considered for admission to Frostburg State University based on the following criteria:

1. High school GPA in academic subjects
2. Scores that would normally predict success in college indicated by the SAT 1 or ACT
3. Completion of a college prep program that includes four units of English, three units of social science, two units of laboratory science, three units of mathematics, and two units of a foreign language

Georgia College

Milledgeville, Georgia 31061
(912) 453-5004 or (800) 342-0471

Founded in 1889, Georgia College has grown into a comprehensive regional institution which offers 100 degree programs. Located in the center of the state, the college attracts students from throughout the region and country. With an undergraduate and graduate enrollment of under 6,000, the college can provide rich, diverse academic programs that are characterized by interactive classes, professional staff and faculty who take an interest in their students, and a caring, welcoming environment. From the first day, when new students meet with their advisors to select classes, to the last semester of senior year, when professors write letters of recommendation for outgoing seniors, students are never alone in the education process. They receive the guidance, encouragement, and challenge necessary to succeed.

Academics

Degrees Offered: Bachelor's, Master's, Specialist

Undergraduate Majors: 50+

Student/Faculty Ratio: 23 to 1

Number of Faculty: 290 full and part time

Georgia College has all the advantages of being part of the University System of Georgia: the faculty, research facilities, and state funds. But it is not your typical state university. There are no mega-dorms, gigantic lecture halls, or scientific labs and equipment that are reserved for graduate students only. Instead, Georgia College has a caring, welcoming environment where students can be academically inspired by a community of learners.

There are over 200 full-time faculty members teaching here, and their primary focus is teaching undergraduates. While they hold high credentials within their academic specialty, they are approachable, concerned, and involved in their students' education and very much a part of the college environment—from sports to cultural events, they support their students. But that's not all. Georgia College offers more than 100 major programs from areas as traditional as English, mathematics, and physics, to areas as unique as music therapy and logistics systems.

The college has definitely made academics a priority. Bright students can accelerate their degree program and complete college in three years, or complete a dual degree in four years. Students who are interested in pursuing a specific avenue of study related to their major, but not offered at the school, can develop an independent-study contract with one of the professors and work on issues and elements that interest them. Some students have even designed their own major by combining elements from several academic departments.

The college's commitment to excellence in academics goes beyond the classroom. Georgia College has instituted off-campus programs like internships, cooperative learning programs, and study abroad where students can put what they have learned into action. For a state college, Georgia has a lot of programs catering to individual students.

Students and Student Life

5,700 students from 32 states and 40 foreign countries
22% are students of color
2% are international
1,200 live on campus

From fine arts to competitive sports, professional organizations to special interest groups, honor societies, service organizations, and fraternities, sororities and leadership clubs, Georgia College has them all. The acclaimed Georgia College Theater is a regionally renowned company that produces six shows a year and invites professional guest artists to work alongside students.

Students interested in acquiring writing experience can work on the *Peacock's Feet* literary magazine, the college newspaper (*Colonnade*), or the *Spectrum* yearbook. Musical performing groups include chorus, show choir, jazz, concert, and pep bands. Sports-minded students can choose from intercollegiate, club, and intramural sports. There are eight fraternities and six sororities that have chapters on campus, and about 20 percent of students are members.

Athletics: NCAA Division II Peach Belt Conference
Women's Teams: basketball, soccer, softball, tennis
Men's Teams: baseball, basketball, soccer, tennis

Campus and Community

The appealing southern campus is spacious and provides comfortable facilities. Most of the buildings are the traditional red brick connected by walkways criss-crossing the campus. The Russell Library interfaces with 12 online bibliographic services so students have research capabilities that reach beyond the campus. Computer access is available in most of the classroom buildings, laboratories, and residence halls. Georgia College is located within walking distance from Milledgeville's downtown historic district, 30 miles from Macon and 90 miles from Atlanta.

Georgia College Academic Offerings

Accounting • Art • Art Ed. • Art Marketing • Biology • Chemistry • Computer Science • Criminal Justice • Early Childhood Ed. • Economics • French • General Business • General Studies • Health Ed. • History • Information Systems • Instrumental Music • Journalism • Legal Assistance Studies • Logistics Systems • Management • Marketing • Mathematics • Middle Grades Ed. • Music • Music Therapy • Office Adm. • Physical Ed. • Political Science • Psychology • Public Adm. • Sociology • Spanish • Special Ed. • Voice

Secondary Teacher Certification: English • Foreign Language • History • Mathematics • Political Science • Science • Social Science

Green Mountain College

Poultney, Vermont 05764-1199
(802) 287-8208 or (800) 776-6675

For over 160 years Green Mountain College has been educating men and women in an environment that creates community, individual responsibility, and lifelong learners. It was the first college in Vermont to admit women, and one of the few colleges in the country to define itself as an environmental liberal arts college. Innovation and leadership are characteristics of this small New England school. As one student says, "It's a place where you can try out a lot of things, where you learn by doing."

Academics

Degrees Offered: Bachelor's
Undergraduate Majors: 19 majors
Student/Faculty Ratio: 14 to 1

Green Mountain College is an ideal setting to explore the union of the liberal arts and environmental studies. The diverse ecosystems found in Vermont play an important role in the education of Green Mountain students. The college has an academic focus that blends the study of liberal arts and the environment within its core curriculum, major course offerings, and elective courses. The "E-Core," as the core curriculum is called, is a three-course sequence organized around environmental themes and issues. All first-year students take Perspectives on the

Environment in tandem with freshman English. Sophomores through seniors enroll in two additional E-Core classes plus another 12 to 15 courses in liberal arts distributive requirements.

As students progress through the academic curriculum and choose a major, they are strongly urged to participate in an externship or other field experience within their major. This hands-on experience develops skills and role models while achieving a better understanding of career options. Field experience is a vital component of almost all the programs at Green Mountain College.

Community service and leadership are two important elements of a Green Mountain education. Starting with first-year student orientation, incoming students participate in Bridges, a community-service project that integrates them into the college and town of Poultney. Throughout the four years, students have opportunities to work with the Poultney community through the Friends Outreach Programs and GMC Cares, two service oriented activities. For those students who want to develop or improve their leadership skills, the college holds an annual student leadership conference and offers Introduction to Leadership, a two-credit course, each year.

Students and Student Life

550 students from 30 states and 15 foreign countries
95% live on campus

The students at Green Mountain College come from all over the country. For a small college with about 550 students, only about 10 percent come from Vermont! International students comprise about 10 percent of the population, and the rest of the students come from all over the United States.

Sports, outdoor club, community service, intramurals, and special-interest activities keep the students at Green Mountain college busy during their after-school hours. The campus is more like a community: Students know one another and work together on class projects and student organizations.

One of the most popular organizations on campus is the Student Government. Representation from residence halls, college committees and elected officials of the Student Council work together toward the improvement of campus, academic, and co-curricular life. Green Mountain has a long history of including student representation on most college committees. One student comments, "We really do have a say in creating the rules by which we live. The administration, from the President to the Dean of Students, listens to what we have to say."

One activity students share is athletics, and the college sponsors both intramural and intercollegiate teams. Twenty-five percent of the students participate in intercollegiate sports! In the past five years almost all of the teams have made it to district, regional, or national finals. Outdoor activities like mountain biking, rod and gun club, snow boarding, and hiking are also popular with Green Mountain students. The area offers opportunities for all types of activities all year round.

For the more cultural-minded student, the college sponsors an active drama club that produces two to three productions per semester, a literary magazine, visual arts clubs, and a music guild. Because of the diverse student population, the college really makes an effort to provide activities, clubs, and organizations for everyone.

Athletics: NAIA Division II

The college fields teams in basketball, lacrosse, skiing, soccer, softball, and volleyball.

Campus and Community

The 155-acre campus is a picture-book New England college with 25 Georgian-style red brick buildings joined by walking paths and park areas. Located right in Poultney, a small Vermont town, the college lies in the heart of ski country and in one of the most picturesque and artistic areas of the state. Griswold Library is a national depository for Welsh and rare Early American books in addition to a unique American decorative-art exhibit.

The six residence halls on campus offer a variety of living accommodations, including a freshman-only wing and a substance-free dorm. The college has just completed construction on a new area of the ceramic studio that includes a kiln for firing large pottery and clay sculptures. The Waldron Athletic Center provides ample space and facilities for all kinds of indoor sports, including an Olympic-size swimming pool. While Poultney is not a big town, it does provide walking access to restaurants, a few stores, and the local pizza shop. Rutland, the second largest city in Vermont, is 20 miles away and New York, Boston, and Montreal are only a few hours away by car.

Green Mountain College Academic Offerings

Accounting • Adventure Recreation • Art • Arts Management • Behavioral Science, with specialization in anthropology, psychology, or sociology • Business Management, with specialization in economics, finance, international business, or marketing • Communications • Elementary Ed. • English • Environmental Studies, with specialization in humanities, recreation, science, or policy • History • Leisure Resource Facilities Mgt. • Liberal Studies • Recreation and Leisure Studies • Self-Designed Major • Special Education • Therapeutic Recreation • Visual & Performing Arts • Writing

Admissions Statement

Admission to Green Mountain is based upon a comprehensive appraisal of each applicant's academic record, personal character, aptitude, and motivation. School recommendations and test scores also play a part in determining the extent to which standards are met.

University of Hartford

West Hartford, Connecticut 06117
(203) 768-4255 or (800) 947-4303

The University of Hartford is a modern, private institution that offers associate, bachelor's, master's, and doctoral degrees in more than 100 areas of study. The university is composed of the College of Arts & Sciences, the Barney School of Business & Public Administration, the College of Education, the College of Engineering, Hartford College for Women, the Hartt School of Music, Hillyer College, and Ward Technical College. All have their own distinct character and bring a wealth of opportunities to the university.

The Art School has received accolades for its professional curriculum, outstanding facilities, and noted faculty. The Hartt School of Music is recognized as a professional conservatory. The Barney school of Business has alumni who have made an impact in Fortune 500 companies, local and state government, and the legal profession. Hartford College for Women is one of only three or four women's colleges that remains women-centered yet is part of a larger coeducational university. For more than 65 years, HCW has educated successful women.

Academics

Degrees Offered: Associate, Bachelor's, Master's, Doctoral

Undergraduate Majors: 70+

Number of Faculty: 783 full and part time

While its academic offerings are numerous and diverse, the university provides a student-centered education that incorporates small classes, faculty involvement in and out of class, and high-tech facilities. No student is just another number at this university! The well-trained faculty and staff takes a personal interest in the total development of the individual student. Each of the nine undergraduate colleges is a small community of learners who share the experience of working with and learning from one another.

At the University of Hartford students can personalize their degree program by incorporating one or several different opportunities into their curriculum. Students who participate in the Washington Semester can pursue a course of study in American politics, foreign policy, economic policy, justice, conflict resolution, or art and architecture while living in Washington, D.C.

Students can also concentrate on the government and politics of other countries by studying in London, Brussels, Vienna, Madrid, Copenhagan, Rome, Beijing, or Buenas Aires. Cooperative education, which integrates academic study with related professional training, is also offered at U of H on an alternating plan (in which a semester of full-time study alternates with a semester of full-time work) or a parallel plan (in which a student works and studies part time).

While enrolled at U of H, students have access to five other academic institutions in the Hartford area (Hartford Graduate Center, Hartford Seminary, St. Joseph College, St. Thomas Seminary, and Trinity College). Through the Hartford Consortium for Higher Education, students can enroll in courses at other institutions without additional charge. A shuttle bus runs frequently among the five institutions. In addition to courses, the libraries at all five institutions are open to students at U of H. It is opportunities like this that take the students beyond the classroom and campus, and allow them to design the college experience they want.

Students and Student Life

5,200 undergraduates and 2,000 graduates students from 39 states and 62 foreign countries
More than 65% are from out-of-state
10% are students of color
5% are international
3,500 live on campus

Think of a club, organization, activity or sport and chances are you can join it, play it, or do it at the University of Hartford. This is just a sampling of co-curricular opportunities: drama groups, musical groups, choral groups, opera, fraternities, sororities, professional clubs, environmental clubs, religious organizations, intramural sports, campus radio station, television station, university newspaper, symphony, outdoor club, honor societies, political organizations, and much more.

Athletics: NCAA Division I
Women's Teams: basketball, cross country, golf, soccer, softball, tennis, volleyball
Men's Teams: baseball, basketball, cross country, golf, lacrosse, soccer, tennis

Campus and Community

The 320-acre suburban campus is located in a pleasant residential area of West Hartford. The spacious campus includes more than 28 academic and residential buildings in a park-like setting—complete with a wooden foot bridge over the Park River. Almost all the academic buildings are located on the front side of campus, with the sprawling residential complex and athletic facilities on the back side.

Residential facilities include six suite complexes and seven village apartment complexes, which together accommodate more than 3,000 students. The oldest building on campus was erected in the late 1960s and new construction continues almost every year.

In addition to some of the finest science, art, music, theater, and engineering facilities, the campus is home to more than 3,000 men and women. There are picnic benches, an outdoor sculpture garden, an on-campus grocery store, fitness center, swimming pool, tennis courts, and some of the best live entertainment any campus can offer. Each year more than 400 performances take place on the U of H campus. You really have to see the campus to appreciate all it has to offer.

University of Hartford Academic Offerings

Accounting • Acoustics—Music • Actuarial Science • Art • Art History • Audio Engineering Technology • Biology • Biology/Chemistry • Biomedical Engineering • Business • Ceramics • Chemical Engineering Technology • Chemistry Civil Engineering • Cinema & Theater • Communications • Composition • Computer Engineering • Computer Engineering Technology • Computer Science • Criminal Justice • Dance Performance • Dance Teaching • Drawing • Early Childhood Ed. • Economics • Economics & Finance • Education • Electrical Engineering • Electrical Engineering Technology • Elementary Ed. • Engineering • Engineering Technology • English • Entrepreneurial Studies • Environmental Engineering • Environmental Science • Environmental Studies • Experimental Studio • Finance & Insurance • French • German • Foreign Language & Literature • Graphic Design • Health Sciences • History Human Services • Illustration • Insurance • Interdisciplinary Engineering • International Studies • Italian • Jazz Studies • Judaic Studies • Legal Assistance • Liberal Arts • Management • Manufacturing Engineering • Marketing • Mathematics • Mathematics/Mgt. Science • Mechanical Engineering • Mechanical Engineering Technology • Medical Technology • Music • Music Ed. • Music History • Music Performance • Music Production & Technology • Music Mgt. • Music Theater • Occupational Therapy • Painting • Performing Arts Mgt. • Philosophy • Photography • Physical Therapy • Physics • Political Economy • Politics & Government • Printmaking • Professional & Technical Writing • Psychology • Radio-logical Technology • Respiratory Therapy • Science • Sculpture •

Secondary Ed. • Sociology • Spanish • Special Ed. • Technology • Theater Arts • Video • Women's Studies

Admissions Statement

The Admissions Committee considers the following factors: The strength and composition of the student's secondary record, especially in relation to the applicant's desired program of study, rank in class, character and leadership activities, and SAT 1 or ACT scores.

Hawaii Pacific University

Honolulu, Hawaii 96813-2882
(808) 544-0239 or (800) 669-4724

Hawaii Pacific University is a comprehensive school with two distinct campuses, one right in the heart of Honolulu and the other in the green foothills of the Koolau mountains. Besides being able to study on either campus, students at Hawaii Pacific participate in a dynamic international community that offers more than 30 liberal arts and career-oriented majors, and a curriculum that includes classroom theory and practical, real-world experience. With more than 7,000 students from 50 states and 70 foreign countries, the university is big enough to offer versatile experiences and diverse course offerings, yet personal enough to have a student/faculty ratio of 18 to 1 and an average class size of 22.

Academics

Degrees Offered: Bachelor's, Master's

Undergraduate Majors: 35

Student/Faculty Ratio: 18 to 1

Average Class Size: 22

Number of Faculty: 200 full and part time

Hawaii Pacific University has developed a strong liberal arts curriculum that is part of every major offered, and builds a foundation for almost any career choice. This 45-credit core curriculum affords basic knowledge in the liberal arts, develops important communications skills, and stimulates the students' interest in a broad range of areas. Students can choose from options like cooperative education, internships, university scholars programs, and more than 20 minor areas to design or tailor a more personal degree program.

At Hawaii Pacific, many degree majors are career based and take advantage of the unique locations of the university. While students can major in traditional liberal arts areas like economics, humanities, and social sciences, many students enroll in degree programs in Pacific studies, international business, oceanography, teaching English as a second language, and travel-industry management. After all, where would you rather learn about and work in tourism, international finance, and ocean research…in New England, or Hawaii?

The student population at Hawaii Pacific is very diverse, and students come from different academic backgrounds. To meet the academic needs of its student body, the university offers an extensive network of support services. Professional counselors provide academic assistance through the Advising Center. The International Students Office helps students from foreign countries deal with their unique needs and concerns. The Tutoring Center provides free, individualized peer and faculty tutors in a host of academic subjects. The Learning Assistance Center is a state-of-the-art, multi-use, multimedia facility providing all forms of interactive educational resources.

Hawaii Pacific may be big, but small classes, individual attention, and an active classroom environment are the norm!

Students and Student Life

7,000 students from 50 states and 70 foreign countries

Students come from all over the world to attend Hawaii Pacific University and therefore there is no majority population. The diversity of the student body provides first-hand experience and knowledge about other cultures.

The university offers two types of housing. Residence halls with cafeteria service are available on the Hawaii Loa campus, while university-sponsored apartments are available in the Waikiki area. While the majority of students live in apartments off campus, the school does have on-campus housing for about 400 students.

Hawaii Pacific University sponsors more than 30 clubs and organizations, including student government, social and professional organizations, and honors societies. The university has an active theater group and produces a student literary magazine. There are special interest groups, like the Japan club and the international student organizations, and many opportunities for leadership development. The tropical island location is a haven for students who love the outdoors. Area recreational activities include surfing, bicycling, snorkeling, deep-sea diving, and hiking.

Athletics: NAIAC
Women's Teams: cross country, soccer, softball, tennis, volleyball
Men's Teams: baseball, basketball, cross country, soccer, tennis

Campus and Community

The university has two distinct campuses located eight miles apart and linked by shuttlebus service. Students can take courses at either the downtown campus, located in the business and financial center of the Pacific, or on the 133-acre Kaneohe campus, located amid the lush green foothills on the windward side of the island.

The downtown campus consists of six buildings, including the Meader Library, with Internet access to libraries throughout the nation; The Learning Assistance Center, which provides tutorial assistance and the latest in interactive computer and CD-ROM technology; and classroom facilities.

Residential halls are on the Kaneohe campus along with classrooms, laboratories, and the Cooke Academic Center. Students at Hawaii Pacific University have the best of both worlds—an exciting city campus in the heart of a tropical island and a serene, lush campus tucked away in the foothills.

Hawaii Pacific University Academic Offerings

Accounting • American Studies • Asian Studies • Business Economics • Communications • Computer Information Systems • Computer Science • Corporate Communications • Economics • Entrepreneurial Studies • Finance • History • Humanities • Human Resource Development • Human Resource Mgt. • Human Services • International Business • International Relations • International Studies • Justice Adm. • Literature • Management • Marine Biology • Marketing • Mathematics • Nursing • Oceanography • Pacific Studies • Political Science • Psychology • Public Adm. • Social Sciences • Sociology/Anthropology • Teaching English/Second Language • Travel Industry Mgt.

Henderson State University

Arkadelphia, Arkansas 71999-0001
(501) 230-5135 or (800) 228-7333

Henderson State University is a public university that has many of the advantages of a private college. It is a midsize university with 4,000 students. The 187 professors who teach at the school are dedicated instructors and scholars within their fields. Small classes of about 30 students foster classroom environments where students can ask questions and propose ideas.

The 125-acre campus sits at the foot of the Ouachita Mountains in the community of Arkadelphia, Arkansas. The 52 collegiate buildings range in style from the Civil War/plantation era to ultra-modern structures. The gorgeous campus is enriched with scenic landscaping, nature trails, and a temperate southern climate that makes outdoor recreation a year-round sport. In addition, the university is located just a half-hour drive from Hot Springs National Park, and an hour from Little Rock, so there is plenty to do and see in the surrounding areas.

Academics

Degrees Offered: Associate, Bachelor's, Master's

Undergraduate Majors: 45

Student/Faculty Ratio: 19 to 1

Henderson State University offers a vast array of educational opportunities built into its 45 academic majors. The three divisions that offer undergraduate programs are the Ellis College of Arts and Sciences, the School of Business, and the School of Education. More than 500 courses are offered within these three schools each year, in addition to independent-study options and internships.

The professors who teach at the university do more than just instruct their students. Many act as mentors and assist their students with research projects, or take on the role of academic advisors. They are interested and involved in their students' education. Most of the faculty provide individual attention to their students while they employ interactive teaching methods within the classroom.

While each of the three undergraduate schools offers an extensive curriculum in specific subject areas, all students enrolled at the university complete approximately 50 credits within the general education program. These courses encompass areas in English, social sciences, mathematics, humanities, oral communication, natural science, non-Western culture, and physical education. In most cases a student will complete these courses during the first two years of study. From there they will choose a major from one of the three undergraduate schools.

The Ellis College of Arts and Sciences is the largest of the undergraduate colleges, yet it provides an open, caring environment where students are encouraged to think logically and critically, communicate effectively, appreciate the diversity of world cultures, and become lifelong learners.

In the School of Business students complete a group of courses (approximately 40 credits) called "the business core." These courses cover a broad range of topics and are the foundation for additional study in the various business fields. The school is a member of the prestigious American Assembly of Collegiate Schools of Business.

The School of Education's curriculum was developed to prepare competent teachers for elementary and secondary schools. It is one of the oldest schools within the university, yet one of the most innovative.

Students and Student Life

3,500 students from 38 states and 17 foreign countries
Less than 10% are from out-of-state
17% are students of color
1% are international
900 live on campus

Henderson State University attracts both traditional and nontraditional students to its undergraduate programs. Almost one quarter of the men and women are over the age of 25. They bring to the campus a wealth of life experience and diverse interests.

On campus, the university provides more than 70 different clubs and organizations where students can become involved. There are also six sororities and six fraternities that have chapters on campus. The Garrison Activities and Conference Center is the heart of student activities. The campus radio station, KSWH-FM, and the *Oracle* (student newspaper) are housed here, along with fitness rooms, racquetball courts, and lounge areas. In the evening students can be found here scarfing down a snack and kicking back with friends.

About 900 students live on campus in seven residence halls. New students usually occupy Smith and Newberry Halls, so it's easy to meet other first-year students and get used to college life. The university sponsors several annual events that bring together all the students on campus. Homecoming, Spring Fling, and Parents Weekend are popular, and there are also weekly lectures, coffeehouses, and concerts. Sports enthusiasts can cheer for the "Reddies" at a number of intercollegiate sporting events.

Athletics: NCAA Division II and the Gulf South Conference
Women's Teams: basketball, cross country, diving, swimming, tennis, volleyball
Men's Teams: baseball, basketball, diving, football, golf, swimming, tennis

Campus and Community

The 125-acre campus of Henderson State University has 52 academic buildings spread out among groves of pine trees, lush gardens, and walking paths. The campus architecture reflects several different eras and over 100 years of history, but it has been designed to blend together harmoniously. The physical facilities of the campus are modern and well kept, and most of the older structures have undergone major renovations.

The seven residence halls provide three different lifestyle options: three are set up as traditional dormitories, three are suite-style, and one is apartment-style housing. All residence facilities include lounges, laundries, room phones, and cable access. Special campus facilities include the Russell Fine Arts Center, which provides studios, work areas, and labs for art majors; the Carpenter-Haygood Stadium, where over 9,000 fans can watch "Reddies" football; and the Child Service Center, which is operated jointly by the Departments of Elementary Education and Home Economics and provides work-related experience for students in these majors.

The campus is located in the community of Arkadelphia, with a population of about 10,000. The community has been ranked as one of the "50 Fabulous Places in America to Live." It is a culturally diverse community that offers many of the best aspects of small town life along with some of the finest recreational sites. The nearby Ouachita Mountains provide parks, trails, and camping opportunities while De Gray Lake is a favorite site for swimming, fishing, golfing, and picnicking. Henderson's central location also ensures that students will not feel isolated. They can easily get to any of these places, or travel a little further to Texarkana or Little Rock.

Henderson State University Academic Offerings

Associate Degrees: Child Care • Office Administration

Bachelor of Arts: Communication • English • Family and Consumer Science • History • Mass Media • Political Science • Psychology • Public Administration • Sociology • Spanish • Theater Arts

Bachelor of Fine Arts: Art

Bachelor of Science: Aviation • Biology • Chemistry • Computer Science • Human Services • Mathematics • Nursing • Physics • Recreation

Bachelor of Music: Composition • Instrumental • Vocal

Bachelor of Science in Education: Art • Elementary Education • Physical Education • Social Science • Teacher Certification in biology, chemistry, English, mathematics, physics, Spanish • Vocational Business • Vocational Home Economics

Bachelor of Business Administration: Accounting • Business—Computer Sciences • Business Administration

Admissions Statement

Henderson State University has two types of admissions.

1. Unconditional Admission: Students must be graduates of accredited high schools and have a GPA of at least 2.5 and have scored at least 19 on the ACT (or equivalent score on the SAT 1).

2. Conditional Admission: A first-time entering freshman who does not meet the criteria for unconditional admission may be admitted if the applicant has graduated from high school or completed a GED. A person admitted conditionally must have a GPA of 1.25 after 12 semester hours of course work. Supplemental application material may be required.

High Point University

High Point, North Carolina 27262-3598
(800) 345-6993

This attractive Piedmont Triad school was founded as a college in a cooperative venture between the United Methodist Church and the city of High Point in 1924. In 1991 the college expanded many programs and took on a more comprehensive profile. Throughout its 75-year history, High Point has provided an academic atmosphere and curriculum that "encourages communication skills, critical thinking, and personal integrity" in the belief that students who possess these skills "are equipped to succeed in life, in work, and in graduate or professional school."

Academics

Degrees Offered: Bachelor's, Master's

Undergraduate Majors: 35+

Student/Faculty Ratio: 16 to 1

Number of Faculty: 199 full and part time

High Point University offers the bachelor of arts and bachelor of science degrees in traditional liberal arts areas like English, French, and in philosophy and professional areas like home furnishings marketing, medical technology, and sports medicine. At the heart of every major is a general education core that reflects the university's mission to provide a strong liberal arts education in which students can grow into responsible citizens in a multi-cultural world.

In addition to providing a foundation for lifelong learning, the general education curriculum is developed along a thematic line. Freshman year the focus is human images; sophomore year is self and society; junior year is self, society, and world; and senior year is self, world, and vocation. Students choose courses each year that meet the theme requirements and conclude with a senior seminar in a student's major area.

High Point University makes the curriculum and programs more personal and reflective of students' individual academic goals. These include self-designed majors, double majors, independent study, an honors program, and teaching certification. Students can expand their High Point education with three off-campus programs. The university promotes exciting study-abroad opportunities in England, France, Germany, Mexico, and Spain.

Internships with businesses, industries, schools, and agencies in and around the Piedmont Triad area can provide work experience and 15 credits. Each year more than 70 upperclassmen participate in an internship experience. The university has also developed an exchange program with Oxford University in England, and a dual degree program in forestry/environmental studies with Duke University.

Students and Student Life

2,500 students from 31 states and 34 foreign countries
55% are from out-of-state
9% are students of color
2% are intenational
850 live on campus

Campus life at High Point University includes more than 50 clubs and organizations. There are professional clubs where students can network with professionals in their academic majors, a large and active drama club that produces several major productions each semester, and many special interest clubs. One of the largest groups on campus are the "Greeks." More than 30 percent of students are members of one of the eight national fraternities and sororities. Another very popular activity on campus is community service. The Campus Connection office coordinates many of the student activities and each year High Point students contribute more than 10,000 hours to community service projects.

Athletics: NCAA Division II
Women's Teams: basketball, cheerleading, cross country, soccer, tennis, volleyball
Men's Teams: baseball, basketball, cross country, golf, soccer, tennis, track

Campus and Community

High Point University occupies 80 wooded acres in the city of High Point, North Carolina. The university is located in a quiet residential area about one mile from downtown High Point. Most of the 28 campus buildings are traditional red brick, flanked by groomed lawns and connected by walkways that criss-cross the campus.

Roberts Hall, one of the first buildings on campus, was totally renovated in 1991 and houses administrative offices and classrooms. The four-story Smith Library, the academic heart of the university, has an automated, integrated library system, audio-visual lab, and satellite receiver.

Classroom facilities are located in several buildings and all of the classrooms and laboratories are modern and provide comfortable learning areas. Indoor recreational facilities are located in the Millis Athletic/Convocation Center, completed in 1992. There is an eight-lane Olympic pool, court facilities and gymnasium. Eight residence halls are located throughout the campus and provide a variety of living arrangements.

The city of High Point has a population of more than 70,000 and is part of the largest metropolitan area in the state. Educational, cultural, and social activities are all accessible to High Point students. Within a 60-mile radius, students can visit more than 14 area colleges.

High Point University Academic Offerings

Bachelor of Arts: Art • Art Ed. • Elementary Ed. • English, with concentrations in media studies, literature, writing • French • History • Human Relations • International Studies • Middle Grades Ed. • Philosophy • Political Science • Religion • Sociology, with concentrations in criminal justice, cultural studies, general studies, social work • Spanish • Special Ed. • Theatre Arts

Bachelor of Science: Accounting • Biology • Business Administration, with concentrations in accounting, economics, finance, international mgt., management, marketing • Chemistry, with a concentration in chemistry/business • Computer Information Systems • Exercise Science • Forestry • Home Furnishings Marketing • International Business • Mathematics • Medical Technology • Physical Ed. • Physicians Assistant • Psychology, with concentrations in industrial/organizational, mental health • Recreation • Sports Management • Sports Medicine

Admissions Statement

Students seeking admissions to High Point University should have completed a college prep program in high school and received acceptable scores on the SAT 1 or ACT. In addition to academic credentials students should submit letters of recommendation and information about their civic and co-curricular activities.

Iona College

New Rochelle, New York 10801-1890
(914) 633-2502 or (800) 231-IONA

Iona College was founded by the Christian Brothers in 1940. Since its beginnings the curriculum has been based upon the liberal arts, while the philosophy of the institution has focused on providing students the opportunity to develop their full potential. The college welcomes students of diverse backgrounds and provides a campus atmosphere that is characterized by challenging and relevant academic offerings, a community environment where faculty, students, and administrators work together in the pursuit of knowledge, and an educational climate where each area of learning is pursued according to its own principles, with liberty of inquiry.

Academics

Degrees Offered: Associate, Bachelor's, Master's

Undergraduate Majors: 37

Student/Faculty Ratio: 17 to 1

Number of Faculty: 431 full and part time

A degree from Iona College includes a lot more than attending classes, passing exams, and perhaps completing an internship. The college has established several important learning opportunities that can be incorporated into most degrees offered at the school: these include the Mentorship Program, service learning projects, and study abroad. Each one can personalize a degree program and enable students to fulfill personal and career goals in conjunction with getting a great education.

At Iona, students have a unique opportunity to become involved with the arts, work one-on-one with a professor, and interact with people from different cultures. The Mentorship Program is a year-long experience in which students come together in small groups under the tutelage of a mentor and prepare for and attend numerous cultural programs (ballet, symphony, opera, theater) in New York City. The program introduces students to the full breadth and scope of the arts, and provides a venue for discussion and interaction along with the guidance of a mentor.

Service learning is another program that can be a part of any degree program. Service-Learning coursework intensifies a student's critical inquiry into the individual's relationship with society. Funded by the federal "Learn and Serve America" program, Iona sponsors an after-school center for at-risk children and also places Iona students in volunteer work positions at 20 local service agencies within the community. The college coordinates service learning with specific on-campus courses like moral philosophy and the Judeo-Christian philosophy. Students go on site on a weekly basis to perform service. Students can also participate in credit-bearing "service intensives" offered in Appalachia and Central America, and a semester-long "Iona in Florida" program, in conjunction with the Christian Brothers, where service is provided to migrant workers in Bonita Springs, Florida.

Iona also sponsors study abroad programs in Ireland, Belgium, France, England, Spain, Italy, Mexico, and Morocco. The programs are designed to broaden students' educational experiences and gain cultural perspective. Iona participates in the Inter-Institutional Cooperation, which enables students to study art, classical languages, literature, and communication arts at the College of New Rochelle, and ecology at Concordia College.

Students and Student Life

4,250 students from 21 states and 42 foreign countries
27% are students of color
600 live on campus

The Iona College campus is a busy place. While the majority of the students are commuters and about a quarter of the students are over the age of 25, they are very involved in campus activities. Many of the top students are members of one or more of the 18 honor societies. The college has several outstanding theatrical and music-based organizations, like the Iona Players and the Vocal Ensemble, which provide performance and production opportunities.

Campus Ministry coordinates worship, education, outreach, and social programs, and Iona students work in many community volunteer activities. The campus radio station broadcasts a variety of news, sports, and music and the student newspaper keeps students informed about what's happening on campus. There are also local and national fraternities and sororities, a large intramural program, special interest clubs, and academic organizations. In all, the college sponsors more than 70 clubs.

Athletics: NCAA Division I football Division I-AA
Women's Teams: basketball, crew, golf, softball, swimming and diving, tennis, volleyball
Men's Teams: baseball, basketball, cross country, football, golf, ice hockey, rugby, soccer, swimming and diving, track & field, water polo

Campus and Community

The 35-acre suburban campus is located in New Rochelle, New York in a quiet residential community. The more than 40 campus buildings provide modern equipment and outstanding learning facilities. Many of the college buildings reflect a Georgian architectural style. Since its founding in 1940, the college has grown substantially: New buildings have been added and older ones have been totally renovated.

The Murphy Science and Technology Center houses the Joyce auditorium and classrooms, laboratories, conference rooms, a student lounge and computer labs. The Mass Communication Department is housed in this building along with a complete television studio, two radio stations, journalism lab, and theater for film and video. The Ryan Library has open-access stack areas and more than 235,000 volumes. Online reference and information retrieval service to major data bases is available, and Iona students have open access to the library at the College of New Rochelle.

Walsh Hall is home to the Department of Psychology, and the building has several laboratories for the study of animal and human learning, one-way mirror observation rooms, physiological bio-feedback recording systems, and statistical on- and offline research facilities. The Mulcahy Center is the home court for the Iona basketball team, and also houses the swimming pool, fitness center, sauna, and lockers. Rice Hall and Loftus Hall provide residential facilities on campus while additional housing is available at the College of New Rochelle.

Students who attend Iona College are only a train or bus ride from New York City and within a half-hour's drive of approximately 10 other colleges and universities.

Iona College Academic Offerings

Accounting • Area Studies • Biochemistry • Biology • Business Adm. • Chemistry • Communication Arts • Computer and Information Sciences • Computer Applications and Information Systems • Computer Science • Criminal Justice • Ecology • Economics • Elementary Ed. • English • Finance • French • History • Interdisciplinary Humanities Studies • Interdisciplinary Science Studies • International Business • International Studies • Italian • Management Information Systems • Marketing • Mathematics • Medical Technology • Philosophy • Physics • Political Science • Psychology • Religious Studies • Social Work • Sociology • Spanish • Speech and Dramatic Arts

Admissions Statement

Applicants for admission to Iona must be graduates of a secondary school, or demonstrate an equivalence of preparation. The college prefers applicants who are in the upper half of their high school class and who have four units in English, one unit in U.S. history and one in social studies, two units in a foreign language, one unit in natural science, and three units in mathematics.

Johnson State College

Johnson, Vermont 05656-9405
(802) 635-2356 or (800) 635-2356

If you love the outdoors, are eager to learn, prefer small classes with active discussions, and see yourself as a rising star, Johnson State may be just the college for you. This small, liberal-arts college in Vermont has everything a student needs to be successful, including dedicated faculty, an active learning environment, a comprehensive Learning Resource Center, and a 100-year tradition of educating men and women!

The informality of the college can be seen in the fact that many professors go on a first-name basis with students, and mentoring relationships develop between faculty and students. The professors are sensitive to the needs of the average student and provide opportunities for academic and social growth both in and out of the classroom. In turn, the students who come to Johnson State make it a special place through their participation and desire to learn in an environment that requires respect, acceptance, and energy!

Academics

Degrees Offered: Associate, Bachelor's, Master's

Undergraduate Majors: 18

Student/Faculty Ratio: 18 to 1

Number of Faculty: 120

For a small New England state college, Johnson State has a lot to offer. It has just completed construction of a state-of-the-art library and Learning Center that has an online database system providing full-text journal access, a 24-hour study room, and a top-of-the-line computer center. The college recently upgraded its computer information and phone system, allowing greater access to the WWW and providing voice mail and e-mail for every student.

The college offers 25 associate, bachelor's, and master's degree programs, and a curriculum that combines experiential learning and classroom theory. The degree programs are designed to be relevant, practical, and professional, whether a student chooses one of the standard liberal-arts majors like psychology, history, or biology, or one of the specialized majors like hotel/hospitality management, performing arts, or environmental science. Students can choose majors, minors, concentrations, and certificate programs to design the type of education they want.

The faculty members at the college work closely with their students. They call it "education by engagement, putting ideas and ideals into practice." This teaching style underscores all academic programs at Johnson State. Many majors require a hands-on internship, and even in the few majors that don't, students are strongly encouraged to seek out an externship or practicum.

In some ways Johnson State is more like a private college. The low student/ faculty ratio, seminar- and discussion-focused classes, and the modern facilities all reflect a strong commitment to education at its best. Even the general education program required in every major is designed to help students develop into critical thinkers. It provides 12 credits in fundamental skills courses like oral communications, expository writing, and mathematics; nine credits in interdisciplinary courses; and 13 credits in discipline-based introductory courses. An upperclass student commented that, "The general education courses made me think beyond my major. Now that I took them I'm glad I did."

The most popular academic programs are environmental and health sciences, education, and business; over half the student body selects a major in one of these areas. Many times students will combine a major in business and a minor in hotel/ hospitality management or a major in biology and a minor in natural resources, to get an edge in the career market.

Because Johnson State is dedicated to helping all students reach their potential, it has developed a comprehensive Learning Resource Center. Here students can receive peer tutoring, take a workshop in study skills, or receive assistance in writing or mathematics. In addition, bright students who have proven their mastery of a subject can tutor or work in another capacity, or investigate academic resources in areas they would like to perform better in. The center is for all students.

While most students at Johnson State remain on campus for all four years, the college does offer the opportunity for students to study abroad. The college sponsors a London Semester Program and a Quebec/New England exchange where students may study at one of 25 New England colleges or 12 Canadian Colleges. In 1996 the college joined the National Student Exchange (NSE), a program offering students the opportunity to study at one of 125 other universities and colleges around the country for a semester or academic year.

Students and Student Life

1,500 students from 23 states and 6 foreign countries
30% are from out-of-state
4% are students of color
2% are international

The common thread for most students at the college is their need to be engaged in life's activities. They find success and fulfillment in many ways, like skiing, mountain biking, hiking, outdoor sports, community service, and part-time work. The community of students at Johnson State is made up of both traditional and non-traditional students. About 35 percent are over the age of 22, and more than 50 percent live on campus.

In addition to the vast array of outdoor activities, students are also involved in over 30 different clubs including an active drama organization that puts on several productions each semester. Students can participate in LEAD (Leadership, Education, And Development), a comprehensive leadership program, and another club that combines leadership training and outdoor education. As one student says, "The kids here are involved in campus life. The college provides opportunities for us to be leaders, and for me it was the first time anyone ever put that much trust in me. I like doing things, and I really like to do things for other people."

It seems as if a lot of students at Johnson State enjoy participating in community-service programs. The SERVE program (Students Enriching and Responding through Volunteer Efforts) acts as a clearinghouse for over 150 volunteer opportunities and organizes specific programs and projects like Little Brother/Little Sister, and Break Away, an alternative break program designed to promote service on a regional, national, and international level during scheduled vacations. More than 300 students at Johnson State are involved in SERVE.

Athletics: NAIA and NCAA Division III, Nordic and Alpine Ski is NCAA Division I
Women's Teams: basketball, cross country, soccer, tennis
Men's Teams: basketball, cross country, soccer, tennis

Campus and Community

The 350-acre hilltop campus is located in the hills of Vermont, just outside the village of Johnson. The campus Quad is picturesque, with 12 academic and residential buildings forming the heart of the college. The Dibden Center for the Arts houses a 550-seat theater with proscenium stage, dance studios, practice rooms, and the Julian Scott Memorial Gallery.

There are four residence halls on campus offering single, double, and suite-style accommodations, and college apartments are located at the north end of campus. There are two alcohol-free halls, and an international living/learning suite area where American and international students reside and actively participate in cultural experiences, special programs, and discussions on global issues.

The Visual Art Center on campus has recently been renovated and greatly enlarged to include studios for drawing, painting, sculpture, ceramics, and a wood shop. All the buildings are modern and overlook the gorgeous Vermont terrain. The campus is a very inviting place. You can easily walk from residence hall to class and probably stop many times along the way to say hi to your friends, classmates, and professors.

The college is located about 12 minutes from Stowe, a busy little resort town with shops, restaurants, entertainment, and a world-class ski area. When Johnson State students want to leave campus for an afternoon or evening they can head there or visit friends at UVM in Burlington (about an hour away).

Johnson State College Academic Offerings

Anthropology & Sociology • Art • Biology • Business Management • Education • English • Environmental Science • Health Sciences • History • Hotel/Hospitality Management • Journalism • Liberal Arts • Mathematics • Music • Performing Arts • Political Science • Psychology • Writing and Literature

Admissions Statement

No formula is used to determine who is admitted to Johnson State College. Our admissions counselors consider a range of information about each individual candidate, carefully evaluating each student's academic preparation as reflected by transcripts, course selection, letters of recommendation, SAT or ACT scores and class rank. They also look closely at personal qualities such as motivation, ambition, activities, and community service.

Keene State College

Keene, New Hampshire 03431
(603) 358-2276 or (800) KSC-1909

Keene State is a small, dynamic state college making its mark on the educational horizon. Don't let its quaint New England campus fool you—this is an up-and-coming academic institution with a curriculum based on the educational needs of the 21st century. While other state colleges and universities throughout the country are increasing class size, postponing major construction, and marketing more programs for the older student, Keene State College has ventured upon a Vision 2000 quest in which the college will be seen as the public undergraduate college of choice in New England by the year 2000.

So far the college is right on track. It has finished construction of new residence halls, automated the Mason Library, completed major renovations on eight college facilities, including the Adams Technology Building and the Science Center, enhanced access for students with disabilities, put a computer on every faculty desk, and constructed the new Thorne-Sagendorph Art Gallery. With all that going on Keene

State has continued to be a student-centered institution with small classes, involved faculty, and a strong community atmosphere.

Academics

Degrees Offered: Associate, Bachelor's, Master's
Undergraduate Majors: 40
Student/Faculty Ratio: 19 to 1
Number of Faculty: 343 full and part time

The college has provided outstanding facilities, a cadre of faculty who are experts in their fields and dedicated teachers, and student services that can rival many private colleges. The college's commitment to student success is evident in the services developed and performed by the Instruction Innovation Center (IIC). The center focuses on improving the teaching and learning environment at Keene State. It consists of Media and Technology Services, the Instructional Innovation Laboratory, and the Learning Center.

IIC provides media and technology support for classroom instruction and integration of new technologies into instructional programs. The center also supports special programs on campus, including the Freshman Year Experience and the Interactive Television Project, and oversees the developmental studies, writing center, math center, study groups, and supplemental instruction. For faculty, the IIC provides development opportunities, workshops, teleconferences, and seminars on teaching and learning.

The college has also developed an honors program that consists of 12 credits of special honors level interdisciplinary courses in the arts and humanities, social sciences, and natural sciences, an upper division capstone course and advanced honors work. Students invited into the program have access to many challenging and enriching opportunities both on campus and through off campus programs. Many students in the program participate in one of several exchange programs that exist with institutions in England, France, Ireland, Japan, Ecuador, Quebec, and Russia.

Students and Student Life

3,950 undergraduate students from 26 states and 21 foreign countries
39% are from out-of-state
4% are students of color
1% are international
2,000 live on campus

More than 100 academic, sports, and social organizations, societies and clubs provide leadership opportunities and learning experiences for Keene State students. There are more than 22 academic clubs like physics society, ecology club, and music educators national conference, 12 honor societies, and 13 fraternities and sororities.

Religious organizations include the Newman Club, Hillel, and Keene State Christian Fellowship. Students participate in community service through organizations like Habitat for Humanity, Student Volunteer Organization, and Amnesty International. The campus radio station, WKNH, and the *Equinox*, the student newspaper, keep students well informed about the happenings on campus. Students at Keene State College enjoy outdoor activities like skiing, hiking, and club sports—and the college is in the ideal area for all-season recreation.

Athletics: NCAA Division II
Women's Teams: basketball, cross country, field hockey, soccer, softball, swimming & diving, volleyball
Men's Teams: basketball, cross country, soccer, swimming & diving

Campus and Community

Keene State College has a wonderful 150-acre campus located down the street from the center of Keene, New Hampshire. This safe, small New England city provides an ideal environment for students. The 70 historic and contemporary buildings that make up the campus are all designed with students in mind. The campus is technologically advanced, yet pleasantly comfortable. The numerous ivy-covered brick buildings, grassy commons, and winding walkways reflect the serenity of a typical New England college. Three of the buildings are registered as National Historic Landmarks, and the whole area has a significant historical background.

The city of Keene was founded in 1753, and while it has treasured and protected its historical features it is also the home to more than 22,000 people, several large manufacturing corporations, numerous small businesses, and educational opportunities that include public schools, a regional vocational school, and Antioch-New England Graduate School. Within walking distance from shopping areas, restaurants, shops, and businesses, the campus is ideally located. Residence facilities are outstanding. Pondside, the newest residence hall, accommodates over 100 students and overlooks the Brickyard Pond. There are several different housing options including traditional dorms, apartment-like townhouses, and four-person suites.

Keene State College Academic Offerings

Associate Degrees: Applied Computer Science • Chemical Dependency • Chemistry • Driver & Traffic Safety • Early Childhood Development • General Studies • Safety Studies • Technology

Bachelor Degrees: American Studies • Applied Computer Science • Art • Biology • Chemistry • Chemistry/Physics • Computer Mathematics • Economics • Education, options in elementary, middle/junior high mathematics ed., elementary special ed., secondary special ed. • English • Environmental Studies, options in environmental policy, environmental science • French • General Technology, with specialization in computer electronics or electronics management, industrial management, manufacturing technology • Geography • Geology • Graphic Design • History • Home Economics, options in dietetics, early childhood development, health teacher certification, home economics ed., individualized • Individualized Major • Industrial Chemistry • Industrial Technology & Safety, options in drafting & design technology, with specializations in architectural technology & design, mechanical technology & design • Journalism • Management • Mathematics • Mathematics/Physics • Music, options in history & literature or theory & composition • Music Education, option in instrumental or vocal/choral • Physical Education, options in teacher certification or sports management with specializations in health & fitness, sports & leisure administration, sports medicine • Political Science, options in U.S. politics, international/comparative politics • Psychology, with options in developmental, experimental, industrial/social, personality/counseling, honors program • Safety Studies, options in industrial safety or occupational safety • Social Science • Sociology • Spanish • Technology Ed. • Theater Arts, Speech, and Film, options in film studies with specialization in film production or critical studies; theater arts with specialization in acting/directing, dance, design/technical/theater • Vocational Ed.

Admissions Statement

Applicants should have graduated from an accredited high school, completed a solid college preparatory program with a "C" or better and attained acceptable scores on the SAT 1.

Lake Superior State University

Sault Sainte Marie, Michigan 49783
(906) 635-2231 or (800) 682-4800

With a student population of 3,500, Lake Superior is the smallest university in the Michigan State System. It is this smallness that makes it an ideal university for men and women who want a personal, student-centered institution. At Lake Superior students also enjoy many of the quality characteristics found at large institutions. These include a solid academic reputation, 28 areas of study, more than 700 courses offered each year, an Honors Program, a comprehensive learning center that assists academically challenged students, a career planning and placement center that provides services for graduates and alumni, and a 120-acre campus that is a great place to live and learn!

Academics

Degrees Offered: Associate, Bachelor's, Master's
Undergraduate Majors: 40+
Student/Faculty Ratio: 19 to 1
Number of Faculty: 106 full time

Lake Superior State University provides an environment where students can work closely with their professors, learn cooperatively from other students, and participate in relevant and exciting learning activities. The professors at the university are skilled instructors who encourage students to assimilate new ideas and reach their academic and personal potential. Classroom theory is enhanced through student use of the latest technologies, involvement in individual and group research projects, and inclusion of field ventures and experiential learning.

One school within the university that deserves special notice is the School of Engineering Technologies and Mathematics. All of the engineering technology programs at LSSU are accredited by the Accreditation Board for Engineering and Technology, and the university provides some of the finest facilities for its technology majors. Students use sophisticated electrical, mechanical, and computer instruments, work in an automated manufacturing technology lab with 11 industrial robots, and conduct experiments and scientific calibration in special thermal-science labs and echo-free labs.

Other professional departments with academic programs are criminal justice and fire science. Students receive a broad introduction to the criminal justice system that includes law, psychology, legal procedures, correctional case studies, and specialized courses in their major area.

The university also offers a Michigan Law Enforcement Officers Training Council degree track that incorporates a six week mini-academy component and prepares successful graduates for employment with Michigan law enforcement agencies. Almost all of the programs in criminal justice and fire science combine classroom theory with actual work experience. The university even has its own criminalistics laboratory, pistol firing range, computer center, and fire-science laboratory.

Students and Student Life

3,000 students from 18 states and 9 foreign countries
22% are from out-of-state
9% are students of color
19% are international
1,000 live on campus

Lake Superior State University enrolls approximately 3,000 students from many different backgrounds. More than 19 percent of the men and women come from areas outside the US and more than 6 percent of the students are Native Americans. Sororities, fraternities, athletics, pep band, theater group, radio station, campus newspaper, and environmental awareness club are just a small sampling of the 40 school sponsored activities and clubs at Lake Superior State University. Many of the college-sponsored activities take place right on campus.

The nine fraternities and sororities provide social events and community service projects for students while the theater group and musical organizations sponsor performance activities. The college has 20 professional and honor societies in addition to a full component of recreational and varsity sports.

Athletics: NCAA Division
Women's Teams: basketball, cross country, softball, volleyball
Men's Teams: basketball, cross country, hockey, tennis, track

Campus and Community

The campus of Lake Superior State University is located on 120 acres of land just outside downtown Sault Ste. Marie, Michigan. All of the facilities on campus enhance the learning environment and provide opportunities for students to use the latest equipment and technology. There are two large academic computer centers that provide all students with access to IBM and IBM compatible microcomputers, in addition to eight other computer laboratories with software related to specific fields of study.

The Crawford Hall of Science contains fully equipped laboratories for the study of biology, chemistry, geology, and physics. No wonder science is such a strong major at Lake Superior State! The Applied Science and Engineering programs offer top of the line technology right on campus. The Center for Applied Science and Engineering Technology houses specially designed manufacturing and metals labs, computer-aided design (CAD) and computer-aided manufacturing (CAM), digital electronic facilities, and PUMA and IBM industrial robots.

There are seven residence facilities on campus that offer a variety of living accommodations. Students can choose to live in traditional single-sex dormitories, coed apartment complexes, townhouses, historic homes, and even a mobile-home park nestled in the woods adjacent to the campus.

The university is located in an area rich in natural beauty, outdoor recreation, and cultural activities. The campus is less than a mile from the downtown area of Sault Ste. Marie, which has a population of 15,000, and right across the river from Sault Ste. Marie Ontario, which has a population of 81,000. The twin cities provide a wealth of social and cultural activities like plays, concerts, festivals, night spots, and shopping areas. The campus is also located amid the eastern upper peninsula and the Algoma Region of Ontario, a natural outdoor playground characterized by superb down hill skiing areas, some of the best snowmobiling trails in the midwest, uncrowded beaches, and thousands of acres of forests. Students at LSSU have access to it all—city life and rural beauty.

Lake Superior State University Academic Offerings

School of Arts, Letters, and Social Science: English Language and Literature • History • Human Services • Legal Assistant Studies • Liberal Arts • Political Science • Psychology • Public Administration • Social Sciences • Sociology • Teacher Education: elementary and secondary

School of Business: Accounting • Business Adm. • Economics • Finance

School of Engineering Technologies and Mathematics: Automated Manufacturing Engineering Technology • Computer Aided Drafting • Computer and Mathematical Sciences • Electrical/Electronics Engineering • Electrical Engineering • Environmental Engineering • Mechanical Engineering • Mathematics • Teacher Education in Mathematics • Telecommunications Engineering

School of Health and Human Services: Criminal Justice: specialities in corrections, criminalistics, law enforcement, loss control, public safety • Exercise Science, with concentrations in athletic training • Fire Science: specialities in engineering technology, hazardous materials • Nursing: four-year BSN and completion program for RN students • Recreation Management, with concentration in parks & recreation management • Therapeutic Recreation

School of Science and Natural Resources: Biology • Environmental Chemistry • Environmental Geology • Environmental Science • Fisheries & Wildlife Mgt. • Geology • Medical Technology • Teacher Education in geology and biology

Admissions Statement

The primary factor in evaluating an application for admission is the individual's GPA. Secondary factors which may also influence the admissions decision are the number of academic courses an applicant has completed, the trend from year to year of the applicant's grades, class rank, and recommendations. Seventy-five percent of the freshmen admitted to LSSU have an overall high school GPA of 2.50 or higher.

Lewis University

Romeoville, Illinois 60441
(312), (708) or (815) 838-0500

Lewis University is a midsize Catholic university and is one of seven colleges and universities founded by the Christian Brothers. Since its establishment in 1932, the school has offered a value-based education that combines liberal arts education and real-world professional preparation. The university is comprised of three schools: The College of Liberal Arts, The College of Business, and The College of Nursing, and offers over 50 academic majors that prepare students for 21st-century careers as well as admission to graduate and professional schools. Internships are a part of almost all programs and with the city of Chicago within a 30 minute commute, students have an almost unlimited choice of site placements.

Academics

Degrees Offered: Associate, Bachelor's, Master's

Undergraduate Majors: 50

Student/Faculty Ratio: 16 to 1

Number of Faculty: 183 full and part time

With undergraduate programs in more than 50 majors, students can explore academic areas as diverse as the humanities and the sciences and receive a quality education in either. The success of Lewis University's academic programs is linked to its 60+ year history and affiliation with the Christian Brothers, the founders of the school. They have influenced the nature of the curriculum, making it career directed and well grounded in the liberal arts. Each degree program consists of general education requirements, a major, and elective courses, similar to many other small universities. But at Lewis the course selection and choice of majors is quite extensive. There aren't too many schools that offer courses in abnormal psychology, hydraulics, pneumatics, macroeconomics, and Shakespeare!

In addition to a large course selection, the university offers several rather unique majors. Lewis's programs in Aviation have received national recognition. The university has created degree programs in aviation administration, flight management, maintenance avionics, and maintenance management. The state-of-the-art White Aviation Center and Lewis University Airport are two good reasons why the university is an acknowledged leader in the aviation field.

The program in radio/television broadcasting is one of the. best in the region because students are trained to use the latest video/sound equipment and work in professional studios right on campus. Whether you choose a major in human communication, management information systems, public administration, or any of the other areas, you will be well prepared with any degree from Lewis University.

Students and Student Life

3,600 undergraduate students from 19 states and 19 foreign countries
18% are students of color
1% are international
800 live on campus in eight residential halls

The 800 residential students. at Lewis University have the best of both worlds—a suburban campus that offers more than 40 student-sponsored activities and organizations, and the plethora of social, cultural, and recreational opportunities of Chicago only 30 minutes away.

On campus, students can participate in creative pursuits like theater, campus ministry, a full schedule of intramural sports, more than 15 professional clubs and 15 sororities and fraternities, campus radio and television stations, and student newspaper. Campus life is active with classes and activities scheduled days and evenings.

Athletics: NCAA Division II, Great Lakes Valley Conference
Women's Teams: basketball, cross country, golf, soccer, tennis, track & field, volleyball
Men's Teams: baseball, basketball, cross country, golf, soccer, tennis, track & field, volleyball

Campus and Community

The Lewis University campus is an outstanding community in which to live and learn. The academic facilities are technologically enhanced and students work with equipment that is modern and leading edge. The video/sound studio for communications students is similar to those found in large on-the-air stations. The renowned Philip Lynch Theater and Ives Recital Hall are terrific facilities for performing arts majors.

The Lewis Airport, located within walking distance of campus, houses 17 university owned planes and is a designated Chicago reliever. The airport has more than

500 aircraft and is the site of flight-training and management programs. The White Aviation Center next to the airport is a new $2.5 million facility. The campus also contains modern computer laboratories in almost every academic area.

Lewis University Academic Offerings

Associate Degrees: Aviation Maintenance • Aviation Maintenance Mgt.

Bachelor of Arts: Accounting • Art • Biology • Business Adm. • Business Studies • Chemistry • Computer Science • Criminal/Social Justice • Economics • Economics for Social Science • Elementary Ed. • English • Finance • History • Human Communication • Human Resource Mgt. • Journalism • Liberal Arts • Management Information Systems • Marketing • Mathematics • Music • Music Merchandising • Philosophy • Physics • Political Science • Psychology • Public Adm. • Radio/Television Broadcasting • Religious Studies • Social Work and Human studies • Sociology • Speech Ed. • Theater

Bachelor of Science: Airway Science • Applied Science • Aviation Adm. • Aviation Flight Mgt. • Aviation Maintenance • Aviation Maintenance & Avionics • Aviation Maintenance & Non-Destructive Evaluation • Aviation Maintenance Mgt. • Biology • Chemistry • Computer Science • Nursing • Physics

Admissions Statement

Students interested in applying to Lewis University should be high school graduates who have completed a solid college preparatory program with a minimum 2.0 GPA. They should rank in the top half of their class and have obtained acceptable scores on the SAT 1 or ACT. Factors considered include secondary school record, test scores, class rank, recommendations, essay, and extracurricular activities.

Long Island University— Southampton College

Southampton, New York 11968
(516) 283-4000 or (800) LIU-PLAN

Southampton is one of three campuses that makes up Long Island University. While it shares the resources and reputation of one of the largest private universities in the country, it has developed its own character and academic focus. Southampton is the smallest unit of the LIU system, and because of this smallness it is a place where students come first, where the individual matters, and where a strong community of learners exists. Faculty are not only teachers, but also friends. There are no large dormitories, lecture classes, or lines in the dining commons. Classes are student focused and challenging. Throughout the four years, students receive the attention and recognition necessary to succeed.

Academics

Academic Offerings: Bachelor of Arts and Science in 34 academic areas, and Master's degrees in two areas

Student/Faculty Ratio: 16 to 1 and most classes have less than 20 students.

Teaching Staff: 74 faculty members

At Southampton College, students take an active part in the education process. Beginning freshman year, they complete an academic plan they'll use throughout their degree program. Students can choose a four-year traditional track, which may include one experiential education option; a four-year experiential track, which includes a minimum of two experiential learning opportunities; a five-year experiential track, which includes a minimum of three experiential learning options; or an accelerated track of eight semesters of study in $2\frac{1}{2}$ years. Once their choices are made, students have abundant opportunities to make their degree program fit their individual career goals.

Since experiential learning is part of a Southampton College degree, the college offers several ways for students to fulfill this requirement. The college's Career Development Office has 3,000 co-op positions for which students can apply. These positions are located not only in the New York area, but literally all over the world.

SeaMester, a special Southampton program in which students spend nine weeks during on a research voyage aboard the 125-foot schooner *Spirit of Massachusetts*, is also an option. The schooner sails from the United States to the Caribbean, and students in the program receive 16 credits in courses that include literature of the sea, field work in coastal ecology, and ichthyology. In January, the college runs a tropical marine biology research program in the South Pacific, and in the summer, the college conducts an environmental science research program in Australia.

Southampton College places a great deal of emphasis upon experiential learning but not at the risk of diminishing formal classes. The college has uniquely blended both aspects of education. On campus, classes are small with a lot of student interaction. Discussions are encouraged and faculty work closely with students to help them fulfill their academic plan, encourage them to pursue their goals, and support them at both academic and social activities.

Students and Student Life

1,200 undergraduate and 250 graduate students from 40 states and 7 foreign countries
18% are students of color
3% are international
800 students live on campus

The college funds 30 clubs and organizations that include recreational clubs like scuba diving, frisbee, sailing and ski club; professional clubs like law society and geology club; and special interest groups like recycling committee, campus parish, and the club for gender issues. The university has an active theater company and two student-run radio stations, WLIU-AM and WPBX-FM.

Athletics: NCAA Division II
Women's Teams: basketball, soccer, softball, volleyball
Men's Teams: basketball, lacrosse, soccer, volleyball
Coed Teams: tennis

Campus and Community

The 110-acre campus is located in Southampton, Long Island. It is only minutes from some of the best beaches on the east coast, and the commuter train stops just outside the North Gate on its way into New York City. Who could ask for more?

The campus is beautiful and most of the buildings are set back from Tuckahoe Road. When you enter the campus it feels like you are coming into a small community. The 30 buildings are located around grass areas, winding pathways, and gentle, sloping hills. The 275-year-old windmill sets the gentle, relaxed tone for the whole campus. In addition to academic and residential buildings, the campus has a lovely outdoor swimming pool and a greenhouse.

The library is networked with other facilities within the Long Island University system and also participates in a computerized network with 4,000 other libraries. The fine-arts building, one of the largest structures on campus, has outstanding studio facilities. It also houses the Fine Arts Gallery, where students and local artists exhibit their works, and the theater where student productions take place.

There are 16 different residence halls on campus and each offers small, friendly, living arrangements. Residence halls are arranged in four-bedroom suites, each with its own bath and living room. The campus is about three miles from the village of

Southampton, where students can find some of the best shopping on Main Street or Job's Lane. There are a number of fine restaurants and cultural activities in town and near by Sag Harbor and East Hampton. And of course, New York City is only a train ride away.

Southampton College Academic Offerings

Business: Accounting • Marketing/Management

Fine Arts: Art • Art Ed. • Arts Mgt. • Communication Arts • Graphic Design

Humanities: Writing and Literature

Natural Science: Biology • Chemistry • Environmental Science • Geology • Marine Science

Social Science: Environmental Studies • History/Political Science • Interdisciplinary Psychology/Biology • Psychology • Social Studies • Sociology

Teacher Education: Art • Elementary • Secondary

Admissions Statement

Incoming freshmen are evaluated on their performance in high school, SAT 1 or ACT scores, recommendations from counselors and teachers, and interviews with an admissions counselor at Southampton.

Lyndon State College

Lyndonville, Vermont 05851
(802) 626-9371 or (800) 225-1998

"Small, personal, and student centered" is the way students at Lyndon State describe their education. Established in 1911 as a teacher preparatory school, the college has undergone vast changes in the past 80 years. Today it is situated on the former grounds of the Theodore N. Vail estate in Lyndonville, Vermont and offers 18 bachelor, five associate, and two master's degree programs. While it is the smallest of the four state colleges and universities in Vermont, it has a variety of majors like ski resort management, meteorology, sports medicine, and traditional majors like English, education, and psychology.

Academics

Degrees Offered: Associate, Bachelor's, Master's

Undergraduate Majors: 16+

Student/Faculty Ratio: 17 to 1

Number of Faculty: 65

At Lyndon State, each degree program is composed of a general education core of liberal arts courses, experiential learning programs, and professional courses in the major. The general education courses make up approximately one third of every degree program, and while internships are not required they are strongly suggested. More than 85 percent of the students participate in at least one experiential learning program.

Some of the more popular majors at Lyndon State include education, with teacher certification in preschool through high school, communications arts and sciences, and meteorology. The meteorology major is well known throughout New England, and graduates have gone on to positions with the National Weather Service, the Environmental Protection Agency, and the U.S. Air Force.

The communication major offers concentrations in TV-news producing, news reporting and anchoring, telecommunications production, and graphic design. This popular program is built around liberal arts and professional courses that prepare students for graduate study or for careers in television (as reporters, anchors, writers, and producers) or in graphic design. The campus radio and TV studios allow all students access to hands-on training.

The small class size is just another way students get individual attention. The professors who teach at the college are known for their expertise in their field and also for their teaching skills. One student says, "Classes are challenging and interesting. The professors do more than just read from their notes or the book. They teach, through discussions, asking questions and involving the whole class in the material."

Students and Student Life

1,000 students from 18 states and 4 foreign countries

40% are from out-of-state

3% are students of color

1% are international

50% live on campus

The student life at Lyndon is active, diverse, and centered on the outdoors and community service. The campus is located in the heart of ski country and only minutes away from downhill slopes, cross-country trails, and snowboarding facilities. But those aren't the only activities in which students participate. The college fosters a strong sense of community and develops within each student the desire to give something back to the community. All first-year students participate in a community service project that takes place during the first semester on campus. Through a coordinated effort of the college and Lyndonville business people, many students continue to be involved in community renewal projects throughout their four years.

While the surrounding area provides many outdoor activities, students do not have to leave campus to find things to do. The campus has a professional radio station and a complete television studio that broadcasts daily shows. There's an entertainment club that schedules weekly performances of bands, DJs, comedians, and other entertainers. There are also several professional clubs like the National Press Photographers Association, the Sports Medicine Club, and the American Meteorological Society/National Weather Association. With over 30 campus clubs and organizations there are activities for just about everyone. There's even a women's rugby club!

The students at Lyndon State come from diverse backgrounds. Because of its location in the beautiful mountains of Vermont, the college attracts students from small rural areas of New England and big metropolitan cities like Boston and New York. The college prides itself on being a place where students of all backgrounds can live together in one community. As one student said, "There are kids here from small towns in Vermont who graduated from classes with less than 30 kids and others from places like Providence and a class of 300. We have skiers and writers, jocks and photographers, conservationists and smokers. That's what's great about this place. It's small enough to know everyone, yet big enough to give everyone their space."

Athletics: NAIA Mayflower Conference and fields five men's and five women's intercollegiate teams

Men's and Women's Teams: basketball, cross country, soccer, tennis

Campus and Community

The 175-acre campus is a natural outdoor haven. Located in the mountains of Vermont, the view from any direction is beautiful. Since all of the buildings were built after 1950, the college presents a rather traditional image with red brick buildings, walking paths and acres and acres of green space.

The seven residence halls on campus, which offer singles, doubles, a few triples, and suites, give students a variety of living accommodations from which to choose. The indoor recreational facilities include an Olympic-size swimming pool, racquetball courts, squash and tennis courts, a well-equipped exercise and fitness room, and weight-training facilities. All are housed in the Rita L. Bole Center.

And of course there is the beauty and challenge of the outdoors. Lyndon State is only a short distance from Burke Mountain Recreation Area where skiing can become a daily form of exercise. In addition, Lyndon students can enjoy the cultural and social events at the nearby Catamunt Film and Arts Center, or the Fairbanks Museum and Planetarium. Activities at other colleges like Trinity, Saint Michael's College, UVM, and Johnson State are within a 90 minute drive.

Lyndon State College Academic Offerings

Accounting • Allied Health Sciences & Physical Education • Business Adm. • Communication • Education • English • Human Services/Counseling • Liberal Studies • Mathematical Sciences • Meteorology • Natural Science • Psychology • Recreation Resource & Ski Mgt. • Small Business Management & Entrepreneurship • Social Science • Teacher Certification

Admissions Statement

While recognizing the importance of previous academic performance, we believe the most important criteria in considering applicants are ability, character and motivation. Lyndon's rolling admissions policy means applicants are accepted throughout the year and decisions are generally reached within two weeks. This assures that students are spared unnecessary delay and may plan their futures with certainty.

Lynn University

Boca Raton, Florida 33431-5598
(407) 994-0770 or (800) 544-8035

Lynn University is a young and growing institution that has already achieved an international reputation. The university is committed to student-centered learning, where faculty and staff work with students, providing the guidance, encouragement, and support necessary for each student to reach his or her potential. The university has developed a challenging and enriching honors program for academically talented students, and a comprehensive academic assistance program for students whose academic skills have not been fully developed.

The university has embraced the concept of pluralism and provides a campus environment that reflects the multicultural nature of our society. Students are encouraged to try out what they have learned through internships and practicum experiences both in the United States and throughout the world.

In every way, Lynn University has developed academic programs that provide a balance between theory and practice, programs that prepare students for careers and future learning, and programs that meet the changing needs of our global society. Lynn University may only be 35 years young, but its graduates are known for the success they have encountered in their careers and in their lives.

Academics

Degrees Offered: Associate, Bachelor's, Master's

Undergraduate Majors: 30+

Student/Faculty Ratio: 19 to 1

Number of Faculty: 119 full and part time

Lynn University has several comprehensive programs for students of differing educational backgrounds. The Honors Program is designed to create a dynamic environment where intellectually curious students can be academically challenged. The program includes honors level courses, seminars, and special leadership activities that promote inquiry and stimulate creative discovery.

The Freshman Frontier Program provides specialized assistance and support for new students including tutorials and workshops where they can acquire good study habits, and weekly meetings with mentors who help them adjust to college life. The Advancement Program (TAP) is designed for high school graduates who have diagnosed learning problems, but who have the motivation and intellectual capacity for college level work. This comprehensive yet flexible program incorporates tutorial and guidance services and alternative teaching strategies.

Lynn University is also committed to providing a global perspective as part of its academic offerings. Students have the opportunity to participate in three special study abroad programs: at the American College in Dublin, Ireland; Trident College in Nagoya, Japan; or the University of Stockholm in Sweden.

There are also many international studies on campus. The International Diploma Program provides course work and a plan of study designed specifically to prepare international studies for undergraduate students at American colleges and universities. The two-semester program includes three advanced level ESL courses, an ESL study skills seminar, and three undergraduate college courses. It is a transitional year in which foreign students can perfect their English speaking and writing skills, complete several college courses, and become comfortable in an American college before tackling a bachelor's degree.

Another important aspect of a Lynn education is the integration of learning with doing. Opportunities for internships are plentiful and almost every major at the university is designed to include a senior level seminar, portfolio/exhibit, project, or experiential learning component within the curriculum. Liberal arts majors complete a senior seminar in which they synthesize and assess knowledge gained in the major. Education majors spend a semester student teaching. International business majors participate in a study-abroad program.

Students and Student Life

1,500 students from 30 states and 42 foreign countries
70% are from out-of-state
10% are students of color
20% are international
55% live on campus

Campus life at Lynn University is, for many students, another way of learning. Through campus and community activities students make friends, learn about other cultures, participate in volunteer activities, try out new skills, and have fun! The culturally diverse student body adds to the energy of the campus. In addition to international students pursuing a degree at Lynn University, the IES Program (Intensive English Studies) and the International Diploma Program attract college-age students from all over the world to the campus.

The university sponsors more than 25 student organizations. A national sorority and two national fraternities have active chapters at the university and approximately 10 percent of the students are members. The university has a weekly newspaper, several religious organizations, service clubs, and an active student government. Many academic majors have corresponding professional clubs, like the hospitality club or the aviation club, where students can network with professionals in the field and plan and develop activities and events associated with their major.

A complete fitness center is located in the Lynn Residence Center. The McCusker Sports Complex has an outdoor swimming pool and tennis and basketball courts, and there is a large gymnasium in the Sports and Cultural Center.

Athletics: NCAA Division II
Women's and Men's Teams: basketball, golf, men's baseball, soccer, and tennis

Campus and Community

Lynn University is located on a beautiful 123-acre campus in Boca Raton, Florida. The oldest building on campus was constructed in 1962, and several facilities including the Lynn Library, Lynn Residence Center, and the International Center were constructed in the 1990s. There are spacious areas of grass, seven lakes, and shaded areas with flowers and shrubs. The four residence halls provide housing for more than 650 students in private and double rooms and the campus is a wonderful place to live.

The city of Boca Raton has a population of 200,000 and is midway between Palm Beach and Fort Lauderdale. In addition to miles of beautiful beaches, the area is a mecca for shopping, recreational and cultural activities.

Lynn University Academic Offerings

Associate Degrees: Art & Design • Fashion Merchandising • Liberal Arts • Pre-Primary Education

Bachelor of Arts: Behavioral Science/Psychology • Communications • History/Political Science • International Communications • International Studies • Liberal Arts • Sociology

Bachelor of Science: Health and Human Service • Natural Science

Bachelor of Science in Business Administration: Accounting • Aviation Mgt. • Fashion Marketing • International Business • Management • Marketing • Small Business Mgt.

Bachelor of Science in Hospitality Administration: Food Service Adm. • Hotel and Resort Adm. • Sports and Recreational Mgt. • Tourism and Travel Adm.

Bachelor of Science in Design: Design • Fashion Design • Graphic Design • Interior Design

Bachelor of Science in Education: Elementary • Pre-Primary • Secondary Education: English/humanities • Secondary Education: Social Studies

Admissions Statement

Admission to the University is based upon a review of a student's high school transcript, scores on the SAT 1 or ACT, and recommendations from school counselors and teachers.

MacMurray College

Jacksonville, Illinois 62650-2590
(217) 479-7056

MacMurray College is a small private institution affiliated with the United Methodist Church. The curriculum offered at the college is based upon a liberal education enhanced by pragmatic training for a career. The educational atmosphere is supportive, and faculty and students share ideas, experiences, and good times, making a MacMurray education personal, interesting, and challenging. The college has a core curriculum that emphasizes the central ideas of civilization—history, philosophy, politics, economics, science, and the arts—in a single coherent program.

Campus activities are looked upon as another avenue of learning, a place where students can try out the lessons and theories they learned in class while enjoying and interacting with their peers. Since the goal for many students who attend MacMurray is a career, the college begins the career-development process during freshman year, and follows through each following year with internships, professional speakers, resume assistance, and on-campus career fairs. The services of the career office are available to all graduates, even after they graduate and land their first job. MacMurray College is not just a place students attend for four years; it is an experience that will last a lifetime.

Academics

Degrees Offered: Associate, Bachelor's
Undergraduate Majors: 30+
Student/Faculty Ratio: 12 to 1
Number of Faculty: 81 full and part time

MacMurray is the type of college where bright students are challenged and average students are provided with the academic attention they need to develop into articulate, proficient graduates. Because classes are small and students tend to work together, they share, reinforce, and learn from each other. The college can make provisions for both types of students so that their educational goals are met. The faculty who teach at the college are active in their disciplines and bring their professional involvement and enthusiasm into the classroom. They have a keen interest in their students' development and a deep love of teaching.

The sequential General Education Program is another educational aspect that provides both challenge and support for MacMurray students. It is designed to ensure that all students receive a broad liberal arts education, develop writing and research skills, and gain familiarity with computers and proficiency in mathematics.

In the freshman year students take courses in writing and communication. Sophomore, junior, and senior years include courses from the Ideas in Perspective sequence, an integrated approach to understanding the major ideas that have shaped the Western World, and a series of liberal arts courses from the social sciences, natural sciences, mathematics, humanities, and fine arts areas. Altogether the General

Education Program makes up about one-third of a student's curriculum and provides a common purpose and insight for all students.

The college has established several other programs that focus on bringing out the best in each student. January Term provides a more limited, yet intense learning experience where students concentrate on one three-hour course during the month. Often this course will be an overseas study tour, or a special experimental course not ordinarily offered at other times during the year. Students can also expand their educational experiences through independent study, where they concentrate on special topics outside of the regular curriculum, or field practicum options, which combine classroom theory with active participation in the professional world of business, industry, or government.

The college also offers a College Success Program for students who may experience academic difficulty. This program includes a strong counselor-student relationship, opportunity to take structured skills courses, and tutorial assistance.

Students and Student Life

715 students from 23 states and eight foreign countries
11% are from out-of-state
10% are students of color
1% are international
70% live on campus

MacMurray College is a residential school that is alive with student activities, social clubs, professional organizations and religious and community service opportunities. The campus activities reflect the interests of all students and include religious organizations like the Newman Club, the Fellowship of Christian Athletes, and the Holy Fools, a clown ministry group that visits the hospital and nursing homes of Jacksonville. Although the college is affiliated with the United Methodist Church, students of all religions are in attendance and share in the community atmosphere.

The college offers a large selection of professional clubs or activities like *The Daily Other*, an independent student newspaper sponsored by the journalism program (the only small-college daily newspaper in the United States), the Community Symphonic Band, sponsored by the Music department, and the Concert Choir, which tours places like New York, Washington DC, Denver, New Orleans, and Florida annually. There is a chapter of Big Brother/Big Sister and a Circle K club on campus so students can participate in community service projects.

Athletics: NCAA Division III, St. Louis Intercollegiate Athletic Conference
Women Teams: basketball, softball, soccer, tennis, volleyball
Men's Teams: baseball, basketball, golf, soccer, tennis, wrestling

Campus and Community

The focal point of the 60-acre MacMurray College campus is the Annie Merner Chapel, the center of campus religious life and a community landmark. This stately building has a seating capacity of 1,200 and is used for all major events including concerts, lectures, and recitals and sets the tone for the rest of the campus. Most of the 16 academic and residential buildings are of Georgian style and are spaciously placed among lawns and walks that criss-cross the campus.

The largest building is the Education Complex, which houses learning space for many of the liberal arts and education departments in addition to being the headquarters for the college's athletic program. The complex is outfitted with a competition-size swimming pool, a smaller special-education pool, three basketball courts, and seating for 1,400 people. Next to the complex is the Campus Center, located midway between north and south campuses. It is here where most of the student organizations meet and have their offices. The six residence halls provide a variety of living arrangements for over 700 students. Four of the halls are located on south campus close to the tennis courts and recreational areas.

The town of Jacksonville, Illinois is only a 30-minute ride from Springfield, the state capitol, so students have easy access to the cultural and social opportunities of the city, and the quiet beauty of a suburban campus.

MacMurray College Academic Majors

Accounting • Art • Biology(*) • Business • Chemistry • Computer Electronics • Computer Science • Criminal Justice • Deaf Studies(*) • Elementary Ed.(*) • English(*) • History(*) • International Studies • Journalism • Learning Disabilities • Management Information Systems • Marketing • Mathematics(*) • Modern Languages(*) • Music(*) • Nursing • Philosophy • Religion • Physical Ed.(*) • Physics • Political Science • Psychology • Secondary Ed. • Social Work • Sports Management

(*) Programs also offered in teacher education

Admissions Statement

Admission to MacMurray College is dependent on a candidate's academic preparation, personal attributes and overall potential for the successful completion of college level work. The principal factor in the admissions process is the high school record. While MacMurray does not require a specific distribution of subjects, it does recommend four years of English, two years of algebra, one year of geometry, two years of laboratory science, two years of social science, and two years of a foreign language. Test scores from either the ACT or SAT 1, class rank, and counselor recommendations are also important in the admission process. A personal interview with an admissions counselor is strongly recommended.

Mansfield University

Mansfield, Pennsylvania 16933
(717) 662-4243

Located in northern Pennsylvania, this small, friendly, rural school may be in the hills, but its educational programs reach around the world. Established in 1857, this state university has over 100 years of experience and over 13,000 alumni. Noted for its small classes, outstanding faculty, and supportive atmosphere, Mansfield U offers degree programs leading to careers in business, education, and the liberal arts.

The university's strong commitment to educating students from diverse academic backgrounds is reflected in the numerous student centered programs, including an Honors Program for academically talented students and a Summer Development program for academically challenged students. In addition, the college offers 60 clubs and activities where students can build self-esteem, develop leadership skills, and put their academic knowledge to use in a fun way.

Academics

Degrees Offered: Associate, Bachelor's, Master's

Undergraduate Majors: 60+

Student/Faculty Ratio: 18 to 1

Number of Faculty: 185 full time

The undergraduate degrees at Mansfield University are built upon a four-year course sequence that combines core liberal arts courses, professional preparations courses, and specific courses in a major subject. During the first year, most students complete core general arts and science courses. In the second year students add professional preparation courses, and in the third and fourth year students concentrate on courses within their major area of study.

Many of the degree programs incorporate internships or semester abroad programs, enabling students to integrate an off-campus experience into their career preparation. As a member of the College Center of the Finger Lakes and the

Pennsylvania State System of Higher Education, students at Mansfield University can take classes at other member colleges and universities including Bucknell, Lock Haven, and Susquehanna Universities, or they can double major, design a self-developed major, or participate in independent study or individualized instruction. The academic options are almost unlimited. Because the university offers more than 70 majors and 35 minor areas of concentration, a student can easily combine a pre-professional and liberal arts education.

Classes at Mansfield University are discussion oriented and interactive. The majority of courses have less than 30 students per class and less than 5 percent of all the classes offered have more than 50 students. One student comments, "At Mansfield all of my professors know who I am and how I am doing in their course. Professors at Mansfield take an interest in their students, they teach, they don't just lecture."

Mansfield University works hard at placing incoming first year students in classes that are appropriate for them. Students are evaluated in mathematics, study skills, and written communication through placement tests or SAT scores, and placed in appropriate courses. Each year approximately 100 incoming freshmen participate in a summer development pre-college experience that gives them a head start on success for the fall semester. The university has also developed preparatory courses in English, mathematics, and ACT 101 for students who may be lacking a strong academic background.

Academically talented students who come to Mansfield University may be invited into the Honors Program. This is an intellectually intense program that focuses on taking bright students beyond the realm of the regular classes and into the learning and discovery process.

Students and Student Life

3,000 students from 20 states and 21 foreign countries
15% are from out-of-state
7% are students of color
1% are international
70% live on campus

The Mansfield University campus is an energetic, bustling place seven days a week. There are more than 60 campus activities including a popular weekly news-paper, FM radio station, and equestrian club. The student body is large enough to support diverse cultural, social, professional, and recreational activities, yet small enough to provide special interest clubs for students. The university sponsors bus trips to the Arnot Mall in Elmira and the Clemens Performing Arts Center, along with ski trips to the nearby mountains and sailing excursions to the area lakes. On campus the more than 10 performance clubs provide concerts, jazz sessions, dance performances, and plays.

Almost two-thirds of the students live on campus, so campus life is active and interesting. Two of the most popular groups are the fraternities and sororities. About 20 percent of the students belong to the six national fraternities or four national sororities.

The university has a strong athletic tradition that dates back to 1891 when it became the first college to initiate spring practice for football. For the past 30 years the men's baseball team has been nationally ranked and posted winning seasons. Since 1970, 30 players have been drafted by major league teams.

Athletics: NCAA Division II men's and women's varsity sports
Women's Teams: basketball, cross country, hockey, softball, swimming, track & field
Men's Teams: baseball, basketball, cross country, football, track & field, tennis, wrestling

Campus and Community

The 205-acre campus is located in north-central Pennsylvania. The region is noted for its year-round outdoor activities and beautiful scenery. On-campus students have modern facilities that offer 32 academic and residential buildings. Approximately 1,800 men and women live in the five residence halls that include both coed and single-sex halls and traditional dormitory and suite-style living.

The academic buildings on campus are a combination of traditional and modern architecture and are set within areas with trees, walkways, and large expansive lawn areas. The Grant Science Center has a planetarium, solar collector, and science museum. The athletic center or Decker Gymnasium has an Olympic-size pool. Allen Hall is equipped with high-tech lecture rooms and a modern TV studio.

Mansfield University is located 22 miles from the New York state border in an area that includes the natural setting of the Endless Mountains of Pennsylvania. Outdoor recreation includes skiing, rafting, hiking, and picnicking. The Tioga-Hammond Dam offers miles of unlimited camping areas, marinas, and boating opportunities. Other colleges within an hour's ride of Mansfield University include SUNY Binghamton and Elmira College.

Mansfield University Academic Offerings

Accounting • Actuarial Science • Art • Biology • Broadcasting • Chemistry • Computer Science • Criminal Justice • Earth and Space Science • Economics • Education • English • Environmental Science • Exceptional Persons • Foreign Languages • Geography • Geography-Mapping Technology • History • Human Resource Mgt. • International Business • International Studies • Journalism •

Liberal Studies • Marketing • Mathematics • Media Specialist • Medical Technology • Music • Nursing • Nutrition and Dietetics • Philosophy • Physics • Political Science • Professional Writing • Psychology • Public Relations • Radiology Technology • Regional Planning • Respiratory Therapy • Social Work • Information Systems • Sociology/Anthropology • Speech Communication • Theater • Travel and Tourism

Admissions Statement

Applicants for admission should have graduated from an accredited secondary school, completed a college prep program, attained a combined score of 920 or better on the SAT 1 or 19 or better on the ACT, and rank in the top three fifths of their class.

Marian College of Fond du Lac

Fond du Lac, Wisconsin 54935-4699
(414) 923-7650 or (800) 2MARIAN

Established in 1936, Marian College is a comprehensive Catholic college offering graduate and undergraduate degree programs in liberal arts and professional areas. The college concentrates on educating the whole person through a strong liberal arts core curriculum, specialized courses in major areas, and integrating classroom theory with practical work experiences. Students have extraordinary opportunities to learn from and work with over 100 dedicated faculty in classes that are small and student centered.

The campus is modern and provides excellent resources and facilities where students can engage in educational pursuits, make life-long friendships, and have fun. In the past 60 years, thousands of men and women have graduated from the college and taken their place in careers throughout the United States.

Academics

Degrees Offered: Bachelor's, Master's
Undergraduate Majors: 30+
Student/Faculty Ratio: 16 to 1
Number of Faculty: 113 full and part time

Marian College provides a wide range of learning opportunities for undergraduate students. In addition to small interactive classes, the college offers study abroad, independent study, practicums, clinicals, supervised teaching, and cooperative education programs. Each of the six academic divisions that make up the college has incorporated some form of experiential learning into its curriculum, and students are encouraged to integrate what they learn into how they live. In the truly educated person, self knowledge and actualization are just as important as English, mathematics, and science.

The Division of Arts and Humanities provides courses and career preparation on both liberal arts and professional career tracks. The Division of Business Administration offers undergraduate programs in five major and five minor areas, and a unique graduate program in Quality, Values, and Leadership. All business majors are required to complete a cooperative education or internship program. The Division of Educational Studies is a professional department with primary emphasis on preparing talented teachers and educational leaders for careers within the American school system. The program at Marian College utilizes the Preservice Teacher Perceiver Interview, which enables Marian students to enter the teaching profession with a keen understanding of how to use their talents to achieve success in teaching.

The Division of Mathematics and Natural Science offers six major and six minor areas of concentration including majors in health care areas like cytotechnology, medical technology, and radiological technology. The Nursing Studies Division provides a baccalaureate program of study in professional nursing and is accredited by the National League for Nursing. The major and minor areas of studies within the Division of Social and Behavioral Sciences focus on the historical and contemporary development of interpersonal, social, political, and economic forces that are part of our world. Each of the six majors offered within this division provide opportunities for cooperative education or internships.

Students and Student Life

2,000 students from 13 states and 5 foreign countries
15% are from out-of-state
7% are students of color
1% are international

The student body of Marian College is made up of both traditional age and adult students. Over one third of the men and women enrolled in undergraduate programs are over 25. Many are drawn to the college because of its strong reputation for preparing students for careers. Because of the extensive clinical and co-op work experiences Marian graduates receive, the college has established an excellent reputation among business, industry, and human resource personnel.

Marian College provides an environment where all students can feel comfortable, learn from each other, and enjoy activities, events and organizations that build a sense of community. Facilities on the campus have been constructed with the needs of both traditional and non-traditional age students in mind. The four residential facilities include traditional dormitories, a townhouse village complex that provides apartment-style living, and a new courtyard facility (built in 1993) that has three types of housing arrangements for up to 150 students. The college also runs an early childhood center right on campus.

The Student Senate is the most important student organization on campus. It represents student interests in the governance of the college and is responsible for initiating and supervising the 25 college clubs and organizations that provide spiritual, intellectual, personal and social development of the students. These clubs include campus ministry, intramural activities, professional societies, subject/career related clubs, and a national fraternity and sorority. The college has a student newspaper, active drama club, and numerous performance groups including choral and musical ensembles.

Athletics: The Sabres compete in the NAIA Lake Michigan Conference.

Women's Teams: basketball, cross country, soccer, softball, tennis, volleyball

Men's Teams: baseball, basketball, cross country, golf, hockey, soccer, tennis

Campus and Community

The 58-acre campus of Marian College is located in Fond du Lac, Wisconsin, a picturesque city of 38,000 on the south shore of Lake Winnebago. The campus has 12 academic buildings, including the large circular Cardinal Meyer Library; the Courtyard, a new and modern residential complex; the Hornung Student Union; and the Dorcas Chapel, the center of religious activity on campus, noted for its beauty and unique design. The residential halls on campus are modern and provide a variety of space for student living. The oldest hall was constructed in 1962 and has undergone periodic renovations. The Courtyard is the newest residence facility and was completed in 1994.

The Marian College campus is located in a safe, comfortable neighborhood with easy access to shopping areas, movies, theaters, and restaurants. Because of the natural terrain and the changing seasons, the Fond du Lac area supports a host of year round recreational activities. Lake Winnebago is ideal for swimming, sailing, and water-skiing in the summer and ice fishing, skating, and cross-country skiing in the winter. Fond du Lac is within easy driving distance of all the big-city glitter of Madison, Milwaukee, and Green Bay, yet it provides a serene campus environment surrounded by natural beauty.

Marian College Academic Offerings

Arts and Humanities: Art • Art Ed. • Communication • English • English Ed. • English/Language Arts Ed. • Foreign Language Ed. • Music • Music Ed. • Philosophy • Theology • Women's Studies

Business Administration: Accounting • Business Economics • Business Ed. • Management • Marketing • Sports & Leisure Mgt.

Educational Studies: Early Childhood • Elementary K-12 Programs • Middle • Secondary •

Mathematics and Natural Science: Biology • Biology-Cytotechnology • Chemistry • Computer Science • Mathematics • Environmental Science • Medical Technology • Natural Science • Radiological Technology

Nursing Studies: Nursing

Social and Behavioral Sciences: Administration of Justice • Army ROTC • History • Human Relations • International Studies • Psychology • Social Studies • Social Work • Sociology

Admissions Statement

In judging an applicant's eligibility, Marian College gives consideration to the entire secondary school record, including ACT or SAT 1 scores. The best indication for success in college is a strong high school record. Students with at least a "C" average who have completed high school in the upper half of their graduating class are strongly encouraged to apply.

Mayville State University

Mayville, North Dakota 58257-1299
(701) 786-2301 or
(800) 342-4583 in-state, or
(800) 437-4104 out-of-state

Mayville State University's motto is 'The School of Personal Service,' and it lives up to this description with a 15 to 1 student/faculty ratio, a peer mentor program for first year students, and a faculty that is dedicated to meeting the academic needs of all students. The college offers Associate and Bachelor's degree programs in 18 different areas, and has a strong education curriculum that provides teacher certification in areas from early childhood through secondary level.

The 55-acre campus is located in the Mayville-Portland communities, adjacent towns where students can shop, take in a movie, or enjoy an evening out at one of the restaurants. Mayville is one of six state universities in North Dakota, and has been providing a quality education for more than 100 years.

Academics

Degrees Offered: Associate, Bachelor's

Undergraduate Majors: 14+

Student/Faculty Ratio: 15 to 1

Number of Faculty: 60 full and part time

Mayville is a student-centered college where classes are small, professors work with their students, and the learning environment is challenging yet supportive. A cooperative learning model is used within the classroom and students learn from one another in an interactive environment. The faculty take an active interest in their students. One student comments, "All of my professors know me by name and have a good idea of the type of work I can do. If I need extra help they're always available. There are no large lecture classes here. Mayville is not your typical, big, state university. It is small, and the kids here really get to know each other."

Mayville offers a liberal-arts curriculum with majors in traditional subjects like English, history, and biology. Students can put together a diverse career related education by selecting a minor in fields like accounting, coaching, or computer information systems. Many of the degree programs incorporate experiential learning into the curriculum. The college's cooperative education/internship program places students in private industry, governmental agencies, and nonprofit organizations throughout the state. Students can either participate in the co-op on a full-time basis, alternating a semester of job placement with a semester of college courses, or they can combine a job with a local business/agency with full or part time studies. Either way students earn college credit and are paid for their work experience.

The teacher-education program at Mayville is one of the oldest in the state. It provides certification in early childhood and elementary education and nine subjects areas in secondary education. Other popular majors are business administration and computer information systems. Every degree program at Mayville incorporates 42 credits in general education requirements and includes courses in public speaking and computer information in addition to the more traditional liberal arts offerings.

Students and Student Life

    777 students from 17 states and 2 foreign countries
    30% are from out-of-state
    5% are students of color
    8% are international
    400 live on campus

The cornerstone of a Mayville education is the individual attention students receive from the time they enter as freshmen until the day they graduate. One way new students become initiated and involved in the college is through the Mentor Program. Upperclass students and faculty are paired with new students to give support, encouragement, and advisement. Because the college is small (with about 777) students, there is a strong sense of community on campus. Friendships are not limited to students in your classes or to students on your hall. The many activities, cultural clubs, and professional societies bring all students together.

    Many of the campus activities are centered around residential life. There are four residence halls offering a variety of living accommodations including an over-21 residence building that has single rooms and several apartments. Each residence hall has its own student board that sets policies and plans activities for the house. In addition, the college has a Student Senate that meets weekly to discuss issues, plan events, and work with the faculty and administration on college wide committees.

Athletics: The Comets compete in the NAIA, and are members of the North Dakota College Athletic Conference.
Women's Teams: basketball, softball, volleyball
Men's Teams: baseball, basketball, football

Campus and Community

The 55-acre campus is like its own little town. Academic buildings, residence halls, and recreational areas share the campus with the Child Development Center, playground, and faculty apartments. The major academic buildings are joined by connecting corridors, so students do not have to actually go outside between classes on cold wintry days.

    Sports and recreational facilities include tennis and racquetball courts, a football stadium and baseball diamond, practice fields, and a track & field area. The modern Student Center houses an indoor swimming pool, meeting rooms, and the university cafeteria. Students can watch their favorite show on the big-screen TV, or just hang out in one of the lounges. It's not unusual to see one of your professors at a performance in Old Main Theater or watching a game in the football stadium.

    For a change of scenery, students can easily go into Portland just a few minutes away, or head out toward Fargo or Grand Forks, both only an hour away.

Mayville State University Academic Offerings

Administrative Office Services • Biology • Business Adm. • Chemistry •
Computer Information Systems • Elementary Ed. • English • General Studies •
Health Education • Mathematics • Physical Education (Sports Science/Athletic
Training) • Physical Science • Social Science • Teacher Certification

Admissions Statement

Mayville State University welcomes applications from both in state and out-of-state
students. In order to be eligible for admission a student should be a graduate of an
accredited high school and should have completed the following courses with a "C"
or better average; four units of English; three units of mathematics (Algebra I or
higher); three units of laboratory sciences; three units of social science; and have
taken either the ACT or SAT 1.

McMurry University

Abilene, Texas 79697
(915) 691-6226 or (800) 477-0077

McMurry University is a small private university that is supported by the United
Methodist Church. The 1,400 men and women who attend the university experience
a liberal arts education that includes small classes, experimental and innovative
courses, cross registration at two other major universities in Abilene, and a student/
faculty ratio of 13 to 1. Because of its Christian heritage, the university attracts students from many different religious affiliations including Catholic, Baptist, and other
Christian denominations.

The student government, composed of executive, judicial, and legislative branches,
affords student representation on all major university committees and entrusts many
important aspects of college life to the students themselves. McMurry University
provides outstanding facilities, talented faculty, and a campus atmosphere in which
students can expand their educational ambition and fulfill their personal goals.

Academic Statistics

Degrees Offered: Associate, Bachelor's
Undergraduate Majors: 40

Student/Faculty Ratio: 13 to 1 with an average class size of 166

Number of Faculty Members: 145 full and part time

McMurry University offers seven specialized undergraduate programs including the Bachelor of Arts, Fine Arts, Business Administration, Bachelor of Music, Music Education, Bachelor of Science, and Bachelor of Science in Nursing. All majors include a liberal arts core curriculum that combines interdisciplinary courses in written and oral communication, health and fitness, fine arts, humanities, science, mathematics, and social sciences.

The university has an atmosphere in which students can grow and develop educationally and socially, while faculty, staff, and administrators work with them every step of the way. The Academic Enrichment Center, staffed by professional and peer tutors, offers tutorial assistance in basic and advanced courses and coordinates programs for students who may need additional assistance. An Honors Program challenges and stimulates the academically advanced students. Bright students can also accelerate their degree program and graduate early, or they can engage in an independent study in an area of interest.

McMurry is committed to providing academic opportunities that will educate and prepare students to become active citizens. Students can participate in internships in business, industry, and the private sector, take courses at Hardin-Simmons University, or study abroad. May Term at McMurry University gives students a chance to travel abroad, do an internship, or take courses where they can explore academic areas not usually offered during regular semesters.

Students and Student Life

1,400 students from 18 states and 2 foreign countries
19% are students of color
2% are international
51% live on campus

Campus life is filled with social, professional, recreational, performance, and community service clubs and organizations. The university has 13 fraternities and sororities on campus and approximately 38% of the students are members. There is a large Service Club that contributes hundreds of hours of community service in the city. Outstanding fine arts programs bring theater, concerts, and artists to campus for performances and exhibits. Several intramural clubs and activities allow students to participate in recreational sports. Some of the other 40 student organizations are campus ministry, jazz band, musical ensembles, Fellowship of Christian Athletes, year book, literary magazine, and musical theater.

Athletics: NAIA
Women's Teams: basketball, tennis, volleyball
Men's Teams: basketball, football, golf, tennis

Campus and Community

The 41-acre campus is located in Abilene, Texas. The city is home to the Abilene Zoo, the Philharmonic Orchestra, civic ballet, and several museums, shopping malls, movie theaters, and restaurants. Students have ample opportunities to develop internship sites in the city, acquire part time employment and socialize with students from several other colleges and universities.

The McMurry University campus has a fully equipped science center containing laboratory facilities for biology, chemistry, geology, and physics. Performance facilities include two theaters, a large recital hall, and rehearsal rooms. There is a physical education center, field house, football field, indoor swimming pool, and track and tennis courts.

McMurry University Academic Offerings

Associate Degrees: Humanities • Liberal Arts • Nursing

Bachelor's Degrees: Accounting • Art • Biology • Business Adm. & Mgt. • Ceramics • Chemistry • Clinical Laboratory Science • Communications • Computer Information Sciences • Computer Science & Computational Mathematics • Criminal Justice • Drama/Theater Arts • Elementary Ed. • English • Economics • Finance & Banking • History • Human Services • Mathematics • Marketing • Music • Music: Piano & Organ Performance • Music: Voice & Choral/Opera Performance • Nursing • Painting • Paralegal/Legal Assistant • Philosophy • Physical Ed. • Political Science & Government • Psychology • Religion • Religious Ed. • Religious Music • Secondary Ed. • Sociology • Spanish • Teacher Education: Multiple Levels

Admissions Statement

To be considered for admission to McMurry University students should be graduates of an accredited high school, have completed a college prep program, and received adequate scores on the SAT 1 or ACT. High school grades, class rank, test scores, extracurricular activities, and leadership potential are all considered in the admissions decision.

Menlo College

Atherton, California 94027-4301
(415) 688-3753 or (800) 556-3656

Menlo is a small, private, residential college nestled in the hills of Atherton, California, about 30 minutes south of San Francisco. But don't let its size and appearance fool you. This is a college where academic goals are attained, where students and faculty work together in a community of shared interests, and where technology and leadership underscore all academic endeavors. The mission of the college is "to educate men and women for eventual leadership in modern organizations, and for useful and fulfilling lives as individuals and citizens." Through small classes; experienced professors; a strong, coherent curriculum; and a concern for global issues, the college accomplishes these goals.

Academics

Degrees Offered: Associate, Bachelor's
Undergraduate Majors: 11
Student/Faculty Ratio: 10 to 1

The signature of a Menlo education is the personal attention each student receives. The college is more than an institution of learning. It is a community of learners, where students and professors foster each other's creativity. The 40 professors and 550 students work together in the learning process. Classes are small and characterized by student interaction. Most classes incorporate frequent out of class learning encounters, and interdisciplinary learning is stressed. Every student learns to work with the latest technology.

The college offers three distinct degree programs in management, mass communications, and liberal arts. Students can choose one or possibly two areas of major concentration from fields like environmental resource management, media studies, humanities, psychology, or human resource management. In addition they may pursue a minor in one of 13 areas including French, Spanish, or computer information service.

The curriculum at Menlo is designed to be flexible yet encompassing, so students can integrate liberal arts and career-oriented programs. The foundation of every degree program is a core curriculum which emphasizes a broad base of knowledge in science, mathematics, social sciences, humanities, computer fundamentals, critical thinking, and oral and written communications.

Internships play a major role in all degree programs, and the college has an impressive record of internship placements. Students have been placed in work experiences at Fortune 500 companies, global corporations, and international companies in Japan, India, Italy and Germany. A short list of companies where Menlo students interned includes Apple Computers, Hewlett-Packard Company, Merrill Lynch & Co., the San Francisco Giants, and the Walt Disney Corporation.

One special characteristic of the Menlo curriculum is the emphasis on global learning. The Menlo campus is quite international, with about 20 percent of students coming from 28 countries. The college offers concentrations in international management or international policy studies, and opportunities for all students to spend a semester or year in England at Oxford College. The college also sponsors International Travel Courses to foreign countries where students investigate and experience first-hand the culture, language, politics, customs, and international relations of a specific nation.

Students and Student Life

550 students from 20 states and 29 foreign countries
40% are from out-of-state
20% are students of color
15% are international
75% live on campus in five residence halls

Ask any student about life on campus and they'll probably tell you that the students all know one another, but they're not all alike. The campus is a close-knit, intimate community, and the learning doesn't all take place in class! They learn from each other through the activities, clubs, and organizations sponsored by the college. In addition to the usual clubs and activities that encourage the development of leadership skills, Menlo provides a leadership training program for students. It's called the Leadershop Series. Monthly workshops focusing on the different aspects of leadership are offered to all club officers and other students.

The college is a busy place with more than 40 clubs and organizations in which to participate. Athletics are a favorite interest, and more than 30 percent of the students are members of one or more of the 13 men's and women's NCAA division III teams. Intramurals and the Outdoor Club are also very popular. Since the weather is nice most of the year, flag football, frisbee golf, sand volleyball, and inner-tube water polo attract fun-loving sportsmen and women.

Athletics: NCAA Division II
Women's Teams: cross-country, softball, tennis, track & field, volleyball
Men's Teams: baseball, basketball, cross country, football, golf, soccer, tennis, track & field, volleyball

Campus and Community

The 62-acre campus is located in one of the most attractive and exciting areas in the country. Nestled in an upscale residential community, the college is within walking distance to Menlo Park (a town of about 25,000 people) and less than a half-hour from San Francisco. The campus reflects the beauty of the northern California scenery and enjoys the mild weather of the San Francisco Bay area.

The college property is beautiful. The five residence halls offer students singles, doubles, and suite accommodations, and are located in park-like settings. The outdoor recreational facilities include pool, tennis courts, walking paths, and gardens. Students can easily get into San Francisco for internships, shopping, and cultural events, and visit friends at the 15 colleges in the area.

Menlo College Academic Offerings

Management: Environmental Resources Mgt. • General Management • International Management • Management Information Systems

Mass Communications: Electronic Communications • Media Management • Media Studies

Liberal Arts: Humanities • Human Resource Mgt. • International Policy Studies • Psychology

Admissions Statement

The Menlo College Admission Committee seeks to attract a very diverse group of students, both freshmen and transfer students. The committee reviews each application individually, and grants admission to those who are most likely to benefit from and contribute to the many programs and activities at Menlo College.

Missouri Valley College

Marshall, Missouri 65340-3197
(816) 886-6924

Missouri Valley College is a place where educational opportunities turn into scholastic success. It is a campus where students are not only educated in academic areas but also learn to become leaders and build community spirit. For more than 100 years the college has been offering liberal arts and career-focused majors, exciting internships, and interactive classroom environments where professors take an interest in their students. Affiliated with the Presbyterian Church since its founding in the late 1800s, the college is committed to preparing young people to become active and contributing members of society.

Academics

Degrees Offered: Associate, Bachelor's

Undergraduate Majors: 20 +

Student/Faculty Ratio: 17 to 1

Number of Faculty: 70

The emphasis at Missouri Valley College is on a personalized liberal arts education with a focus on career preparation. The college awards both Bachelor of Science and Bachelor of Arts degrees and has developed a curriculum that includes more than 20 majors within the Divisions of Arts/Humanities, Business, Education, Social Sciences, Human Service, and Mathematics/Science. The faculty members at the college are actively involved in teaching. They know their students by name and are aware of their abilities. Since most classes are not large, the faculty have the time to engage their students in a more individualized learning environment and can provide the encouragement, challenge, and mentoring relationship that brings out the best in every student.

The foundation for all degrees offered at the college is a core curriculum that includes courses in communication skills, language and literature, mathematics and science, social sciences, civilization, fine arts, and physical activities. This traditional core curriculum assures each student a solid base upon which to choose a major. From here students can develop a curriculum that includes major, minor, and elective subjects. Because the focus of the college is on career preparation, the majors have been designed to meet professional standards and to develop marketable skills.

Within the Division of Business, the major in actuarial science prepares students to become actuarial professionals, a highly respected and financially rewarding profession. In today's global world the need for actuarials far surpasses the number of trained people within the field, and the program at Missouri Valley is designed so that students can take the first set of qualifying exams required by the Society of Actuaries prior to graduation!

Alcohol and drug studies is a career-based major that comes out of the Division of Social Sciences. Students who choose this major will prepare for careers within the criminal justice, probation, and law enforcement/public service area, and will gain the specific knowledge and training necessary to take the Examination of the

Missouri State Substance Abuse Certification Board and become Certified Substance Abuse counselors.

Students who choose one of the liberal arts majors can incorporate a minor in a career focused area or pursue teacher certification is a specific area. No matter what major a student chooses, she or he will be well prepared to move out into the world of work.

Students and Student Life

1,200 students from 33 states and 16 foreign countries
29% are from out-of-state
20% are students of color
3% are international
1,000 live on campus

One reason students select Missouri Valley College is the school's reputation as a place where opportunity, leadership, tradition, and friendships are developed. With more than 75 percent of the students living on campus, the residential community is strong and active. Three national fraternities and three national sororities have houses on campus. Almost a third of all students belong to the Greek system. But Greeks are not the only ones who are busy on campus. The college sponsors about 40 different clubs, organizations, and activities, so there is usually a lot going on during the school year.

Volunteerism is an area where most students are involved. The close relationship between the campus and the city of Marshall is built upon student involvement in the community. The campus television and radio stations produce weekly shows that are created, directed, and feature Missouri Valley students and are broadcast weekly over the Marshall Cable TV System. Students interested in print media can write for the campus literary arts magazine, student newspaper, or be on the staff of the year-book.

If you are interested in the performing arts, Missouri Valley sponsors a comprehensive music and theater program that includes Valley Players, Musical Theater, Show Choir, Gospel Singers, Dance Concerts, and Children's Theater. As one student says, "There's always something to get involved in here on campus. I would say that almost all of the students at Missouri Valley are 'do-ers'—not couch potatoes!"

Athletics: NAIA and the Heart of America Conference
Women's Teams: basketball, cross country, softball, soccer, track & field, volleyball
Men's Teams: baseball, basketball, cross country, football, soccer, track & field, wrestling

Campus and Community

The 100-acre campus is located in the city of Marshall, Missouri. The college's main campus area is quite traditional, with redbrick buildings, winding pathways, and a large, picturesque central campus green. The five residential halls and six Greek houses are located around the perimeter of the academic quad, and the expansive modern athletic and recreational areas are located on the south part of the campus.

The 900 students who live on campus have a variety of residential accommodations to choose from, including Greek houses; suite, double, and single dorm rooms; and several house and apartment residences. The relatively new Georgia Robertson Burns Multi-Purpose Athletic Center is an all-inclusive athletic complex that includes a 40-acre recreation area, practice fields, horse barn, tennis courts, and other recreational/athletic facilities. Baity Hall, the oldest building on campus, is on the National Register of Historic Places.

Marshall has a population of about 15,000 people. It is a friendly midwestern city that offers shopping, entertainment, and opportunities for internships and community service projects. It is located 80 miles east of Kansas City and 180 miles west of St. Louis in an area of Missouri rich in history and outdoor opportunities. Missouri Valley College is an hour or less away from several other state and private universities, and is a member of the Kansas City Regional Council on Higher Education. If you are looking for a Christian college with a traditional campus and midwestern friendliness, take a good look at Missouri Valley.

Missouri Valley College Academic Offerings

Accounting • Actuarial Science • Agri-Business • Alcohol & Drug Studies • Art • Biology • Business Adm. • Computer Science • Criminal Justice • Economics • Education • English • History • Human Services Agency Mgt. • Mass Communication • Mathematics • Physical Education • Political Science • Public Adm. • Psychology • Recreation Adm. • Religion/Philosophy • Social Studies Ed. • Sociology • Speech Communication and Theater

Admissions Statement

Applications for admission to Missouri Valley College are reviewed individually; the college desires to select freshmen and transfer students who will benefit from the college's full-service program, and who demonstrate the potential for academic and personal success.

Monmouth University

West Long Branch, New Jersey 07764-1898
(908) 571-3400

Monmouth University is a midsize suburban university composed of the graduate division, the School of Business Administration, the Wayne D. McMurray School of Arts and Sciences, the School of Education, and the Edward G. Schlaefer School. It attracts students from diverse educational backgrounds. The campus, once the estate of F.W. Woolworth, is gorgeous and continues to be updated and expanded. The neoclassical architecture of the past is blended with the new state-of-the-art facilities to provide a traditional yet innovative campus environment.

In the past 60 years, Monmouth has grown from a small regional college to a comprehensive teaching university where teaching and technology go hand in hand. The university has 17 computer laboratories, in addition to terminals in the residence halls. The student-to-computer ratio is 11 to 1. Every student receives an e-mail account. Monmouth University's undergraduate curriculum is built upon an innovative, interdisciplinary, general-education program; comprehensive preparation in a major area; and opportunities to develop collaborative problem-solving skills, leadership, and responsibility. Small classes, interactive student-faculty exchange, and cooperative learning are all dimensions of the Monmouth degree.

Academics

Degrees Offered: Bachelor's, Master's

Undergraduate Majors: 45

Student/Faculty Ratio: 16 to 1

Average Class Size: 21

The Edward G. Schlaefer School, one of the five divisions within the university, was established to provide extra support and a more structured learning environment for students who have not met regular admission requirements, but who appear to have the potential for college. Through a combination of small class sections limited to Schlaefer students, additional class time, trained faculty and perhaps even a reduced course load, students are provided with the assistance and opportunity they need to succeed. When Schlaefer students complete college English II and have a GPA of at least a 2.0, they can move into the major of their choice.

Monmouth University has also developed a rigorous honors program for students at the other end of the spectrum. Freshman Honors is comprised of a series of honors courses integrated around a theme. During subsequent years, students can choose selective honors courses or pursue the entire honors program.

All students at Monmouth can study abroad through the College Consortium for International Studies, which offers a semester or year of study in Spain, Ireland, France, and England; and the Partnership for Service-Learning which combines academic study and community service in several countries including England, Jamaica, and The Philippines. Monmouth University participates in the Washington Center program which provides on-the-job experience with academic study in Washington, D.C.

Students and Student Life

2,400 undergraduate students from 19 states and 43 foreign countries
11% are students of color
140 are international
1,200 live on campus in seven residential halls and two garden-apartment complexes

Monmouth University takes a holistic approach to education and provides opportunities for students to develop academically, socially, and personally. Through a co-curricular program that includes sports, professional associations, lecture series, comedy shows, and cultural celebrations, the university encourages students to define what they like and do it. More than 70 campus organizations are offered. Things like campus publications, WMCY-FM radio station, honor societies and special interest groups are all available to everyone who wants to participate. There are also eight national fraternities and five national sororities that have chapters on campus.

Athletics: NCAA Division I, Northeast Conference
Women's Teams: basketball, cross country, lacrosse, soccer, softball, tennis, track
Men's Teams: baseball, basketball, cross country, football, golf, soccer, tennis, track

Campus and Community

The stately 140-acre campus is located in a quiet residential community on the Jersey Shore. The campus, with its 49 buildings, estate gardens, and lawns, is truly spectacular. Woodrow Wilson Hall, the main building on campus, is a beautiful example of neoclassical French architecture. Its 130 rooms now serve as the university's administrative center. The Guggenheim Memorial Library, once the summer home of Murray and Leonie Guggenheim, hold the university's extensive reference and book collection. Both structures are in the National Register of Historic Places.

In contrast to these remarkable stately mansions, the campus also houses a new modern Business Administration building, fitness center, and garden apartments. All are tastefully blended into the serene campus environment. West Long Branch and the surrounding communities provides an abundance of internship sites, shopping opportunities, and recreational events. The town is located an hour and a half from both Philadelphia and New York City, and close to nearly 10 other colleges and universities.

Monmouth University Academic Offerings

The School of Business Administration: Accounting • Economics • Finance • Management • Marketing

The Wayne D. McMurray School of Arts and Sciences: Anthropology • Art (studio & computer design) • Biology • Chemistry • Communications • Computer Science • Criminal Justice • Education • English • History • History/Political Science • Mathematics • Medical Technology • Music • Nursing (transfer RN only) • Physics/Computer Science • Political Science • Psychology • Spanish • Social Work • School of Education

To earn certification as an early childhood and elementary teacher, students are required to simultaneously complete the requirements of both a B.A. program in education and one of the B.A. or B.S. programs in the College of Arts and Sciences.

To earn certification in a K-12 subject area, students are required to simultaneously complete the requirements for both the B.A. program in education and one of the B.A. programs in the College of Arts and Sciences, or complete the B.S. program in education and one of the B.S. programs in the College of Arts and Sciences.

Admissions Statement

Admission to Monmouth University is based upon many factors. Previous academic achievement, test scores, extracurricular activities, work experience, and personal qualities all play a part. Recognizing that each student is different, Monmouth makes every attempt to ensure that its selection process is as fair to each student as possible. A personal interview is encouraged and a campus tour is strongly recommended.

Morehead State University

Morehead, Kentucky 40351
(606) 783-2000 or (800) 262 7474

Morehead State University has a proud history spanning over 100 years. Started as a small private school known as Morehead Normal School in 1887, the institution has changed significantly during the past century, but it has never abandoned its commitment to providing a comprehensive, quality, affordable education. Today the midsize state university enrolls over 8,400 students in associate, bachelor's, and master's degree programs. Located in the northeast section of Kentucky, Morehead State University has a 500-acre campus which includes a nine-hole golf course, a 320-acre experimental farm, and some of the finest academic and recreational facilities in the area.

Academics

Degrees Offered: Associate, Bachelor's, Master's
Undergraduate Majors: 96
Student/Faculty Ratio: 18 to 1
Number of Faculty: 350 full and part time

Morehead State is a comprehensive state university that offers more than 96 different undergraduate majors. The university is small enough to provide an educational environment that can meet the needs of its students and large enough to offer more than several hundred courses each semester in a variety of learning formats.

The university is made up of four undergraduate colleges: the College of Business; the College of Education and Behavioral Sciences; the Caudill College of Humanities; and the College of Science and Technology. The academic offerings at the university represent traditional majors like business, psychology, art, nursing, and some very unique majors like computer information systems, ornamental horticulture and manufacturing/robotics technology.

The foundation for all bachelor degree programs is a 42-credit general education requirement that combines 15 credits in communications and humanities, 12 credits in natural and mathematical sciences, 12 credits in social and behavioral sciences, and three credits in health and physical education.

Students at Morehead State come from different academic backgrounds and the university offers educational advantages for a range of students. The cooperative experience combines alternating semesters of supervised course-related work with on-campus classes. Students receive academic credit and a salary for each work experience. In some cases students enrolled in the cooperative education program take five years to complete a bachelor degree. As one student says, "The co-op program required an additional year at Morehead State, but it also gave me job experience and a way to finance most of my college education."

Students can also combine their academic studies with an experiential learning opportunity through the Washington Center National Government Seminar and Internship Program. Students choose an intensive two-week seminar program or a semester-long internship in one of the many senatorial or congressional offices in Washington, D.C. And you do not have to be a government or political science major to participate in this program. It's open to all students.

The Honors Program at Morehead is much more than just enrolling in academically enriching courses. The program combines selected honors-level general-education courses, interactive upper-division seminars, and an independent project in the senior year. Students invited into the Honors Program also receive special opportunities and recognition. They have more flexibility in their major field content requirements, receive special library privileges (including a separate study room and free computer research) and participate in a yearly "seminar week." Special programs like these display to the university's success in providing academic programs for students of varied educational backgrounds.

Students and Student Life

6,800 students from 38 states and 32 foreign countries
12% are from out-of-state
6% are students of color
1% are international
3,400 live on campus

With over 100 organizations on campus, undergraduate students have a large choice of social, recreational, and cultural activities to choose from. The long list of student organizations includes more than 25 academic organizations, five club sports, 13 honors organizations, seven religious clubs, 14 service organizations, and four social organizations!

The university presents at least four major theatrical productions each year, along with numerous concerts that feature the MSU percussion ensembles, jazz ensembles, university chorus, and concert and symphony band. One of the largest and most active campus groups are the Greeks. About 8 percent of the students are members of the 12 fraternities and 10 sororities. They are active in Homecoming activities, sponsor Greek Week in the spring, and provide a number of community service activities on campus and in the community.

Morehead State students and alumni are big supporters of the Eagles and the university puts together a great half-time show during the home football games including performances by the national champion cheerleaders, marching band, and nationally recognized percussion ensemble.

Athletics: NCAA Division I football team is in Division 1AA.
Women's Teams: basketball, cross country, squash, swimming and diving, tennis, track & field, volleyball
Men's Teams: baseball, basketball, cross country, football, golf, soccer, swimming and diving, tennis, track & field

Campus and Community

The campus is composed of nearly 1,000 acres of land. The main campus, which houses the academic, athletic, and residential buildings, is approximately 500 acres and is located adjacent to the Daniel Boone National Forest. On the southern border, the university stretches right to the busy shopping district in the city of Morehead.

The 50 major buildings on campus are a combination of contemporary and traditional architecture. In addition to the main campus the university has a 320-acre experimental farm that is used extensively by those students enrolled in agriculture courses, and a nine-hole golf course. Residential facilities include apartment-style housing, coed dormitories, single-sex dormitories, and freshman-only halls.

When the students at Morehead State want to get away from it all, they can enjoy the beauty and tranquillity of the Daniel Boone National Forest, or sail, swim, or soak up the sun at Cave Run Lake, a 15-minute ride from campus. For those students who want more of a city adventure, Lexington is an hour west and Cincinnati is two hours north.

Morehead State University Academic Offerings

Accounting • Agricultural Ed. • Agricultural Science • Agricultural Technology • Art • Biology • Child Development • Communications • Comprehensive Business • Computer Information Systems • Criminology • Economics • Education • Environmental Science • Finance • Foreign Language • Geography • Geology • Government • Health • History • Human Science • Industrial Technology • Interdisciplinary • Management • Marketing • Mathematics • Medical Technology • Music • Nursing • Office Systems • Paralegal Studies • Philosophy • Physical Ed. • Physics • Radiological Technology • Real Estate • Recreation • Social Work • Sociology • Speech

Admissions Statement

If you are a graduate of an accredited high school, you will be admitted to the University if you meet the Pre-College Curriculum required by the Kentucky Council on

Higher Education and have a minimum admission index of 400. The admission index is computed by adding together your GPA (GPA must be on a 4.0 scale) times 100 and your composite ACT score (or converted SAT) times 10.

Mount Marty College

Yankton, South Dakota 57078-3724
(605) 668-1545 or (800) 658-4552

Founded in 1936, Mount Marty College is one of 19 Benedictine Colleges in the United States and Canada. This small private college offers career-oriented degrees in more than 30 academic areas. Because the mission of the college is to educate the whole person, students are taught more than policy, theory, and a career skill. Cooperative learning, interactive classroom presentations, and experiential learning are all part of the degree programs offered at Mount Marty College, and that is why in recent years almost 95 percent or more of Mount Marty graduates are employed or pursuing further education within several months of graduation.

Academics

Degrees Offered: Associate, Bachelor's, Master's

Undergraduate Majors: 18 majors with more than 30 areas of concentration

Student/Faculty Ratio: 10 to 1

Average Class Size: 20

Number of Faculty: 81 full and part time

The educational process at the college focuses on "developing intellectual competence, professional and personal skills, and moral spiritual and social values." A strong core curriculum is the beginning of this learning process, but that is not the only element. By the time students graduate from Mount Marty College they will have gained insight into the human concerns of contemporary society, examined their value system in light of ethical principles, participated in a primary research experience, developed in-depth knowledge and competency in their major field, and be knowledgeable about and able to use current technology.

The college has developed and initiated academic programs that develop skills, introduce students to the arts, foster leadership, and immerse students in the learning process. Students can design their own major, or take a course as independent study.

They can accelerate their degree program and graduate early or they can spend a semester abroad. As a member of Colleges of Mid-America, a cooperative group of five independent colleges in South Dakota and Iowa, students at Mount Marty can participate in an exchange program for a semester or a year at one of the other schools. Learning is not a static process at Mount Marty, and students have every opportunity to succeed.

Students and Student Life

900 students from 28 states and 5 foreign countries
4% are students of color
1% are international
400 live on campus in three residence halls.

The college offers campus activities that promote leadership development, social interaction, recreation, and community service. Performing arts activities include jazz band, concert band, chorus, theater productions, and talent shows. There is a student government organization, school newspaper, and literary magazine. The college sponsors eight honor societies, like Phi Beta Lambda and Phi Alpha Theta; 10 department and professional organizations, like English Club and Mass Communications Club; 10 recreational sports, including volleyball and Tae Kwon Do; and special interest groups like Spirit Team, Federation of Christian Athletes, and Benedictine Oblates.

Athletics: NAIA
Women's Teams: basketball, cross country, track, volleyball
Men's Teams: baseball, basketball, cross country, golf, track

Campus and Community

The 80-acre campus is located in historic Yankton, South Dakota (population 13,000) just minutes away from Lewis & Clark Lake, one of the state's most popular recreation areas. The campus overlooks the Mississippi River and its facilities include the Bishop Marty Chapel, a Yankton landmark and one of the country's best example of Western Gothic architecture; Laddie E. Cimpl Arena, a modern sports and recreation building that houses volleyball courts, a jogging track, basketball court, and an 1,800-seat stadium; and the Roncalli Center, with dining facilities, Bede Art Gallery, and student government and club offices.

Three residence halls house approximately 400 students in comfortable living arrangements. All of the science laboratories and facilities were totally renovated in the late 1980s and provide modern technology and equipment for student use. New computer laboratories were added recently, giving students 24-hour Internet access in residential halls and academic buildings. The campus is a pleasant and comfortable place to live and study. Recreational activities are close by and students have easy access to the town of Yankton.

Mount Marty College Academic Offerings

Associate Degrees: Accounting • Business Adm. • General Studies • Religious Studies

Bachelor's Degrees: Accounting • Biology • Business Administration, with emphasis in bank management, marketing, management • Chemistry • Communications • Computer Science • Education, including elementary, secondary, special education • English • Environmental Science • Health, Phys. Ed & Recreation • Mathematics Medical Technology • Music • Nursing • Nutrition & Food Science • Religious Studies • Selected Studies • Social Science, with emphasis in criminal justice, history, political science, psychology, sociology, social gerontology

Admissions Statement

Students are considered for admissions to Mount Marty College if they have a high school GPA of 2.0 or achieve an ACT composite score of 18 or above or SAT combined score of 740 or above.

North Adams State College

North Adams, Massachusetts 01247-4100
(413) 662-5410 or (800) 292-6632

Nestled in the northwest corner of the Berkshire Mountains is a small, public liberal arts college that offers students a caring, residential community, academic programs that prepare them for careers or entry into professional and graduate schools, and a faculty that is talented, dedicated, and committed to teaching. The school is North Adams State College. With an enrollment of 1,600 men and women, it offers both a variety of academic options and campus activities, and a personal and challenging learning environment. For over 100 years, North Adams State College has been the educational choice for many New Englanders.

Academics

Degrees Offered: Bachelor's, Master's
Undergraduate Majors: 35+
Student/Faculty Ratio: 17 to 1
Number of Faculty: 113 full and part time

As the public liberal arts college of Massachusetts, North Adams State's curriculum is made up of courses and programs that are relevant, emphasize intellectual versatility, and prepare students for future academic encounters. It has not forsaken more career-oriented majors like business, education, and medical technology, but instead has garnished these and all its academic majors with an extensive foundation in traditional liberal studies.

At NASC, the general-education requirements offer students an opportunity to gain knowledge in a variety of subject areas, while developing and refining their ability to think, analyze, reason, and communicate. The general education program encompasses 47 credits, and students have between 10 and 30 courses to choose from in each of the eight categories, which include basic skills, language and logic, empirical science, arts and humanities, historical studies, individual and society, personal fitness, and cross cultures. How about Introduction to Weather and Climate, Treasures of Ancient America, Culture, Health and Illness, or Search for the Quality of Life? All are available as part of general education requirements.

In all, students have 15 majors and 20 concentrations from which to choose. Students can also combine a major with 26 minor areas to create a more individualized or career-focused program. Some of the more unique minors are Canadian studies, an 18-credit course sequence that covers topics in Canadian history, geography, politics, and culture; health, aging, and society, an 18-credit program that gives students a good background on issues of aging and health; and information systems, a 19-credit major that provides students with a knowledge of computers and information processing.

Another characteristic of NASC is the abundance of experiential learning opportunities available on campus and in the Berkshire community. In the English/Communication major, for example, students can work on the weekly student newspaper, *The Beacon;* an annual literary magazine, *Kaleidoscope*; and the campus radio station, WJJW. Department facilities include a student-operated, full-production television studio located in Murdock Hall. It is equipped with four studio cameras, a video switcher/special effects generator with chroma key, a 16-bus audio mixing board, two three-quarter inch editing systems, and three portable field units. Students work closely with the technical director of the TV studio and take part in actually producing news, sports, entertainment, and live programming seen in the local community. All of these 'extras' provide opportunities for practical experience, and students don't even have to leave the campus.

Students and Student Life

1,600 students from 20 states
20% are from out-of-state
6% are students of color
1% are international
65% live on campus

Students are involved in a variety of pursuits. Many of them participate in one of several volunteer programs sponsored by the college. These include Big Brother/Big Sister, Habitat for Humanity, Hospice of Northern Berkshire, YMCA, and other community organizations. Students run the campus radio station, prepare shows for the local cable TV stations, and are involved in professional organizations affiliated with their major.

The college sponsors an African American student club, a multicultural organization, a Native American club, an outing club, and a women's issues organization. About 20 percent of the men and women at the college belong to one of the four fraternities or four sororities on campus. There are 14 intramural teams like water polo, indoor soccer, and swimming; nine club sports including cycling, skiing, and weight lifting; and seven men's and women's intercollegiate teams.

Athletics: NAAA Division III and the Eastern College Athletic Conference
Women's Teams: basketball, cross country, soccer, softball, tennis
Men's Teams: baseball, basketball, cross country, hockey, soccer

Campus and Community

North Adams State College has a beautiful 80-acre campus that is just a short walk from the center of town. The campus is tucked amid the rolling hills of the Berkshires. It is comfortable, attractive, and spacious. The three residence facilities are all equipped with new telecommunications systems, including Internet access, nationwide library research access, cable TV, and individual telephone lines and voice mail. Berkshire Towers is an eight-story residence hall that accommodates 320 men and women in suite-style rooms. It is used primarily for first-year students. Hoosac Hall, a seven-story building, houses 216 students in suites, and Flagg Townhouse Apartment Complex is designed for 508 men and women.

The Campus Center, a physically imposing building, is the focal point of student activities. It houses the Office of Student Life. The west wing of the building is the athletic complex, complete with swimming pool, gymnasium, and dance complex, and handball, racquetball, and squash courts. The east wing houses two dining areas, the campus bookstore, and a top-of-the-line Fitness Center.

All of the academic buildings have been updated and equipped with modern laboratories, computer facilities, and technology-enhanced classrooms. The Freel Library has online research capacity and shares an electronic circulation system with 80 member libraries.

The city of North Adams is a typical small New England community with quaint Victorian homes and a small downtown shopping area. The Berkshires are home to many cultural sites including the Norman Rockwell Museum, Hancock Shaker Village, and the Berkshire Scenic Railway Museum. There are two excellent ski areas about 30 minutes away, and about a dozen other colleges within an hour's drive.

North Adams State College Academic Offerings

Accounting • Anthropology • Art • Arts Mgt. • Biology • Broadcast Media • Business Adm. • Chemistry • Computer Science • Crime & Delinquency • Cytotechnology • Education Certification • English/Communications • Finance/ Economics Mgt. • Fine and Performing Arts • Health Sciences • History • Information Systems • Interdisciplinary Studies • Journalism • Literature • Marketing • Mathematics • Medical Technology • Music Studies • Philosophy • Physics • Political Science • Psychology • Public Relations • Social Work • Sociology • Sports Medicine • Theater Studies • Writing

Admissions Statement

North Adams State College actively seeks students who exhibit the potential for academic and personal growth. Admissions standards have been designed to assist us in attracting qualified students who can benefit from a liberal arts education along with contributing to the college community. The average GPA of incoming first year students is 2.7 and the average SAT 1 scores are 990.

New England College

Henniker, New Hampshire 03242-3297
(603) 428-2223 or (800) 521-7642

New England College is an independent liberal arts college where international education and professional programs are important components of an education. The college has two academic facilities and environments. At the campus in Henniker, New Hampshire, approximately 900 graduate and undergraduate students are enrolled in more than 15 academic majors and three graduate programs. At the campus in Arundel, England, more than 150 American and international students pursue undergraduate degrees in four areas. The common administration and shared curriculum make it possible for students to attend either campus for a semester or a year, or complete an entire degree program in Arundel or Henniker.

At both campuses, students will enjoy an intimate academic community which features small classes, faculty members whose first concern is the success of their students, and a modern curriculum that incorporates an international focus, experiential learning, and traditional course work.

Academics

Degrees Offered: Bachelor's, Master's

Undergraduate Majors: 15

Student/Faculty Ratio: 12 to 1

Average Class Size: 15

Number of Faculty: 60 full and part time

At New England College, the bachelor's degree curriculum explores the liberal arts through courses in humanities, social sciences, and natural sciences; a comprehensive specialization in a major subject; participation in community service and internships that link academic majors with the world of work; and academic and social encounters that increase students' global awareness and introduce them to multicultural experiences. This education process is very different from programs offered at other colleges.

New England College can offer such a unique program because it is a global college: one college, two countries, many cultures. The Arundel campus, established in 1971, enrolls students from more than 30 countries in bachelor's degree programs in business administration, English, humanities, and international relations. The international and cross-cultural perspectives at the Arundel campus are part of the academic and social environment, adding a global dimension to all the degree programs. New England College is one of only a handful of institutions in the country to provide this type of international opportunity to its students.

At New England College, the vast majority of majors come from the traditional liberal arts and sciences, but the career opportunities are numerous because of the well-defined internship programs and the specialized career emphasis built into many of the liberal arts majors.

Students who major in education can secure teacher certification in most states. Students with a major in kinesiology can concentrate in coaching, athletic training, or fitness leadership. Students who major in art can take a minor in advertising and pursue a career in public relations. Students at New England College can earn up to 15 credits in internship experiences. Some recent internship placements have included the Boston Film Factory; the New Hampshire Conservation Commission; WGBH, Boston; and Turner Broadcasting Systems, Atlanta, Georgia.

Students and Student Life

900 students from 35 states and 25 nations at the Henniker campus
150 students from 33 nations at the Arundel campus
4% are students of color
8% are international
65% live on campus

From activities to professional organizations, the emphasis is on participation, and almost all of the students at New England College do participate in at least one student club. Campus life includes clubs like Adventurebound, Blue Chip Association, Greek Council, Women's Network, fraternities, sororities, and a wildlife rehabilitation program. Almost 50 percent of the student body are members of an intramural or intercollegiate sports team. Another popular activity on campus is community service. Eight different service programs are undertaken each year by New England College students. These include national programs like Habitat for Humanity and Red Cross blood drives, and local programs like Book Buddies and events with local senior citizens.

Athletics: NCAA Division III (Skiing is Division I)
Women's Teams: alpine and Nordic skiing, basketball, field hockey, lacrosse, soccer, softball
Men's Teams: alpine and Nordic skiing, baseball, basketball, ice hockey, lacrosse, soccer

Campus and Community

New England College is located in the village of Henniker, New Hampshire, an area characterized by beautiful scenery, endless outdoor recreational opportunities, and access to big cities like Boston and small cities like Concord, New Hampshire. There are more than six colleges within a 30-minute drive. The 212-acre campus blends classic New England architecture and traditional college buildings to produce an appealing campus and a comfortable living/learning environment.

The 30 buildings include the science building, which is equipped with modern labs, classrooms, and faculty offices, and eight residence halls providing single-sex and coed halls, special-interest housing suites, and apartments. The college has theater facilities that are housed in Carriage House; an art gallery located in Preston Hall; and the Danforth Library, with more than 100,000 volumes and online bibliographic search services.

The Arundel Campus is 25 acres and consists of residential halls, dining room, classrooms and administrative offices, student center, and athletic facilities. It is located 55 miles from London, England, and originally served as a country estate for British royalty.

New England College Academic Offerings

Art • Biology • Business Adm. • Communication • Education • Environmental Science • Kinesiology, with concentrations in athletic training, coaching, fitness leadership • Literature • Philosophy • Physical Ed. • Political Science • Sociology • Special Education • Theater

Admissions Statement

Admission to New England College is based on your academic and personal accomplishments. We have joined several major colleges and universities in eliminating SAT scores from our admission requirements. Your academic record, personal recommendations, extracurricular achievements, work experience, and special talents are more important to us.

New Hampshire College

Manchester, New Hampshire 03106-1045
(603) 668-2211 or (800) NHC-4YOU

New Hampshire College is a small private college that offers programs in business, hospitality administration, and the liberal arts. The classes are small, and faculty make a point of knowing students' names. The programs at NHC blend theory and practice so that students have both textbook knowledge and job experience before they graduate. The college has gained a solid reputation in the East and has alumni working throughout the world. New Hampshire College has recently embarked upon a building campaign which will provide new residence halls and a totally new hospitality center. This is definitely a campus on the rise.

Academics

Degrees Offered: Associate, Bachelor's, Master's

Undergraduate Majors: 35

Student/Faculty Ratio: 17 to 1

Number of Faculty: 239 full and part time

All degree programs at New Hampshire College impart the knowledge, skill, and confidence needed by young adults to lead fulfilling lives and successful careers. The college is dedicated to teaching and has gained a reputation for being innovative and offering challenging, high quality educational programs on the undergraduate and graduate levels.

NHC is also committed to educating the whole person in a caring, friendly environment that fosters learning partnerships among students, faculty, and staff. Students become actively involved in the learning process, which encompasses opportunities for community service and work experience. The faculty bring practical professional experience into the classroom, and students have the great advantage of working with professionals in the field.

At New Hampshire College, students can choose from more than 35 major areas. They can acquire teacher certification, enroll in three-, six-, and 12-credit cooperative learning experiences, or take part in an ROTC program. The choices are wide open, and there are faculty and staff to guide students every step of the way.

Students and Student Life

1,227 students from 31 states and 60 foreign countries
45% are from out-of-state
4% are students of color
18% are international
80% live on campus

The student government association is active and involved in the social, educational, recreational, and community service aspects of college life. The SGA has student representation on all major college committees and oversees most of the happenings on campus. With 40 clubs and organizations, they provide opportunities and activities for all types of students. There are religious organization that promote spiritual, social, and service projects on campus and within the Manchester community. These include the Jewish student association, Protestant student association, Catholic student association, and Campus Ministry.

Fraternities and sororities make up a large part of the social scene on campus, and the college has four national fraternity chapters and four national sorority chapters. Clubs like culinary association, future teachers, and marketing club bring speakers to campus regularly and offer students the chance to attend off campus activities and regional and national conferences. The college also has Camp Synergy, a leadership-development program that utilizes Outward Bound-type activities to build confidence, effective communication skills, and team work.

Athletics: NCAA Division II
Women's Teams: basketball, cheerleading, cross country, running, soccer, softball, volleyball
Men's Teams: baseball, basketball, hockey, lacrosse, soccer

Campus and Community

New Hampshire College is located in Manchester, New Hampshire, the largest city in the state. The College has two campuses. South Campus is more than 200 acres and accommodates 20 major buildings, including classroom/administrative buildings, residence halls, a computer center, library complex, student center, and a large athletic/recreational complex.

North campus is about four miles away, located on more than 500 acres. This campus houses classrooms, administrative offices, dining facilities, graduate school and graduate housing, the Culinary Institute, and the American Language and Cultural Center. Classrooms are comfortable and have the latest in technology. College housing accommodates more than 80 percent of the students in traditional residence halls, town houses, and campus apartments.

The City of Manchester has over 100,000 people, several shopping malls, a number of fine restaurants, and lots of recreational spots. It is also about an hours' drive to Boston, great skiing, and terrific ocean beaches.

New Hampshire College Academic Offerings

Associate Degrees: Accounting • Business Adm. • Computer Information System • Culinary Arts • Retail/Fashion Merchandising • Liberal Arts • Marketing

Bachelor's Degrees: Accounting • Aviation Mgt. • Business Adm. • Business Finance • Communications • Computer Information Systems • Economics/Finance • English Language and Literature • Hospitality Adm. • Hotel Adm. • Humanities • Human Resource Mgt. • International Business • Management Advisory Services • Marketing • Materials Mgt. • Production and Inventory Control • Psychology • Restaurant Mgt. • Retailing • Small Business Mgt. • Social Sciences • Sports Mgt. • Teacher Ed. • Technical Mgt. • Travel and Tourism

Admissions Statement

Candidates for admission are evaluated individually on the basis of academic credentials and personal characteristics. Emphasis is placed on identifying the strengths that each applicant can draw upon to achieve academic success at New Hampshire College. Students should be graduates of an accredited high school, have completed a college prep program and have acceptable scores on the SAT 1 or ACT.

University of New Haven

New Haven, Connecticut 06516-1916
(203) 932-7088 or (800) DIAL-UNH

The University of New Haven is a suburban school that focuses on career-oriented degree programs. It has a strong international reputation and has attracted both graduate and undergraduate students from all over the world. Founded in 1920 as a junior college, the school now has attained university status. It offers degree programs in 75 areas and has an enrollment of approximately 1,500 full-time day students, over 1,000 part-time students, and close to 5,000 graduate students.

The university has remained focused on the academic needs of the student and the professional needs of the New England/greater New York area and has developed successful programs that accommodate both groups. Internships, small classes, professors who are fine teachers as well as working professionals, and a well-established cooperative education program are all part of the university's formula for success.

Academics

Degrees Offered: Associate, Bachelor's, Master's

Undergraduate Majors: 75

Student/Faculty Ratio: 19 to 1

Number of Faculty: 546 full and part time

The University of New Haven is made up of six schools: the School of Arts and Science; the School of Business; the School of Engineering; the School of Public Safety and Professional Studies; the School of Hotel, Restaurant, and Tourism Administration; and the Graduate School. All degree programs at the university combine humanistic and liberal studies that help develop critical-thinking skills and professional and technological training.

The 34-credit core requirement taken by all students has courses in communications, mathematics, computers, social sciences, history, and humanities. Combining this university core with any major gives students skills and conceptual abilities, shared common experiences, and a broad perspective in their discipline.

While the focus of most liberal arts majors within the School of Arts and Sciences is preparing students for a lifetime of learning, students at the University of New Haven can integrate certificate programs or minors in subjects like computer science, marketing, legal affairs, or travel and tourism that can make them more marketable.

The major degree programs offered by the School of Business provide students with a basic knowledge in general business areas, comprehensive knowledge and professional skills in specialty areas, and the opportunity to incorporate a cooperative experience into their program of studies. Students in the School of Engineering are prepared for both professional practice and graduate studies.

The School of Hotel, Restaurant, and Tourism Administration consists of three departments: general dietetics, hotel and restaurant management, and tourism and travel administration. Along with courses in their specialty, students must also complete a 500- to 1,000-hour practicum.

The School of Public Safety and Professional Studies provides a broad professional education in areas of aviation, law enforcement, fire technology, and occupational safety. The curriculum is designed to incorporate classroom learning with laboratory and field experience. The university maintains an office and facilities at nearby Tweed-New Haven airport, and students in the aviation programs can train for and receive a pilot's license.

Students and Student Life

1,500 full-time undergraduates; 1,500 part-time undergraduates; 4,000 graduate students
20% are students of color
10% are international
750 undergraduates live on campus

The university sponsors over 40 student organizations. Many of these clubs, like the international student association, the Latin American student association, and the Black Student Union, reflect the multicultural backgrounds of the students.

Academic associations include the aviation club, fire science club, and travel & tourism club. The University of New Haven also has several chapters of national professional associations like the American Society of Chemical Engineers. There are five fraternities and three sororities, several community service organizations, and several recreational clubs like the ski club. *The Charger Bulletin* is the weekly student newspaper and WNHU, the student radio station, broadcasts in stereo year-round.

Athletics: NCAA Division II, the Eastern College Athletic and New England Collegiate conferences
Women's Teams: basketball, soccer, softball, tennis, volleyball
Men's Teams: baseball, basketball, cross country, football, lacrosse, soccer, track & field

Campus and Community

The University of New Haven is located on 73 acres of land in West Haven. The 22 buildings are characterized by modern laboratories and classrooms, high-tech research facilities, and well-furnished athletic and residential facilities. The majority of the academic buildings are located on south campus; the athletic facilities and fields are on the north campus. The university has four residence halls on campus with suite- and apartment-style living arrangements for 700 students.

University of New Haven Academic Offerings

School of Arts & Sciences: Art • Biology • Biomedical Computing • Chemistry • Clinical Laboratory Science/Medical Technology • Communications • Computer Science • Dental Hygiene • Economics • English • Environmental Science • General Studies • Graphic Design • History • Interior Design • Journalism • Literature • Mathematics • Music • Music Industry • Music & Sound Recording • Political Science • Psychology • Statistics • Writing

School of Business: Accounting • Business Adm. • Business Economics • Communications • Finance • International Business • Managerial Accounting • Management of Sports Industries • Marketing

School of Engineering: Chemical Engineering • Chemistry • Civil Engineering • Computer Science • Electrical Engineering • Engineering • Industrial Engineering • Mechanical Engineering

School of Hotel, Restaurant, and Tourism Administration: General Dietetics • Hotel & Restaurant Mgt. • Tourism & Travel Administration

School of Public Safety & Professional Studies: Air Transportation Mgt. • Arson Investigation • Aviation Science • Correction • Criminal Justice • Fire & Occupational Safety • Fire Protection Engineering • Fire Science Adm. • Fire Science Technology • Forensic Science • Juvenile & Family Justice • Law Enforcement Adm. • Law Enforcement Science • Occupational Safety & Health Adm. • Occupational Safety & Health Technology • Security Mgt.

Admissions Statement

Admissions credentials are reviewed individually by the Admission Committee. A student's overall academic record, class rank, letters of recommendation or reference, extracurricular activities, and scores on the SAT 1 or ACT are all considered prior to an admission decision.

Nichols College

Dudley, Massachusetts 01571
(508) 943-2055 or (800) 470-3379

Nichols is a small independent college offering degree programs in three specific areas: business administration, public administration, and liberal studies. It has earned a reputation for providing a quality education and has stepped to the forefront of higher education by being one of only a few colleges that provide a notebook computer, modem, and software package for each student. Computer application is introduced at freshman orientation and used throughout the four years at college. Nichols is committed to the classroom use of PCs by students and faculty.

The campus is networked via computer connections and phone lines so students can communicate with faculty, staff, fellow students, the library, or use specialized software directly from their classrooms, residence halls, or off-campus homes. While the college is on the cutting edge, it has not abandoned its emphasis on providing personal attention within the classroom. Here, as always, the focus is on teaching. Classes are small (with under 25 students in most classes), and faculty and students work together in the learning process.

Academics

Degrees Offered: Bachelor's, Master's
Undergraduate Majors: 15
Student/Faculty Ratio: 22 to 1
Number of Faculty: 45 full and part time

Nichols College offers three undergraduate degree programs: the Bachelor of Science in Business Administration, the Bachelor of Science in Public Administration, and the Bachelor of Arts. Each degree program combines study in professional areas with a basic grounding in the liberal arts and sciences. Students majoring in business or public administration will complete almost 50 percent of their degree program in liberal studies, and students completing a Bachelor of Arts degree will develop a strong liberal base through courses in English, foreign language, history, social sciences, environmental science, mathematics, computer principles, and humanities.

Another common element in the degree programs is the integration of computer applications into all aspects of education. The Nichols PC Plan was established in 1986 to keep Nichols College in the forefront of education for business management. Since then the program has been so successful that it is hard to imagine how other colleges operate without one.

Incoming freshmen receive their notebook computer at orientation along with the versatile Microsoft Office Professional software programs, color bubble jet printer, and supplies. Students receive eight weeks of hands-on training in the care and use of their computer. Many classrooms are equipped with computer projectors, allowing faculty to display a computer screen to the entire class. Nichols' students learn to use the computer as a tool in data analysis and decision making. By the time students graduate, they have four years' experience that goes way beyond a basic understanding of computer information systems and microcomputer applications.

Through a solid foundation in the liberal arts and the integration of computers in all aspects of the learning process, Nichols' students can handle just about any career in the 21st century.

Students and Student Life

750 undergraduate students from 16 states and 7 foreign countries
400 graduate students
32% are from out-of-state
4% are students of color
1% are international
75% live on campus

The campus is an active place days, evenings, and weekends—it's like its own little community. There is a strong student government that has jurisdiction over club activities, social events, student conduct, and dormitory living. *The Bison*, the school newspaper, and WNRC FM the campus radio station, keep students informed of the current happenings on and around campus.

There are several service clubs, including the Nichols College Fire Department, which is staffed on a volunteer basis by students trained in first response techniques like fire fighting, first aid, and CPR. There are four honor societies; nine professional clubs like the marketing club, psychology club, and economics club; and three student publications. There is a large intramural sports program, a club sport program, and an intercollegiate athletic program. Club sports include men's alpine racing team and rugby, and women's rugby and racquetball.

Athletics: NCAA Division III
Women's Teams: basketball, field hockey, soccer, softball, tennis
Men's Teams: baseball, basketball, football, ice hockey, lacrosse, soccer, tennis
Coed Teams: cheerleading, golf, track & field

Campus and Community

The Nichols College campus is approximately 210 acres and is located in Dudley, Massachusetts. The 44 academic and residential buildings are located amid trees, grass areas, and fields. The Nichols College golf course abuts the property and provides a terrific place for students, faculty, and administrators to improve their game and talk over business.

All the facilities on campus are modern. Older buildings have been renovated and expanded. The four-story Conant Library overlooks the beautiful New England landscape. It's a great place to study or do research. The Chalmers Field House includes swimming pool, workout rooms, basketball courts, sauna, and training room.

One of the newest buildings on campus is Davis Hall, which was completed in 1991, a state-of-the-art academic center that contains classrooms, offices, and seminar rooms and is networked into the campus computer system. There are 13 residence halls on campus with several different living accommodations, including Winston House, where 11 students reside, and Shamie Hall, where 246 students reside.

Dudley, Massachusetts is located in the south central part of the state. The area is rural and offers a lot of opportunities for outdoor recreation. But don't think you'll be out in Nowheresville. Nichols College is just 15 miles from the city of Worcester and 10 other colleges and universities. Boston is about an hour's drive, and Providence, Rhode Island is less than an hour away.

Nichols College Academic Offerings

Accounting • Economics • Finance • Finance/Banking(*) • Finance/Real Estate • General Business • Management • Marketing • Materials Mgt.(*) • Management Information Systems • Small Business/Entrepreneurship

Bachelor of Science: Business Adm. • Public Adm.

Bachelor of Arts: American Studies • History • Industrial Psychology • Psychology • Social Services

(*) Associate degree programs are also offered in these areas

Admissions Statement

Students of good character who have completed a college preparatory program in high school with a minimum GPA of 2.0 and satisfactory scores on the SAT 1 or ACT will be considered for admission.

Northern State University

Aberdeen, South Dakota 57401-7198
(605) 626-2544

An ideal location, a beautiful campus, and a solid reputation are characteristics of Northern State University. This university seems more like a private college with its small classes, outstanding facilities, and supportive environment. But it's not; it is, in fact a comprehensive, multipurpose state institution that offers associate, bachelor's, and master's degrees in over 50 areas. NSU is located within walking distance of Aberdeen (pop. 28,000). It's an interesting college town with a lot of things to do, and businesses and organizations that provide part-time work opportunities for many of the students. The 52-acre campus has some of the newest and finest facilities in the region. No wonder so many students will tell you that Northern is a great place to study!

Academics

Degrees Offered: Associate, Bachelor's, Master's
Undergraduate Majors: 30
Student/Faculty Ratio: 19 to 1
Number of Faculty: 128 full time

At Northern State University the division of Arts and Sciences goes beyond the standard offerings found at other colleges. In addition to traditional courses like biology, psychology, and English, students can broaden their career opportunities with courses in journalism, Chinese, American Indian studies, and gerontology. Arts and Sciences may be the largest division on campus, but a personal quality is still part of all the classes. Course instruction is interactive and students are expected to participate and not just be passive listeners. In addition, all classes are taught by professors and not teaching assistants.

NSU's School of Business and Technologies focuses on combining the theories and information acquired in class with actual exposure and experience in the work environment. Internships are strongly recommended. The university provides on-campus experiential learning opportunities for its business majors through the Small Business Institute and the South Dakota International Business Institute. NSU has developed exchange agreements with Sichuan University in the People's Republic of China and the Universidad del Noroeste in Mexico, providing students, faculty, and the regional business community with access to international forums.

The School of Education has a long-established reputation as one of the best teacher-preparation schools in the nation. In fact, more of South Dakota's teachers have graduated from Northern than any other institution. The latest statistics reveal that almost one-third of all South Dakota's elementary teachers are graduates of NSU!

The School of Fine Arts is home to the departments of art, drama and music. NSU's performance facilities are outstanding. The art department houses some of the finest equipment available, including high-tech graphic computers, lithographic and intaglio printing presses, gas and electric kilns, ceramic labs, and state-of-the-art photographic equipment. Students, area professional artists, and faculty members can display their art work in five galleries. The theater department uses the Johnson Fine Arts Center, with its 1,000-seat auditorium and 250-seat experimental theater. Each year the theater department produces three mainstage productions and an evening of student directed one-act plays.

No matter what major a student chooses, he or she will experience a quality education at NSU.

Students and Student Life

3,000 students from 17 states and 6 foreign countries
Less than 10% are from out-of-state
5% are students of color
1% are international
1,000 live on campus

The NSU Campus is a place where things are happening! The University Programming Council and Student Cultural Affairs Committee develop and schedule about 100 clubs and activities on campus. While some organizations are affiliated with academic areas like the math and science society, others provide an outlet for students to have fun. There are performance groups, student publications, special interest groups, intramural athletics, and religious organizations. The university provides a community atmosphere where involvement, activity, and personal development is encouraged and enhanced.

Athletics: NCAA Division II
Women's Teams: basketball, cross country, golf, softball, tennis, track & field, volleyball
Men's Teams: baseball, basketball, cross country, football, golf, tennis, track & field, volleyball, wrestling

Campus and Community

The 52-acre campus is an inviting place that combines stately redbrick buildings, park-like areas, and outstanding indoor and outdoor sports and recreational facilities. The classroom and administrative buildings are located in the western section of campus and form a traditional campus quad. In the spring and fall, students meander the paths, stopping to chat with friends on their way to classes. Most of the residence halls are located in the southwest corner and form a spacious residential area where students can play frisbee, sit under a tree and read, or soak up the rays. On the other side of campus are the sports fields and the Joseph H. Barnett Physical Education and Convocation Center.

There are a total of 21 buildings on campus. The Beulah Williams Library is the official depository for US Federal Government and South Dakota State publications. It is hardwired into research institutions and libraries throughout the world, giving NSU students global Web access. The Barnett Physical Education and Convention Center is one of the newest and finest athletic centers in the state. It features an 8,000 seat arena, Olympic swimming pool, and 160-meter indoor track. And the Johnson Fine Arts Center provides professional accommodations for every type of performance.

Northern State University Academic Offerings

Accounting • Administrative Systems • Art • Biology • Business • Chemistry Communication Disorders • Community Services • Economics • Education • English • Environmental Sciences • Finance • Fitness • History • Industrial Education • Industrial Mgt. • Industrial Technologies • International Business Mgt. • Marketing • Mathematics • Medical Technology • Music • Physical Ed. • Political Science • Psychology • Sociology • Spanish • Special Ed. • Speech and Drama

Admissions Statement

To be considered for admission to Northern State University, a student should be a high school graduate with a C or better average in the following high school courses: 4 years of English, 3 years of social science, 3 years of advanced mathematics, one-half year of computer science, 3 years of laboratory science, one-half year of fine arts, *and* rank in the top 60% of their high school graduating class *or* obtain an ACT composite score of 18 or above.

Northwest Missouri State University

Maryville, Missouri 64468-6001
(816) 562-1562 or (800) 633-1175

Northwest Missouri State University has combined high tech computer networking with traditional educational goals. The result is a dynamic midsize university that offers bachelor's, master's, and specialist degrees in an environment called "The Electronic Campus." Northwest's computer network has more than 2,400 terminals and 600 microcomputers that put students and faculty in touch with nearly every aspect of campus life—academic and social. The Electronic Campus has made computers as much a part of the college experience as classes, textbooks, and social events. It also links the campus to educational and research facilities throughout the nation and world.

The educational possibilities at Northwest include more than 90 majors. In addition to the more well known majors like accounting, education, and communication, the university offers programs like horticulture, wildlife ecology & conservation, and agriculture on its 700 acres of laboratory farmland. It's a unique university where students get personal assistance and support in their academic programs.

Academics

Degrees Offered: Bachelor's, Master's
Undergraduate Majors: 100
Number of Faculty: 250 full time

The university is made up of three undergraduate colleges: The College of Arts and Sciences, The College of Professional and Applied Sciences, and the College of Education and Human Sciences. Within these three schools, students can choose from over 100 majors. Although enrollment is over 5,000, the university is committed to a personalized education for each student. Every class is taught by one of the 275 faculty members, and most classes have under 30 students.

The most unique academic aspect of Northwest Missouri State University is the Electronic Campus. It is best defined as a total integration of computer technology into the teaching curriculum. Each dorm room is equipped with a computer, so every student has access to the library, the student-activities calendar, every professor, the registrar's office, and friends down the hall from his or her room! Computer-user seminars are presented to all incoming students during orientation, and the college offers free computer workshops throughout the year. In addition, each student receives a copy of the Northwest Computer User's Guide, a complete reference manual to the Electronic Campus. Northwest Missouri was the first state university in the country to institute the Electronic Campus, and continues to be a model with its interactive computer network, user-friendly software, and accessibility.

As a student-focused university, Northwest accommodates students with different styles and backgrounds. Students who attain a GPA of 3.0 and above can accelerate their college program, register for 21 credit hours per semester, and graduate a semester or year ahead of time. Students needing academic support during their college years have a variety of services available to them. The Talent Development Center offers student-led study groups, tutorials, brush-up and catch-up sessions. The university's Writing Center and Math Lab provide tutorial assistance in these two areas. The Assist Program and Student Athletes Success Program offer one-on-one support for qualified students who need additional services.

Whether a student is majoring in accounting or zoology, the university's general studies core will be a part of the degree requirements. It includes courses in composition, oral communication, mathematics, computer literacy, life values, and physical fitness, along with an additional 52 credits in Liberal Studies.

Students and Student Life

5,000 undergraduate students from 42 states and 22 foreign countries
42% are from out-of-state
6% are students of color
3% are international
2,800 live on campus

One of Northwest's greatest assets is the sense of family one encounters while living on campus. The university provides safe, modern residential halls where over 60 percent of the full time students live. The 14 residence halls provide programming which includes intramural sports, hall trips and parties. The Student Senate and Campus Activity Programmers bring concerts, films, speakers, and monthly coffeehouses to campus. In all, there are over 100 clubs, organizations, and activities for students to participate in. Greek life is very popular. Northwest has nine fraternities and six sororities on campus. Their members include 20 percent of the student body.

Athletics: NCAA Division II and the Mid-America Intercollegiate Athletic Association

Women's Teams: basketball, cross country, softball, tennis, track & field, volleyball

Men's Teams: baseball, basketball, cross country, football, tennis, track & field

Campus and Community

The 170-acre campus is located in Maryville, a town of just over 10,000. The campus is spacious, and traditional brick buildings, large grassy areas, and winding paths add to its beauty. There are several favorite spots on campus where students congregate. The W. Jones Student Union, located in the center of campus, houses the five dining service areas, bookstore, and game area.

The 14 residence halls located in three areas of campus provide living accommodations including single-sex halls, coed residences, and special-interest wings. There are several sports facilities, including the Ryland Milner Complex, which contains two gymnasiums, tennis courts, and aquatic center. There is even an elementary school on campus where education majors do their practicums and observations.

Northwest Missouri is a two-hour drive from Kansas City, Missouri and Omaha, Nebraska, and 45 minutes from Saint Joseph, Missouri. But you really don't have to leave Maryville to find things to do. Recreational facilities in the area include the Mozingo Lake project, a 1,000-acre lake with swimming beaches, boating facilities, and a golf course; the Maryville Aquatic Center; and miles of nature trails for hiking and exploring. In town there is plenty of shopping and several great places to eat. Maryville is a small town, but it has a lot to offer.

Northwest Missouri State University Academic Offerings

Agriculture • Art • Biological Sciences • Business • Chemistry/Physics • Computer Science/Information Systems • Education • English • Foreign Languages • Geology/Geography • Government and Economics • Health, PE, Recreation, Dance • History/Humanities • Human Environmental Sciences • Mass Communication • Mathematics and Statistics • Music • Psychology/Sociology • Speech • Theater

Olivet College

Olivet, Michigan 49076-9701
(616) 749-7636 or (800) 456-7189

Olivet College was established in 1844 by a group of innovative missionaries who sought to "define, create, and cultivate the essence of liberal arts education in a people-oriented and community-conscious atmosphere." They were visionaries and heartily believed in the value of education for all people. While most other institutions limited their enrollment to white men from elite families, Olivet became the second oldest college in the country to admit men and women of all races!

This innovative spirit is still present in the college today. Through the comprehensive ability based curriculum, students at Olivet engage in active learning both inside and outside of class, discover how to integrate what they have learned, and become responsible for their own learning process. For over 150 years Olivet has been an institutional community that continues to lead the way in educational advancement and individual development.

Academics

Degrees Offered: Bachelor's

Undergraduate Majors: 30+

Student/Faculty Ratio: 14 to 1

Number of Faculty: 70

Students at Olivet College are encouraged to engage in active learning both in and out of the classroom, and to integrate what they have learned from the full range of their experience. To make this happen, the Olivet curriculum combines traditional aspects that include a broad liberal arts foundation, specialized courses in a major area of concentration, and a series of experiential elements such as first-year experience, portfolio assessment, service learning, and senior experience.

Over the four years, students become knowledgeable through discussion, analysis, integration and performance, and in doing so they place themselves at the center of the learning process. By the time they graduate from Olivet College they will have acquired an education and demonstrated competency in communication, reasoning, developing individual responsibilities, developing social responsibilities, and academic mastery in a major.

The college has a supportive community environment that facilitates the individual interactions and in-depth exploration of ideas that characterizes an Olivet education. Class enrollments are small, so stimulating discussions and meaningful exchanges of ideas take place. The professors who teach at the college are superlative teachers and experts in their subject. The Academic Resource Center provides additional services that center on student success. Here, students participate in academic mentoring programs and student tutoring programs. The center also provides workshops, organizational and study materials, computer and word processing instruction, and analysis and interpretation of learning styles.

Students and Student Life

800 students from 22 states and 6 foreign countries
Less than 10% are from out-of-state
12% are students of color
550 live on campus

The Olivet community consists of individuals from many different religious, cultural, philosophical, and political backgrounds. There is a lively campus atmosphere in an environment that encourages self-confidence, self-worth, and self-respect. Organizations such as Earthbound and Habitat for Humanity provide volunteer and community service projects where students can make a difference.

The six local sororities and fraternities on campus have played an important part in student development at the college. The Soronian, also known as the Iota Kappa Omicron Society, was founded on the Olivet campus in 1847 and is the oldest collegiate society in the continental United States. In addition to social activities, the Greek societies are active in service projects that benefit the school and the community.

The college sponsors a newspaper, literary magazine, and radio station in addition to professional clubs and associations. Performance activities allow aspiring artists to develop their skills in music ensembles, dramatic plays, choir, chorale, and informal musical groups.

Intercollegiate sports are played by over one quarter of the students and athletics have a strong history on the Olivet campus. In 1888, Olivet and three other colleges formed the Michigan Intercollegiate Athletic Association, the oldest intercollegiate athletic association in the nation. Today the school is a member of the NCAA Division III and still competes in the Michigan Intercollegiate Athletic Association. The fighting Comets have won league championships in football, wrestling, basketball, and golf.

Women's Athletic Teams: basketball, cross country, golf, soccer, softball, tennis, volleyball
Men's Teams: baseball, basketball, cross country, football, golf, soccer, wrestling

Campus and Community

At Olivet College, education is an on-going process and every aspect of college life contributes to the process. The 92-acre campus provides a comfortable, intellectually stimulating environment that includes over 30 academic and residential facilities. Stately maple and oak trees hover over the stone and redbrick buildings and walking paths that cut through campus and bring students from one building to the next.

The library in Burrage Hall, originally built in 1889, under went major renovations and additions in 1992 that tripled its size, yet retained all of its beauty and character. In addition to being an outstanding research facility, the library is a wonderful place to study or read. Since so much emphasis is placed upon experiential learning, the college has invested its resources in acquiring and maintaining facilities where students can practice their skills. The Oaks, a movie theater in downtown Olivet, has been renovated and now houses the theater program.

On campus, the Visual Arts building accommodates studios and exhibit areas for students and local artists. The Upton Conservatory of Music includes individual practice rooms, vocal and instrumental rehearsal halls, and a recital hall. It is also equipped with a computer electronic music/recording studio.

Campus housing accommodations offer a variety of unique living arrangements. There are three typical residence halls accommodating more than 500 students in dormitory and suite-style rooms. In addition, the six Greek societies maintain residences for their members and the majorities of society members live in these houses. The college has established three separate theme houses (African-American Cultural Center, Global Cultures Center, and The Brewer Honors House) that provide living-learning centers for students interested in residential facilities with a specific focus.

The Olivet campus is located on a beautiful hillside in the small community of Olivet, Michigan. But in less than a 30-minute bus ride, students can be in Lansing, home of Michigan State University and over 40,000 college students. Students have the serenity, safety, and beauty of a small-town campus and access to all the activities that take place in a bustling college town like Lansing.

Olivet College Academic Offerings

Accounting & Finance(*) • American Studies • Art(*) and Fine Arts • Athletic Training • Biochemistry • Biological Anthropology • Biological Illustration • Biology(*) • Business Administration • Business/ Insurance • Business/ International Studies • Chemistry(*) • Commercial Design • Communications • Computer Science • Economics(*) • English(*) • Health, PE, Recreation(*) • History(*) • Journalism • Language Arts(*) • Management(*) • Marketing(*) • Mathematics(*) • Music Performance(*) • Music Theory/History • Personal Interest • Political Science(*) • Psychology • Social Studies(*) • Sociology • Speech(*) • Theater • 20th Century Studies • Wellness
(*) Elementary and/or Secondary Teaching Certification

Admissions Statement

In order to be considered for admission a student should have graduated from an accredited high school and have a 2.6 GPA in college preparatory courses, and have taken either the SAT 1 or ACT. Individual consideration will be given to students who do not meet these criteria but demonstrate potential in other ways.

Pacific Lutheran University

Tacoma, Washington 98447
(206) 535-7151 or (800) 274-6758

Pacific Lutheran University was established in 1890. The Lutheran heritage of the school provides an environment where students work together learning from each other and supporting one another. Students at Pacific Lutheran University are serious about their education and enjoy the opportunity to strengthen their academic horizon.

Academics

Degrees Offered: Bachelor's, Master's

Undergraduate Majors: More than 50 areas

Student/Faculty Ratio: 16 to 1

Number of Faculty: 320 full and part time

Pacific Lutheran University is the type of school where students can explore academic areas and career opportunities beyond the confines of the classroom. The university has opportunities which make learning more than just listening to a professor teach. Students are actively engaged in discovering knowledge, applying what they have learned, and sharing ideas.

A large and diverse study-abroad program allows students to live and learn in more than 40 countries throughout the world including Norway, Kenya, Ecuador, Tanzania, and Australia. Another indication of Pacific Lutheran's commitment to providing a global education is the school's extensive and comprehensive foreign language and culture programs. Students can take courses in French, German, Norwegian, Spanish, Greek, and Latin, and can major and minor in areas like Chinese studies, global studies, Scandinavian Area Studies, and international business. Pacific Lutheran sponsors international service learning programs in six countries.

Strong student faculty relationships afford research opportunities for students to work and publish with faculty members. It is not uncommon for seniors to accompany their professors to national symposiums and present papers or independent research. The academic environment supports cooperative learning, and students are encouraged to apply what they have learned in independent study, internships, and service/work programs.

Many of the majors offered at the university include some type of knowledge integration project, like student teaching, senior seminars, clinical rotations, and production of an individual project into the curriculum. Pacific Lutheran College also has on-campus sites where students practice their theory. At the Family and Children's Center, sociology, education, psychology, and other human service-related majors work with children, adults, and senior citizens. KPLU-FM the university's own radio station, operates a full-power National Public Radio station; Pacific Lutheran is the only independent university in the Northwest to do so. Communication majors have terrific on-air and production opportunities.

Students and Student Life

3,500 students from 34 states and 27 foreign countries
21% are students of color or international
60% live on campus in 12 residential halls

There are more than 55 college-sponsored clubs and activities at Pacific Lutheran University that provide recreational, leadership, social, and educational opportunities for the students. There are 14 musical groups, including Opera Workshop and University Symphony Orchestra; 12 professional clubs that are related to academic majors; and an active theater production organization. The university has a student-run radio and television station, a campus newspaper (*The Mast*), and several service clubs like Circle K and Habitat for Humanity.

Athletics: NAIA
Women's Teams: basketball, cross country, soccer, softball, track & field, volleyball
Men's Teams: baseball, basketball, football, soccer, swimming, wrestling
Coed Teams: golf, tennis

Campus and Community

The 133-acre suburban campus has terrific living and learning facilities. All of the academic buildings, science labs, sports facilities, and residence halls are top notch. The Ricke Science Center surpasses most undergraduate facilities and provides the latest scientific equipment. The 12 residence halls are also spacious and comfortable and accommodate 1,700 students. The university is located seven miles from Tacoma, giving students easy access to a major city.

Pacific Lutheran University Academic Offerings

Accounting • Anthropology(*) • Art(*) • Biology(*) • Chemistry(*) • Chinese Studies • Classics • Computer Science • Computer Engineering • Computer Science • Earth Science(*) • Economics • Electrical Engineering • Engineering Science • English(*) • Finance • French(*) • German(*) • Global Studies • Health & Fitness Mgt. • History(*) • Honors • Human Resource Mgt. • International Business • Latin(*) • Legal Studies • Management Information Systems • Marketing • Mathematics(*) • Music(*) • Music and Music Ed., with concentrations in piano, organ, vocal, instrumental, theory & composition, church music • Norwegian(*) • Nursing • Operations Mgt. • Philosophy • Physical Ed.(*) • Physics(*) • Political Science(*) • Psychology(*) • Recreation Administration • Religion • Scandinavian Area Studies • Science(*) • Social Studies(*) • Social Work • Sociology(*) • Spanish(*) • Special Ed.(*) • Speech(*)

(*) Teacher certification programs offered

Peru State College

Peru, Nebraska 68421
(402) 872-3815 or (800) 742-4412

Peru State College provides a friendly, relaxed atmosphere that encourages students to gain confidence, develop leadership skills, and work toward academic success. Established in 1867 as the first college in Nebraska, Peru has been educating and shaping young people's lives for nearly 130 years. Through the intellectual, social, and physical activities, new students are welcomed into the Peru community and are treated as individuals, not just numbers. The college's philosophy, " . . . that each person is entitled to the opportunity to succeed at the collegiate level," is reinforced through the personal involvement administrators, faculty, and staff take in regard to the students, and the outstanding academic opportunities the college has initiated for students of all educational backgrounds.

Academics

Degrees Offered: Bachelor's, Master's

Undergraduate Majors: 14 with 46 areas of concentration

Student/Faculty Ratio: 16 to 1

Number of Faculty: 80 full and part time

Peru State is committed to providing high quality instruction, personalized attention, and a supportive learning environment. The college builds a strong foundation in the liberal arts as a cornerstone for the four academic divisions (business, education and psychology, humanities, and science and technology) that make up the college.

While the college may be small, with about 1,300 undergraduate and 600 graduate students, the academic offerings are broad. Students have 14 undergraduate majors with 46 concentrations to choose from, including teacher certification in 20 areas. A major like music offers specialization in music performance, music education, or music marketing. The natural science major provides concentrations in areas like wildlife ecology, biological sciences, or even nuclear technology.

The college also has established educational programs for students with diverse backgrounds. The comprehensive Honors Program consists of 15 credits in specific honors seminars taken over the course of four years. Each year several innovative and interesting honors seminars, like Science and Society or Ethics and Social Justice, are introduced to engage academically talented students. Academically challenged students who need additional assistance with college studies can become involved with the developmental studies program and receive individualized computer-assisted instruction and one on one tutoring in English composition, mathematics, and reading.

Other academic advantages offered at the college include a Cooperative Education Internship Program where students explore valuable work experience while earning academic credit, and independent study, where students work one on one with a faculty advisor or conduct independent research.

Students and Student Life

1,300 students from 28 states and 10 foreign countries
15% are from out-of-state
5% are students of color
1% are international
600 live on campus

The college has an elected Student Senate that is the governing body for all students. The Student Senate is the link between the college faculty, administration, and students. Members of the senate also serve on many campus committees. Cultural events are scheduled several times each week and include theater productions, concert bands, classical films, and dance troupes. The college funds professional organizations that bring in speakers to present college wide programs on social issues, political happenings and national trends. Service clubs provide volunteer activities where students share their talents and skills with members of the community.

Athletics: The Peru State Bobcats are members of the NAIA Division II.
Women's Teams: basketball, softball, volleyball
Men's Teams: baseball, basketball, football

Campus and Community

The 103-acre campus has been called the "Campus of a Thousand Oaks." Everything students need for a complete, well-rounded college experience can be found in this beautiful hilltop environment. The center of campus is the academic quad where most of the classrooms and department buildings are located along with the Student Center. The quad is inviting and surrounded by huge stately oak trees. It's almost impossible to walk from the library across the green to the Fine Arts building without stopping to chat with friends. That open, friendly atmosphere seems to be everywhere.

There are three residence halls, one housing complex, and one apartment-style facility on campus. The Centennial Complex is the largest and is located in the southwest corner of campus. It provides coed and single-sex accommodations. Morgan Hall is located in the northwest corner of campus next to the Student Center and it houses over 150 female students in traditional dorm style rooms. Delzell Hall is an all male dorm located by the athletic field and Oak Hill are student apartments with one and two bedroom units.

The city of Peru is in the southeast corner of Nebraska where Nebraska, Iowa, Kansas, and Missouri come together. The city provides access to shopping, entertainment, and cultural activities. The college is about an hour's drive from several other colleges and 65 miles from Omaha.

Peru State College Academic Offerings

Art • Business • Computer Science • Elementary Education • English • Industrial Technology • Mathematics • Music • Natural Sciences • Physical Education • Psychology/Sociology • Social Science • Speech and Drama • Teacher Certification

Admissions Statement

Peru State College welcomes applications from students who wish to pursue their educational and vocational goals. Students should be graduates of accredited high schools, attain a minimum cumulative grade point average of 2.0 or "C", and score at least a 14 composite on the ACT or 650 on the SAT.

Plymouth State College

Plymouth, New Hampshire 03264-1600
(603) 535-2237 or (800) 842-6900

Plymouth State is a midsize public institution. With an undergraduate population of about 4,000, more than 80 academic areas of study, and a faculty committed to teaching, the college is recognized throughout New England for its quality education and community atmosphere. Whether students choose to major in art or social work, or any major in between, they work with professional faculty, use 21st century technology, and receive an education that will prepare them for their career and for the rest of their life!

Academics

Degrees Offered: Associate, Bachelor's, Master's

Undergraduate Majors: 80

Student/Faculty Ratio: 20 to 1

Number of Faculty: 200

Plymouth State College is a learning community which offers students an opportunity to explore their potential within a safe, friendly, caring environment.

At Freshman Orientation, students take Introduction to the Academic Community, a specially designed course emphasizing student success, study skills, student-life issues, and academic support services. At graduation, the staff at the Career Center send out student references for job interviews or applications to graduate school. Throughout, the college has people, programs, and activities that will work with you, prepare you for, and help you achieve your career goal.

As a learning community, Plymouth State College also provides a curriculum and course selection that gives students variety, substance, and knowledge. The general education curriculum is designed to instruct students in communication skills and global, scientific, social, and psychological perspectives. Courses with a major are designed to give students an in-depth knowledge and preparation within a subject field.

The college has designed many of its degree programs to incorporate diverse career opportunities. For example, students who major in health education can prepare for careers in coaching, research, academia, or in rehabilitation clinics by taking specialized courses within the department. Humanities majors can choose an interdisciplinary option and custom-tailor the degree to suit their own area of inquiry.

Plymouth State offers the only undergraduate meteorology major in the state and one of only two in all New England. It also has the distinction of being one of four institutions in the country listed as a World Wide Web weather server. It provides current electronic weather maps, bulletins, and meteorological information to computer users throughout the world.

In the area of fine arts, Plymouth State again leads the way. It offers the only B.F.A. degree in graphic design in New Hampshire and has recently converted a turn-of-the-century mill into studio space with drafting areas and the latest in electronic design equipment.

Students and Student Life

4,000 students from 20 states and 10 foreign countries.
40% are from out-of-state
1% are international
70% live on campus

Staff, faculty, and administrators at Plymouth State recognize that co-curricular activities are a large part of the learning process. That's why the school offers more than 50 student clubs and organizations and has just finished construction of a new student union. The HUB (Hartman Union Building) opened in 1995 is the center of student activity. It is the building where many student leaders and clubs have their offices and a great place to watch movies, play pickup games with friends, or get a late night snack.

Campus activities include guest speakers, movie nights, intramural sports, fraternity and sorority meetings, play rehearsals and student government sessions. The college has media clubs that include *The Clock* (campus newspaper), *The Conning Tower* (yearbook), *The Continuum* (literary magazine), and WPCR-FM radio station. Musical groups like chamber winds, college chorale, hand-bell ringers, percussion ensemble, and symphonic band give students many terrific performance opportunities. There are also a number of professional clubs, religious organizations, honor societies, and recreational events.

Athletics: NCAA Division III
Women's Teams: alpine skiing, basketball, field hockey, lacrosse, soccer, softball, swimming and diving, tennis
Men's Teams: alpine skiing, baseball, basketball, football, hockey, lacrosse, alpine skiing, soccer, tennis, wrestling

Campus and Community

The 150-acre campus straddles the Pemigewasset River; on one side the academic and residential buildings provide a beautiful campus area, while across the river are the huge physical education center and athletic fields. Most of the buildings are redbrick, a New England tradition.

The college has several outstanding facilities where students work with the latest in technology. The Silver Cultural Arts Center has three performance areas, numerous rehearsal rooms and practice modules, classrooms, and several dance studios. It is the showcase of the arts for the entire northern New Hampshire region. The Child Development and Family Center houses the well-respected preschool and kindergarten that accommodates children from the college and community. This lab-school provides field experience opportunities for students in the early childhood studies program.

Campus housing is available for all four years, and students have a variety of living arrangements. There are two single-sex residence halls and five coed halls. There are fraternity and sorority houses and the White Mountain College Apartment Complex. All the residence halls are self-governing and provide comfortable accommodations.

Plymouth State College Academic Offerings

Associate Degrees: Childhood Studies • General Studies • Public Service

Bachelor's Degrees: Accounting • Anthropology • Applied Computer Science • Applied Economics • Art • Biological Science • Biology • Chemistry • Childhood Studies • Computer Information Systems • Early Childhood Studies • English • Environmental Biology • French • Geography • Graphic Design • Health Ed. • History • Humanities • Interdisciplinary Studies • Local & Regional Planning • Management • Marketing • Mathematics • Medieval Studies • Meteorology • Music • Outdoor Recreation • Philosophy • Physical Ed. • Physical Science • Political Science • Psychology • Public Management • Social Science • Social Work • Sociology • Spanish • Studio Art • Theater

Admissions Statement

Standards for admission vary based on residency. Out of state students may face more competitive admission standards. Most out-of-state students rank in the top half of their class with SAT scores in the 400s.

Rider University

Lawrenceville, New Jersey 08648-3099
(609) 896-5042 or (800) 257-9026

Rider University, through its broad, rich curriculum, provides student-centered education to men and women from 30 states and 25 foreign countries. The university meets students at their academic level and brings them to, and sometimes beyond, their personal and academic goals. All students are and given the means to develop their potential. Faculty members work with them in the classrooms, labs, and co-curricular activities. The university curriculum incorporates programs to build and refine students' interpersonal skills, develop a basis upon which future learning will flourish, and give students the opportunity to combine what they have learned with what they can do.

The Rider University experience includes a comprehensive immersion in an academic area of study along with developing leadership skills, redefining one's environment on a more global basis, and working side by side with faculty, administrators, and students who turn into lifelong friends.

Academics

Degrees Offered: Bachelor's, Master's

Undergraduate Majors: 45

Student/Faculty Ratio: 16 to 1

The School of Business Administration is the university's oldest school. It is one of only three colleges in New Jersey to receive accreditation from the American Assembly of Collegiate Schools of Business. The school offers majors in 11 areas and has included an international business course into its core curriculum. Top-flight facilities and a faculty whose first priority is teaching are two outstanding characteristics of the School of Business Administration.

The School of Liberal Arts and Sciences offers majors as diverse as communication, marine science, and American studies. It has several interdisciplinary programs, like geochemistry, international studies, and environmental studies, which can increase students' options in the career market. The modern science laboratories, spacious and well-equipped fine-arts studios, and high-tech communication facilities are all designed and used for undergraduate study.

The School of Education and Human Services offers teacher certification in programs from Early Childhood through Secondary Education. The School is accredited by the National Council for Accreditation of Teacher Education (NCATE).

In 1992 the Westminster Choir College, renowned for its music programs and performing groups became part of the Rider University School of Music. Since then, the School of Music has stepped to the forefront as an academic institution that provides a broad-based education that focuses on music-related fields. The music school's 7 to 1 student/faculty ratio assures aspiring musicians of individual attention, musical performances, and mentoring opportunities with prestigious musicians.

A consistent element within every Rider degree program is practical experience. The university has a large number of internship sites for students in every major. Places like *Business Week* magazine, Circle Repertory Theater, Warner-Lambert, all of the Big Six accounting firms, General Electric, and Bristol-Myers Squibb all have had Rider University interns.

Students and Student Life

3,500 students from 30 states and 25 foreign countries
18% are students of color
1% are international
75% live on campus

Well over 60 clubs and organizations are available for students. These include national sororities and fraternities with chapter houses; the Student Government Association; Student Entertainment Council; more than seven musical/voice related clubs like jazz ensemble, pep band, and inspirational choir; a weekly newspaper; more than five religious organizations like Hillel and Protestant Campus Ministry; a terrific campus radio station; 25 honor societies; and more than a dozen special interest groups. Weekend trips to New York City are planned, and "Rider's Friday Thing" brings bands, comedians, musicians, and other entertainers to campus weekly.

Athletics: NCAA, Division I
Women's Teams: basketball, cross country, field hockey, indoor track, softball, swimming and diving, tennis, track & field, volleyball
Men's Teams: baseball, basketball, cross country, golf, indoor track, soccer, swimming and diving, tennis, track & field, wrestling

Campus and Community

Rider University's 353-acre campus is located in Lawrenceville, New Jersey, a quiet suburban area five miles south of Princeton and three miles north of Trenton. The modern campus provides a perfect environment in which to study and live. All academic, recreational, and residential facilities are clustered nicely on campus, allowing students easy access from dorms to academic buildings.

Although the university is over 100 years old, there is nothing outdated or old about the campus. Traditional styled buildings have been renovated. Computer labs, science labs, and research and resource equipment are all modern. The Moore Library features an online catalog, seating for 400 students, individual study carrels, and private study and discussion areas. Most courses take place in Memorial Hall, the Science and Technology Center, the Fine Arts Center, Academic Annex, Business Administration building, and Maurer Physical Education building. The School of Music is located in Princeton and has outstanding facilities for music and performance related majors.

Rider University Academic Offerings

School of Business Administration: Accounting • Actuarial Science • Advertising • Business Administration • Business Economics • Computer Information Systems • Finance • Human Resource Management • Management and Organizational Behavior • Management Sciences • Marketing

School of Liberal Arts and Science: American Studies • Biochemistry • Biology • Chemistry • Communications • Economics • English • Fine Arts • French • Geosciences • German • History • Journalism • Marine Sciences • Mathematics • Philosophy • Physics • Political Science • Psychology • Russian • Sociology • Spanish

School of Education and Human Services: Business Ed. • Elementary Ed. • Marketing Ed. • Secondary Ed.

School of Music: Church Music • Music/Liberal Arts • Music Education • Music Theory/Composition • Organ Performance • Piano Pedagogy • Piano Performance • Voice Performance

Admissions Statement

Rider University seeks to enroll students who will benefit from the University's academic resources while bringing diversity, talents, and energy to the campus environment. Applicants should have completed a college prep program in high school which included four units of English, three units of Mathematics, and nine units from academic disciplines of science, foreign language, and social sciences and have attained acceptable scores on the SAT 1 and ACT.

Rocky Mountain College

Billings, Montana 59102
(406) 657-1026 or (800) 877-6259

Rocky Mountain College, founded in 1878, was the first institution of higher learning in the state. Over the past 120 years, the college has undergone many changes. Today it is affiliated with the United Methodist Church, the United Church of Christ, and the Presbyterian Church, and is recognized as an impressive small college offering diverse academic programs that combine liberal arts and practical career training.

Academics

Degrees Offered: Associate, Bachelor's

Undergraduate Majors: 36

Student/Faculty Ratio: 14 to 1

Average Class Size: 16

Number of Faculty: 75

Courses Offered Each Semester: 300

The educational environment at Rocky Mountain College is both supportive and challenging. Faculty work with students as advisors, teachers, friends, and co-workers. Students can easily receive extra help or work cooperatively with a professor on a research project or special program. The college has remained small so that it can continue to offer a more individualized education.

Students receive a strong liberal arts foundation whether they choose a traditional major like English, history, music, or a more career-related major like aviation, computer science, or physician assistant. In addition, students can incorporate career-oriented minors with any major and enhance their career options. With student-centered programs like honors, study away, cooperative education, and internships, Rocky Mountain students have opportunities to build and develop the education they want.

Students and Student Life

800 students from 40 states and 16 foreign countries

5% are students of color

4% are international

45% live on campus in three residential halls

The college sponsors more than 25 clubs and organizations including jazz band, concert choir, professional clubs, and Circle K. Live theater activities are very prominent. During the academic year the theater department produces up to five full-length plays, at least one musical, and several student-directed one-act performances. Rocky Mountain students enjoy one of the highest student-production ratios in the country.

The college publishes a weekly student bulletin called *The Rocky Crest*, which lists campus events, and the *Rocky News*, the weekly student paper which provides news and information. Each year students publish an edition of the *Soliloquy*, the annual literary magazine, and a yearbook.

With over 17 million acres of forest and three million acres of wilderness in the state, students have some of the finest locales for outdoor activities. Groups of students participate in mountain climbing, white water rafting, down hill skiing, hiking, and camping. If you are looking for a college where you study and become involved in great outdoor activities, this may be the place for you!

Athletics: NAIA Frontier Conference
Women's Teams: basketball, ski racing, volleyball
Men's Teams: basketball, football, ski racing

Campus and Community

The 60-acre campus is located in a residential areas of Billings, the largest city in Montana. The area offers many outdoor recreational activities including skiing, hiking, camping, and fishing. The campus has 20 buildings, from the collegiate, Gothic-style Losekamp Hall, built in the early 1900s, to more modern buildings like Rocky Hall, constructed in the late 1980s. Most of the older buildings have been renovated to provide modern facilities for the students. The Bair Family Center for Science provides the major science facilities for the college and includes classroom, laboratories, seminar rooms, and the computer center.

Rocky Mountain College Academic Offerings

Applied Management • Art • Aviation • Biology • Business Adm. • Chemistry • Computer Science • Economics • Education • English • Environmental Science • Equestrian Studies • French • Geology • History • History & Political Science • Individualized Studies • International Studies • Mathematics • Music • Natural Science & Mathematics • Philosophy & Religious Thought • Physical Ed. & Health • Physician Assistant • Psychology • Sociology & Anthropology • Spanish • Speech Communications • Theater Arts

Admissions Statement

Acceptance for admission is offered on the basis of high school transcript, test scores, and recommendations. Each applicant is considered on the basis of potential success at Rocky Mountain College.

Roger Williams University

Bristol, Rhode Island 02809-2921
(401) 254-3500 or (800) 458-7144

The curriculum at Roger Williams University is a fusion of traditional liberal arts and professional studies. The two undergraduate colleges and three professional undergraduate schools that make up the university offer students more than 35 areas of study, from traditional liberal arts majors like English and history to more career-oriented programs like construction management, architecture, and accounting. The core curriculum in the liberal arts and sciences challenges students to develop their minds and prepares them to pursue graduate studies or begin their career.

Located on the beautiful Rhode Island waterfront, the campus of Roger Williams University is visually appealing, functional, and equipped with the latest in technology. Students from throughout New England and the East are attracted to the university for its solid academic reputation and challenging, yet supportive, academic environment.

Academics

Degrees Offered: Bachelor of Arts, Architecture, Fine Arts, Science

Undergraduate Majors: 35

Student/Faculty Ratio: 20 to 1

Number of Faculty: 229 full and part time

The College of Arts and Sciences offers majors in areas that include fine and performing art, natural sciences, and social sciences. It is one of only a few schools to offer a major in marine biology, and is surrounded by varied aquatic-life habitats like Mt. Hope Bay, the Narragansett Bay Estuarine Sanctuary, salt marshes, and the Atlantic Ocean. Another strong major is paralegal studies. The only law school in the state shares the campus with Roger Williams University, and students in the paralegal studies program have the good fortune to be taught by federal and state judges, lawyers in private practice, government prosecutors, and law-enforcement officials.

The School of Architecture offers two majors, a five-year professional program in architecture, and a major in historic preservation. Both majors are highly sought after because of their rigorous curriculum and outstanding faculty. The five-year architecture program is one of only two in the nation that is offered at a small private university and is accredited by the National Architectural Accrediting Board. The program in historic preservation is also singled out as being one of two comprehensive undergraduate historic preservation programs in the nation.

The School of Business Administration prepares students for a wide range of career options from accounting to international business. Business management is one of the school's popular majors and the university is proud of the hands-on instruction that takes place in small classes. Many of the faculty in the School of Business are practitioners as well as competent teachers. They bring the real world into the classroom and give students a quality, relevant education.

The School of Engineering offers a bachelor of science degree in three areas: engineering, environmental engineering science, and construction management. Students enrolled in these majors receive a flexible education that focuses on science, engineering, and the liberal arts, while providing opportunities to minor in broad interdisciplinary areas and participate in an experiential learning program in their senior year.

Students and Student Life

2,000 undergraduate students from 26 states and 45 foreign countries
5% are students of color
6% are international
1,400 live on campus

Campus life includes activities like mural painting, pot-luck suppers, Halloween festivals, weekend brunches, lectures, drama festivals, and parties. The university is filled with community spirit and provides just about any club or activity students could want. *The Hawk's Eye* campus newspaper and WQRI radio station keep residents well informed of the weekly events and activities on campus. Professional clubs, religious organizations, honor societies, and special-interest groups are all represented on campus.

Athletics: NCAA Division III
Women's Teams: basketball, cross country, soccer, softball, tennis, volleyball
Men's Teams: baseball, basketball, cross country, ice hockey, lacrosse, soccer, tennis, volleyball, wrestling.
Coed Teams: equestrian, golf, sailing

Campus and Community

The 125-acre waterfront campus is located in the historic town of Bristol, Rhode Island. The campus overlooks the Mt. Hope Bay and provides a spacious and appealing environment. Three residence halls offer students a choice of coed or single-sex living accommodations, specialty floors, and quiet areas for study. With more than 1,200 students living on campus, something is always going on.

Campus facilities include the award winning Architecture Building and Architecture Library, the outstanding Performing Arts Center, and the Paolino Recreation

Center with multiple courts, weight room, and exercise equipment. The Student Center includes a cafeteria, student organization offices, game room, and book store. The Science and Math building, School of Business Administration building, and School of Engineering building all have modern laboratories and comfortable classrooms. The campus is quite picturesque and the waterfront location is terrific.

Bristol is located within 20 minutes of Providence, the capitol city, and Newport, a wonderful resort area. Students can easily get to both areas and enjoy the sophistication of a big city or the enjoyment of a resort area. In addition, Roger Williams students can be at six college campuses within a half-hour's drive.

Roger Williams University Academic Offerings

College of Arts and Science: Administration of Justice • Art • Biology • Chemistry • Communications • Computer Science • Creative Writing • Dance • English • History • Marine Biology • Mathematics • Paralegal Studies • Philosophy • Political Science • Psychology • Social Sciences • Theater

School of Architecture: Architecture • Historic Preservation

School of Business: Accounting • Business Administration • Computer Information Systems • Management • Marketing

School of Engineering: Construction Management • Engineering • Environmental Engineering Science

Admissions Statement

The university recommends a strong college preparatory program emphasizing course work in humanities, social science, science, mathematics, and four years of English. The committee on admissions pays particular attention to the quality of secondary school courses selected, recent achievement, extracurricular activities, and recommendations

Sacred Heart University

Fairfield, Connecticut 06432-1000
(203) 371-7880

In less than 40 years, Sacred Heart University has gone from a small regional school with 173 students to a comprehensive liberal arts and professional university with more than 5,000 students. The university was able to accomplish this growth and success because of three important elements. From its early beginnings the university has been recognized for its caring approach to students. Throughout its short history, Sacred Heart has continually planned and developed quality academic programs in relative disciplines. And, in response to the academic and social needs of its students, the university has constructed a dynamic modern campus that incorporates state-of-the-art facilities into a student-centered living/learning environment. Sacred Heart is committed to continuing to focus on providing the kind of personal attention that leads to achievement and success for all its students.

Academics

Degrees Offered: Associate, Bachelor's, Master's

Undergraduate Majors: 24 associate and 25 bachelor's

Student/Faculty Ratio: 14 to 1

Number of Faculty: 350 full and part time

In recent years, Sacred Heart University has come to the forefront in education in the Northeast and has expanded its academic programs to meet regional and national demand. It has added new graduate programs, increased undergraduate majors, and incorporated several certificate programs into the curriculum. One of the most futuristic programs the university has implemented, the Student Mobile Computing Program, incorporates technology into the classroom. Sacred Heart is the first university in New England to require entering students to have a computer. At this university, computers are just as important as textbooks and laboratories. At Sacred Heart, the fiber-optic network links all students with professors, academic advisors, other students, residential life staff, and the university's library database.

Another significant accomplishment of Sacred Heart is that even with the heightened technology, the university hasn't lost sight of the individual student and continues to provide a personalized education that meets the academic needs of a variety of learners. The Academic Incentive Program gives academically challenged students personal support and academic courses necessary for success in college. The program runs throughout a student's entire first year and includes: a personal advisor who provides academic counseling on a weekly basis; individual and small-group tutoring in reading, writing, and study skills at the University Learning Center; and a three-credit course in reading and writing.

The university has also developed a challenging interdisciplinary Honors Program for high achievers. The honors curriculum is composed of courses that integrate material from diverse fields or focus on one topic from a variety of perspectives. Students are encouraged to develop their own research or cultural project within the program and, in most cases, the university helps defray the expenses incurred from the project. Regional lectures, national honors conferences, and local speakers are all part of an Honors education at Sacred Heart.

Students and Student Life

2,200 undergraduates and 1,600 graduate students from 20 states and 59 foreign countries
25% are students of color
4% are international
1,250 live on campus

At Sacred Heart it is not easy to just sit in your dorm room because there always seems to be something going on. The university sponsors 70 clubs and organizations, which include 13 academic clubs, like debate society and business club; seven performance groups, like PEP band and drama club; five sororities and three fraternities; nine recreational clubs, including the outing club and karate club; three student publications; six community service/volunteer service organizations; four multicultural organizations; and two political clubs. In addition, New York City is only a commuter-train ride away and there are about 10 other colleges and universities within an hour's drive.

Athletics: NCAA Division II
Women's Teams: basketball, bowling, crew, cross country, equestrian, field hockey, golf, ice hockey, lacrosse, soccer, softball, tennis, track & field, volleyball
Men's Teams: baseball, basketball, bowling, crew, cross country, football, golf, ice hockey, lacrosse, soccer, tennis, track & field, volleyball

Campus and Community

The 56-acre campus is located in Fairfield, Connecticut, one of the most dynamic business and economic areas in the country. Fairfield county is home to many Fortune 500 corporate headquarters and provides outstanding opportunities for internships, career exploration, and networking. Since the university is less than 40 years old, the campus is modern and well designed, with facilities that complement the academic offerings. The Academic Center is a huge building that contains most of the classrooms and faculty offices. All of the classrooms and laboratories on campus are equipped with dot-matrix printers so students and faculty can print material stored in their laptop computers.

There are 10 fully equipped science laboratories. The six chemistry labs and four biology labs include nuclear magnetic-resonance spectrophotometers, gas chromatographs, polarographic analyzer/striping voltameters, differential-scanning calorimeters, tissue respirometer, high-speed centrifuges, TV microprojectors, and dissecting microscopes.

The Ryan-Matura Library is almost totally automated. Students can access the library via the Internet, and the library is networked with data resources throughout the world. Sacred Heart University has professional media studios on campus for video, film, and audio production in addition to WSHU-FM, the campus radio station, located in Jefferson House. This 20,000 watt station is qualified by the Corporation for Public Broadcasting and is one of only two National Public Radio stations in the state. It broadcasts throughout Fairfield and parts of Long Island.

The sports and athletic facilities are growing by leaps and bounds. The university recently added an all-synthetic turf athletic field and running track, as well as six champion-caliber tennis courts and a new softball field. The new Pitt Health and Recreation Center (presently under construction) will house a 2,000 seat basketball arena, weight training room, and racquetball and squash course. It will also include a 4,500-square-foot area for clinical space, examination rooms, therapy laboratories, and spa for the new occupational and physical therapy programs.

The university has nine residential facilities accommodating over 1,200 students. Most have been built within the past six years and all provide clean, spacious, modern living facilities. Students can choose traditional hall-style arrangements, townhouse units, and garden-style apartments.

Fairfield is an ideal place to live and go to school. Surrounding environments include beaches on Long Island Sound, cultural and educational institutions like the Peabody Museum and Yale University in New Haven, one of the largest shopping areas in Stamford, and a 40-minute commuter-train ride into New York City.

Sacred Heart University Academic Offerings

Arts & Sciences: Art • Biology • Chemistry • Communications/Media Studies • Criminal Justice • English • Environmental Chemistry • Environmental Science • Global Studies • Graphic Design • History • Illustration • Mathematics • Painting • Philosophy • Political Science • Psychology • Religious Studies • Social Work • Sociology • Spanish

Business: Accounting • Computer Science • Economics • Finance • International Business • Paralegal Studies/Legal Adm.

Education: Certification programs in early childhood, elementary, middle school and secondary

Health Sciences: Biotechnology • Medical Technology • Nursing • Occupational Therapy • Physical Therapy • Sports Medicine

Admissions Statement

Sacred Heart University is small enough to work with each student individually throughout the admission process. The university is committed to enrolling a diverse, highly qualified, and motivated student body. Criteria for admissions include completion of a college preparatory program in high school and acceptable scores on the SAT 1.

Saint Joseph's College

Rensselaer, Indiana 47978-0850
(219) 866-6170 or (800) 447-8781

St. Joseph's is a contemporary Catholic college that traces its history back more than 100 years. The college is located in Rensselaer, Indiana, a wonderful midwestern community close to big cities like Chicago, Indianapolis, and Lafayette. The 340-acre campus is beautiful and includes features like 40-acre Lake Banet Park, the reflecting pond adjacent to Saint Joseph's Chapel, and the Grotto, built in 1898. The town of Rensselaer offers the friendliness and community of a small town with access to the cultural and social opportunities of the neighboring big cities.

While the primary focus of the college is to provide a total educational experience comprised of sound career preparation and an appreciation for the liberal arts, the college also presents a campus atmosphere where students can develop a strong self image and make life long friendships. Clubs, organizations, and activities like intramural sports, theater productions, homecoming, a campus TV station, and the Little 500 (an annual go-cart race) encourage students to use their creative energy while making their own contribution to the campus community. As one student comments, "St. Joseph's is a great place to go to college!"

Academics

Degrees Offered: Associate, Bachelor's, Master's

Undergraduate Majors: 35+

Student/Faculty Ratio: 14 to 1

Number of Faculty: 88 full and part time

Saint Joseph's College offers bachelor of arts and bachelor of science degrees in 22 individual areas like biology, English, and psychology and 14 combined areas like geo-biology, international business, and mathematics/computer science. Each degree program reflects an integrated curriculum composed of the core curriculum, a major program of study, a minor program of study, and elective courses. The faculty at the college create a classroom environment where students can be active participators in class discussions and projects, and not just observers within the classroom.

One of the many outstanding programs at SJC is the unique core curriculum that focuses on the "human phenomenon" and integrates the development of man, society, culture, and language into a four-year cohesive experience. The Saint Joseph's core is very different from the general requirements at most other colleges. It is a single program of integrated liberal arts education that begins in the freshman year and continues in clear stages of progression toward a well defined goal in the senior year. All courses within the core are team-taught and provide a common academic experience for all students. The core consists of nine specific courses that cover all major disciplines within the liberal arts and complements the more specific knowledge acquired within one's major.

Students and Student Life

1,000 students from 26 states and 2 foreign countries
28% are from out-of-state
9% are students of color
1% are international
800 live on campus

The 1,000 men and women who attend SJC are active, outgoing people. This is reflected in the variety and number of campus activities. The college sponsors more than 40 clubs and organizations in all, ranging from volunteer and service opportunities to Campus Ministry to creative, fun events like the Little 500 go-cart race. Co-curricular activities are an important part of student life at Saint Joseph's College. They help students learn about different people and lifestyles and develop spiritual, moral, and ethical principles that will be with them throughout life. The Office of Multicultural Affairs promotes the value of cultural pluralism through various activities, including the Minority Student Leadership Award for incoming freshmen.

The center of student activities at SJC is the Halleck Student Union, which houses student government and student association offices in addition to the publication center for the college newspaper, yearbook, and literary magazine. But that's not all the college has to offer. Students interested in performance activities can choose from chorus, marching band, Columbian Players, and concert band. Sports enthusiasts have more than 20 intramural activities including ping-pong, pool, and flag-football tournaments to keep them busy.

Athletics: NCAA Division II, Great Lakes Midwest Conference
Women's Teams: basketball, cross country, golf, soccer, softball, tennis, track, volleyball
Men's Teams: baseball, basketball, cross country, football, golf, soccer, tennis, track

Campus and Community

St. Joseph's College offers its students a beautiful, 340-acre campus located in the safe, friendly town of Rensselaer, Indiana. The campus is well designed, comfortably blending classic buildings and modern structures. One example of this harmonious design is the Grotto, which was built in 1898. In 1931 it was enlarged to include the interior shrine containing a Carrara marble statue of Christ in Gethsemane. A short distance from the Grotto is the modern Hanson Recreational Center. Dedicated in 1986, it serves as the center for most sporting events, such as basketball, racquetball, aerobics, baseball, tennis, and track.

The eight residence halls at SJC are designed to contribute to the total development of the student. Like all other aspects of the college, residence life at SJC focuses on promoting intellectual awareness, developing effective self government, exposing the students to group living situations, and providing an environment conducive to study. The single-sex residence halls accommodate more than 900 students and range in size from 26 to 248 students.

The Robinson Memorial Library is located in the Arts and Science Building. In addition to 181,000 volume items, the library staff has online access to many national databases covering a vast array of disciplines and material formats. The Academic Computer Center is state of the art, including four labs for student use, and it's also the center of operations for the campus-wide Ethernet network. All campus computers are networked, resulting in easy communication among students, faculty, and administration. St. Joseph's College is proud to be on the cutting edge of campus computer networking and is continuing to connect more dorm rooms to the network every year.

The town of Rensselaer, Indiana is close by and has areas for shopping, entertainment, and employment. It is also located within easy access to several large cities: it is 73 miles southeast of Chicago, 110 miles northwest of Indianapolis, and 49 miles north of Lafayette.

Saint Joseph's College Academic Offerings

Accounting • Biology • Chemistry • Communication & Theater Arts • Computer Science • Entrepreneurship • Economics • Elementary Ed. • English • English/Creative Writing • Finance • History • Music • Management • Mass Communications • Mathematics • Philosophy • Philosophy/Religion • Physical Ed. • Political Science • Psychology • Sociology

Combined Majors: Accounting/Finance • Accounting/Information Systems • Biology/Chemistry • Finance/Information Systems • Geobiology • Geochemistry • Human Services • International Business • International Studies • Mathematics/Physics • Management/Marketing-Information Systems • Medical Technology • Mathematics/Computer Science • Music/Business Adm.

Admissions Statement

Candidates for freshman standing are selected from applicants who present the following academic credentials: a high school diploma from an accredited school; a minimum of 15 units, 10 of which must be in academic areas and completed with a minimum C average; and SAT 1 or ACT scores.

Saint Joseph's College

Windham, Maine 04062-9986
(207) 892-6766 or (800) 338-7057

A lakefront campus, modern facilities, faculty who connect with their classes, and a curriculum that includes 22 majors and 16 minors are all characteristics of Saint Joseph's College. This small New England College, with more than 80 years of history and tradition, offers associate, bachelor's, and master's degrees in both the liberal arts and career-oriented areas. The strong Catholic influence of the founding Sisters of Saint Joseph's is evident in the college's mission to "build an academic community dedicated to enabling its students to develop their potential by learning to appreciate the harmony that exists between faith and reason and to formulate judgments which embody universal values."

The college offers academic programs that are in tune with the work force of the 21st century and maintains a co-curricular program that fosters leadership, cooperative learning, and self development. Students of all backgrounds and faiths enjoy the small classes, excellent teaching, and supportive, caring environment for which the college is noted. Once you step on campus, you know you've come upon a very special place.

Academics

Degrees Offered: Associate, Bachelor's, Master's
Undergraduate Majors: 22
Student/Faculty Ratio: 15 to 1
Average Class Size: 22

Saint Joseph's College has been providing a student-centered education for well over three quarters of a century. The faculty at the college go out of their way to "connect" with their students. There are no large lecture halls, no graduate assistants teaching the courses, and no professors who fit in teaching during "down time" in research. Students and faculty are here to work with one another. The college does not attempt to be all things to all students. The academic offerings are solid and limited to areas in which the school can do the best job possible. The major offerings reflect traditional liberal arts areas and professional education, health care, and business fields.

Saint Joseph's has expanded its academic offerings by developing several alliances and joint degree programs with other colleges and universities. It offers a five-year program with Massachusetts College of Pharmacy in which students attend SJC for the first two years and spend the final three years in Boston at the Massachusetts College of Pharmacy campus. Successful completion of the program provides students with a bachelor of science in pharmacy.

As a member of the Greater Portland Alliance of Colleges and Universities, SJC students have access to courses, programs and social opportunities at six Greater Portland institutions, including Maine College of Art, Southern Maine Technical College, University of New England, University of Southern Maine, and Westbrook College.

Students at SJC can increase their career options by obtaining a double major, or by coupling any major with one of sixteen minor areas of study, which include career-oriented programs like secondary education, computer systems administration, business administration, and journalism. The college utilizes field work, internships, and seminars in all academic areas, which give another dimension to the learning experience. Elementary Education majors begin classroom observations in area schools in their freshman year. Nursing majors begin a 700-hour clinical rotation in their sophomore year. Human Development majors complete two semesters of field experience in a relevant discipline. These are only a few of the experiential learning experiences SJC students enjoy. A junior year program also is available for students to live and study in Nova Scotia, Canada, or one of the Canadian Maritime provinces.

Students and Student Life

900 students from states and foreign countries
5% are students of color
1% are international
500 live on campus in four residential halls

Saint Joseph's College has earned a reputation as a school where students have the opportunity to achieve their maximum potential both in academics and leadership endeavors. Involvement in activities, clubs, and organizations is a vital part of student life. It acts as an extension of the classroom learning environment, an avenue in which to make friends, and a means of having fun.

At SJC, campus life can include joining a the recreational club for skiing, intra-mural sports, and whitewater rafting. At several professional clubs on campus, like secondary education club, political action club, or biology club, students can meet other students with similar career plans. If you are interested in having your voice heard, SJC has its own radio station (B-91), newspaper (*Spectrum*), yearbook (*Shield*), and literary magazine (*e.g.*).

Students can take a hand in student government, including membership in councils and committees like academic council, judicial council, and student affairs and hall council. In all the college has more than 40 clubs, organizations, and teams to join in and weekly cultural and entertainment activities like lectures, movies, concerts, comedic acts, and magicians.

Athletics: NCAA Division III
Women's Teams: basketball, cross country, soccer, softball, volleyball
Men's Teams: baseball, basketball, cross country, golf, soccer

Campus and Community

The 315-acre lake front campus is a serene and pleasant environment to study and have fun, and yet is less than 20 minutes away from Portland, Maine's largest city. The main campus classroom building is Mercy Hall, which houses biology, chemis-try, and nursing labs in addition to faculty offices and a computer room. Next door is the Heffernan Center, which includes the Wellehan Library, auditorium, and chapel.

The campus has four residence halls with traditional dorm style rooms and two town house complexes. The Currier Gymnasium has indoor recreational and sports areas while outdoors there are tennis courts, soccer field, lighted ball field, and sev-eral cross-country trails. The college also has its own beach on Sebego Lake where students can swim, boat, and enjoy waterfront activities. Saint Joseph's College is home to the largest telescope in the state of Maine: the Celestron 14, with its 24-inch diameter aperture, sits atop the Heffernan Center.

The City of Portland is only 15 miles from campus and is home to the Portland Pirates Hockey Team, Symphony Orchestra, museum of art, theater and dance com-panies, and the Old Port, a cobblestone area rich in historic architecture and renowned for its shops, galleries, and fine dining.

Saint Joseph's College Academic Offering

Biology • Business Administration, with concentrations in accounting, banking, international business, marketing, management • Communications • English • Criminal Justice • Environmental Science • History • Human Development • Mathematics • Natural Science • Nursing • Philosophy • Psychology • Religious Studies • Sociology • Social Work • Teacher Education: elementary ed., physical ed. (K-12), secondary ed. in biology, English, history, mathematics, natural science

Admissions Statement

All applicants receive personalized, careful consideration by the Admissions Committee. Candidates are considered on the basis of their academic record and test scores in relation to their intended major.

Saint Leo College

Saint Leo, Florida 33574-2008
(904) 588-8283 or
(800) 334-5532 in-state
(800) 247-6559 out-of-state

Saint Leo College provides an atmosphere that fosters the total development of the person. Through its well-established mentoring program, small class size, and low student/faculty ratio, the college is able to focus on the varying academic needs of its students. The Honors Program offers stimulating and challenging opportunities for the bright student. The 40 co-curricular activities that take place on campus build a sense of community and teach students to learn from one another, work cooperatively, and develop leadership skills. Located in the Tampa Bay region of Florida, the college has access to hundreds of educational adventures provided by nearby attractions such as the Tampa Museum of Art, the Performing Arts Center, Sea World, and EPCOT Center.

Academics

Degrees Offered: Associate, Bachelor's, Master's
Undergraduate Majors: 25+
Student/Faculty Ratio: 15 to 1
Number of Faculty: 72 full and part time

The academic agenda at St. Leo College is formed by the philosophy that the best preparation for a quickly changing world is a broad educational background rather than narrow technical training. The liberal arts curriculum contained within the

Basic Studies program (like a core curriculum) introduces students to the three major areas of human knowledge—the humanities, natural sciences, and social sciences—through a sequence of 16 courses chosen from a field of more than 60 courses. The college feels that no matter what career path students eventually choose, the liberal arts curriculum in the Basic Studies program will help them develop the skills needed to succeed in the workplace.

At Saint Leo College, all of the major areas of concentration can be directly related to a career path. The faculty works with students individually from their first semester, helping them select courses and educational opportunities that will best meet their educational and vocational goals. The faculty and administrators continue to recognize the needs and goals of students throughout their education. Whether students need additional assistance or are looking for academic challenges beyond regular classes, Saint Leo College can accommodate their needs.

The nationally recognized Honors Program was created for highly motivated and academically talented students. Working closely with a faculty advisor, Honors students enroll in an integrated sequence of six liberal arts courses spread over the first three years of college and complete an Honors project during their senior year. In addition to experiencing the challenge of analytical thinking, independent learning, and intellectual discussion, Honors students receive a half-tuition scholarship for their last semester of study at Saint Leo.

The college has academic support services for students who need additional assistance. The classroom environment enables faculty and students to work together and professors are available for extra help after class. The Computer Instruction Center prepares students to be effective computer-users and the Writing Center staff assists students in all stages of the writing process including the pre-writing, writing, rewriting, and editing process. The residence advisor in each hall coordinates programming activities addressing issues like time management and developing effective study habits, in addition to more recreational events.

Students and Student Life

1,000 students from 30 states and 27 foreign countries
40% are from out-of-state
17% are students of color
4% are international

Saint Leo College attracts students from many different backgrounds. Through its Center for Distance Learning, the college enrolls 7,000 adult learners and military personnel at more than 11 military bases stretching from Virginia to Key West Florida, in addition to the 1,000 traditional students who attend classes on campus who make up the community of Saint Leo College.

Approximately 850 students live on campus in six residential halls. One of the most important organizations on campus is the Student Leadership Coalition, the elected student body government. There are also about 40 clubs and organizations including fraternities, sororities, social clubs, honor societies, student chapters of professional organizations, service and religious organizations, and student life council. The wonderful Florida climate is the perfect environment for outdoor activities, and the campus is the ideal place. Because so many full-time students live on campus, things are happening all week long.

Athletics: Sunshine State Conference of the NCAA Division II
Women's Teams: basketball, softball, tennis, volleyball
Men's Teams: baseball, basketball, soccer, tennis

Campus and Community

The tropical campus is located just off Interstate 75, 25 miles northeast of Tampa and just an hour's drive from Orlando. The 170 acres of rolling hills and wooded grounds are in a safe, peaceful, rural setting on the shore of Lake Jovita. A blending of the old and new create a unique mixture of architecture. Spanish Florida baroque stands side by side with the newer contemporary architecture. The six residence halls are conveniently located throughout the campus. Students can select from different types of residence facilities including single-sex and coed halls, suite arrangements, and standard dorm style. All residence halls are air-conditioned, and since 80 percent of the students live on campus, they are the center of campus activity.

The centerpiece of the academic buildings is the Cannon Memorial Library, which contains 129,157 volumes of material in print, audio-visual, microfilm, and computer-based formats. The library was totally renovated and enlarged about 10 years ago and now includes the Hugh Culverhouse Computer Instruction Center on the lower level. The William P. McDonald Center is the hub of campus social activities and includes both dinning and recreational facilities. The Marion Bowman Activities Center's gymnasium, heated outdoor pool, and other physical-education training facilities provide an area for indoor recreation. The beautiful campus setting, combined with the close proximity to Tampa and its major urban activities, makes Saint Leo College an ideal environment for a college student.

Saint Leo College Academic Offerings

Liberal Arts and Sciences: Biology • English • Environmental Science • History • International Studies • Political Science • Psychology • Religion

Professional Studies: Accounting • Business Administration specializations: computer information services, human resource administration, management, marketing, restaurant & hotel management • Criminology • Elementary Ed. •

Health Care Adm. • Human Services specialization: administrative, social services • Medical Technology • Physical Ed. • Public Adm. • Social Work • Sport Mgt.

Admissions Statement

In accordance with Saint Leo College mission statement, all students who, in the judgment of the college, show evidence of likely success in the academic programs offered at Saint Leo College will be considered for admission. Each applicant will be evaluated based upon all the information in the applicant's admission application. An admission decision will be determined on a combination of the following criteria: graduation from an accredited secondary school or GED certificate; course work completed at the secondary level; results of the SAT 1 or ACT; recommendations from guidance counselor, principal, or headmaster.

Saint Mary's University of Minnesota

Winona, Minnesota 55987-1399
(507) 457-1700 or (800) 635-5987

At Saint Mary's University of Minnesota, your education may begin in the classroom, but it will extend beyond the borders of the beautiful 400-acre campus. Surrounded by high bluffs, crystal clear lakes, and the mighty Mississippi River, the university provides an active environment that incorporates experiential learning into a strong liberal arts curriculum.

Students work alongside their professors on research projects that take place in the Weaver Bottoms wetlands. Theater majors can spend a semester in England studying Shakespeare and his world. Human service majors can study cultural differences while immersed in life in Mexico, and education majors can observe school children and teaching methods in Ireland. Students from any major can spend a semester studying in Florence, Italy. Back on campus international students enrolled in the De La Salle Language Institute bring a multicultural characteristic to the university and provide first hand experience about life beyond Minnesota.

One student described the university by saying, "It's the kind of college that's more than just a place to study and learn. It's a community, where students and faculty work together, learn from one another, and experience new things together!"

Academics

Degrees Offered: Bachelor's, Master's
Undergraduate Majors: 35+
Student/Faculty Ratio: 14 to 1
Number of Faculty: 96

There are four undergraduate divisions: the School of Arts and Humanities, the School of Business and Social Sciences, the School of Education, and the School of Sciences and Mathematics. The core studies program is the single educational experience common to all Saint Mary's undergraduates. It has received recognition from the National Endowment for the Humanities and provides a foundation of interdisciplinary courses, showing students the ways in which the world is interconnected.

Courses begin at the freshman level, are distributed over a four-year period and sequentially expose students to the complex spiritual, aesthetic, and social traditions and issues that will shape their futures. In addition to this unique core, all students complete a 27-credit area program in fine arts, behavioral sciences, literature, science, philosophy, religion, American studies, and quantitative studies. With this comprehensive base students move on to specialized studies in one of the four schools.

Students at Saint Mary's can take up to one half of their courses each semester at Winona State. The university also supports independent study projects in which students work one-on-one with a professor or design an individual project that will be evaluated for credit. Students can take up to eight independent-study courses within the four years they are at Saint Mary's.

The university sponsors several interesting off-campus programs where students can pursue experiential learning opportunities. The Semester in London centers on a 12-week investigation of the art, theater, literature, theology, and history of the United Kingdom. Other off-campus programs include Semester in Mexico; student teaching in private, international English-speaking schools throughout the world; the Washington Center Internship; and the Metro Urban Studies Term. Students can also design their own internship. An education at Saint Mary's University can be a lot more exciting than just going to class and reading the text!

Students and Student Life

1,400 students from 30 states and 12 foreign countries
55% are from out-of-state
6% are students of color
5% are international
85% live on campus

The spirit of community is strong at Saint Mary's University, because of the well defined programs that develop students' interpersonal, leadership, athletic, and spiritual capabilities. The university sponsors about 85 groups and organizations that reflect the interests of the students. Concerts, lectures, art exhibits, and a weekly film series are regular features throughout the school year. Intramural and recreational sports are very popular and more than 85 percent of the students participate.

Volunteerism is part of campus life and more than one third of Saint Mary's students are members of service related organizations like the Sunshine Foundation or Youth Association for Retarded Citizens.

The Student Senate at the university is composed of elected executive officers. It maintains it own budget and coordinates and directs all student activities. Student Senate also provides an active forum for student opinion and a practical means for student participation in the life and governance of the school.

Athletics: NCAA Division III, Minnesota Intercollegiate Athletic Conference

Women's Teams: basketball, cross country, golf, nordic skiing, soccer, indoor track, softball, swimming/diving, tennis, track & field, volleyball

Men's Teams: baseball, basketball, cross country, golf, hockey, indoor track, nordic skiing, soccer, swimming/diving, tennis, track & field

Campus and Community

The university is located in Winona, Minnesota, a beautiful college town with a population of 25,000 adjacent to the Mississippi River. The city of Winona is located 100 miles southeast of Minneapolis/St. Paul, 200 miles northwest of Milwaukee, and 275 miles northwest of Chicago.

The 400-acre campus is surrounded by high, wooded bluffs and is part of the Upper Mississippi National Wildlife and Fish Refuge, which attracts some of the country's largest concentrations of canvasback ducks, tundra swans, and bald eagles. It is also where students spend a lot of their time conducting research and enjoying the outdoors.

The 27 buildings on Saint Mary's campus include 14 residence halls where single and double rooms are available in both single-sex and coed facilities. The university also has a series of student villages which accommodate four persons in three-room furnished apartments, complete with bath and an efficiency kitchenette. Each apartment has its own exterior entrance.

The Recreational Athletic Complex has top-of-the-line recreational and athletic facilities, including a new fieldhouse and aquatic center. The Fitzgerald Library recently completed a $1.5 million McEnery Center addition. Its computerized card catalogue system allows access to over 50 other academic and state agency libraries.

The Performance Center is a shining star on Saint Mary's campus. It includes the 450-seat Page Theater, 135-seat Figliulo Recital Hall, and a smaller studio theater. It is the major performance area for student plays and musical productions. The lobby's large frescos, brass railings, and stained glass windows all add to the artistic beauty of the facility. The College Center is where much of campus life occurs, and houses dining facilities, post office, student government offices, bookstore, and campus radio station.

The entire Saint Mary's campus is designed to enhance student learning and promote a sense of community among the students, faculty, and administrators who make up the college.

Saint Mary's University of Minnesota Academic Offerings

School of Arts and Humanities: Art: electronic publishing, graphic design, studio art • English: English education, literature, writing, electronic publishing • Music: guitar/instrumental, band K-12/classroom music, music merchandising, organ/piano/vocal, classroom music • Modern/Classical Languages: French, Spanish • Theater/Speech: theater/speech education, theater, theater education • Theology: religious education, youth ministry • History • Philosophy

School of Business and Social Science: Business: accounting, international business, management, marketing • Computer Science: management information systems • Criminal Justice • Human Services • Media Communications: electronic publishing, public relations • Political Science: public adm. • Psychology • Social Science • Social Science Education • Sociology

School of Education and Integrated Sciences: Licensures in early childhood, kindergarten, elementary, middle, and secondary

School of Sciences and Mathematics: Biology: allied health, cytotechnology, medical technology, nuclear medicine technology, pre-physical therapy • Chemistry: physical science education • Environmental Biology: geographic information systems • Mathematics & Statistics: mathematics education, physics

Admissions Statement

The pattern of high school courses and performance, while not the sole criterion for acceptance, is of primary importance. Students are expected to have completed four years of English, three years of mathematics, two years of social science and two years of natural science. Rank in class, personal essay, test scores, activities, and school recommendations all provide additional data used in the evaluation of a student's academic potential for college success.

Salve Regina University

Newport, Rhode Island 02840-4192
(800) 321-7124

Salve Regina University is a mid-size Catholic college located on the coast of the Atlantic Ocean in scenic Newport, Rhode Island. Visitors from around the world flock to Newport to experience the glory of the Gilded Age, relive America's Cup, or stroll the Cliff Walk. For a Salve student these attractions are part of everyday life. McCauley Hall and O'Hare Academic Center command ocean views, and student housing ranges from stately mansions to modern structures.

Like the architecture, the curriculum intertwines contemporary and classic ideas. The 48-credit core emphasizes personal growth and social responsibility, while the 35 academic majors combine career-oriented and liberal arts subjects. Internships are encouraged. Med-tech students have the opportunity to intern at Rhode Island or St. Joseph's Hospital, while political studies majors can work for judges or at the House of Representatives in Providence. Opportunities like these provide the experience graduates need to have the edge in today's competitive job market.

Academics

Degrees Offered: Bachelor's, Master's, Doctoral

Undergraduate Majors: 30

Student/Faculty Ratio: 13 to 1

Number of Faculty: 117 full and part time

The core curriculum completed in the first two years is a broad sampling of the liberal arts. Requirements include English, math, history, geography, philosophy, psychology, art, religion, and physical education. Upon completion of the core students can choose 35 majors and 28 minors, and select from over 850 courses offered each year.

Salve Regina University supports the specific needs of the students, both the exceptionally gifted and the academically challenged. The college sponsors nine honor societies and is currently developing an honors program. For the academically challenged student, Salve also extends resources that prevent frustration and discouragement. Note takers, oral exams, untimed tests, and tape recordings of class sessions are all available through the Academic Development Center.

All students in good standing can participate in study-abroad programs sponsored in seven countries including Ireland, Mexico, and Australia. On these trips students learn to understand the culture, language, and customs of specific nations. Hands-on learning is also emphasized and available through the internship program. Students who gain the recommendation of their department head can participate in exciting experiences like working for the DEA, attending an anthropology institute in Mexico, or working with an author on an upcoming book.

Students and Student Life

2,200 students from 36 states and 13 foreign countries
5% are students of color
1% are international
730 live on campus

Activities at SRU are varied. There are 27 social organizations, 15 of which are departmental, including the accounting club, artists guild, and council for exceptional children. Student publications include *Regina Maris*, the yearbook; *Mosaic*, a literary magazine; and *The Newspaper*. Sports clubs include sailing and equestrian as well as six intramural teams open to men and women.

Salve students are involved in service projects in the Newport community. Members of Sigma Phi Sigma honors society are involved in Toys for Tots and Feed a Friend. Other volunteer opportunities include participation in the Ronald McDonald House, Head Start, and the American Cancer Society.

New clubs are always being started on campus and guest speakers visit almost weekly. Salve is willing to develop the interests of small groups of students and make their ideas a reality.

Athletics: NCAA Division III
Women's Teams: basketball, cross country, field hockey, sailing, soccer, softball, tennis, track & field
Men's Teams: baseball, football, golf, ice hockey, rugby

Campus and Community

Salve Regina University's campus shimmers with the splendor of stately mansions, sunken gardens, the Atlantic Ocean, and the vitality of student life. Thirty-four academic and residential buildings are housed on the 100-acre campus. The 10 dormitories are all single sex, alcohol free, have quiet hours, and provide live-in resident assistants. Approximately 50 percent of Salve students live on campus. Recreational facilities include athletic fields, tennis courts, fitness center, and a newly redecorated student lounge.

Off campus there are many social, and recreational activities. Salve is located on the Cliff Walk and bordered by mansions once belonging to American's most prestigious families. Students can tour these "summer cottages" at reduced rates, and in town, they can enjoy international restaurants, boutiques, and a movie theater, or just watch the crowds milling down Thames Street. Transportation off the island is available. Regularly scheduled buses run to Providence and Boston, providing easy access to metropolitan areas and many colleges, including Harvard, Boston College, and Providence College.

Salve Regina University Academic Offerings

Accounting • Administration of Justice • American Studies • Anthropology • Art • Biology • Chemistry • Economics • Education • English • French • History • Management Information Systems • Mathematics • Medical Technology • Music • Nursing • Philosophy • Politics • Psychology • Religious Studies • Social Work • Sociology • Spanish • Special Ed. • Theater

Admissions Statement

Admission to Salve Regina University is an individualized process. We are clearly most interested in a candidate's academic ability, but we are also interested in potential, not just past performance. We consider intellectual curiosity, strength of character, motivation, promise of personal growth, and development along with class rank and SAT scores. We seek a class of committed and interesting individuals who will contribute to our community.

Seton Hall University

South Orange, New Jersey 07079-2691
(201) 761-9332

Seton Hall is a private Catholic university where students have access to a rich curriculum and many degree offerings in liberal arts and pre-professional areas. Classes are interesting and students actively participate in class discussions and projects. Unlike many other universities, most of the classes at Seton Hall have between 20 to 25 students, and less than 7 percent of the classes have 40 or more students.

At Seton Hall, students are educated in an environment that addresses the spirit as well as the mind. Ethics and social responsibility are a part of the curriculum. The Catholic tradition of the university embraces an increasingly diverse family of students, faculty, and staff who form a cohesive community of learners.

Academics

Degrees Offered: Bachelor's, Master's, Law

Undergraduate Majors: 40 undergraduate and 43 graduate degrees

Student/Faculty Ratio: 17 to 1

Average Class Size: 25

Number of Faculty: 350 full and part time

Seton Hall University is comprised of four undergraduate schools: the Stillman School of Business, the College of Arts and Sciences, the College of Education and Human Services, and the College of Nursing. While students affiliate with one particular school when they choose a major, they can and do take courses at all the schools. The largest school is the College of Arts and Sciences; 61 percent of the students are enrolled in this school. As the oldest school within the university, Arts and Sciences has a long, proud history of more than 140 years.

The Stillman School of Business, accredited by the American Assembly of Collegiate Schools of Business, provides a comprehensive and intense foundation for a successful career in any area of business. Through its Institute for International Business, Seton Hall business majors can participate in student exchange programs in China, Poland, France, Russia, and the Dominican Republic. The college also offers a five year BA/MBA program.

The College of Education and Human Services prepares students for careers in elementary and secondary education, health and physical education, and in education for children and adults with developmental disorders.

The College of Nursing focuses on preparing professional nurses with the technological, scientific, and interpersonal skills necessary to succeed in the 21st century health care arena. Classroom theory, interactive computer learning systems, and clinical rotations gained in hospitals, public health, and community agencies are all a part of the Seton Hall Nursing curriculum.

Seton Hall also has three graduate schools. The School of Theology, the School of Law, and the School of Medical Education all provide outstanding professional programs. While the university is affiliated with the Catholic church, students of all religions are welcome and comfortable at the university.

Students and Student Life

4,400 students from 35 states and 51 foreign countries
24% are students of color
2% are international
50% live on campus in six residential halls

Student government, publications, cultural clubs, religious organizations, volunteer programs, academic clubs and fraternities and sororities—Seton Hall has them and more! WSOU, the campus radio station, was named the #1 radio station in the country by *Guitar* magazine. The College Pan Hellenic Council oversees more than 20 fraternities and sororities with chapters on campus, and the students at Seton Hall provide community service and volunteer projects through more than eight service related organizations. Professional clubs are affiliated with almost all of the major academic areas and performance clubs include Gospel Choir, Theater-in-the-Round, and *The Setonian*, the campus newspaper, or *Renaissance*, the literary magazine. In all, the university sponsors more than 60 collegiate organizations!

Athletics: NCAA Division I, Big East Conference
Women's Teams: basketball, cross country, indoor track, outdoor track, soccer, softball, swimming, tennis, volleyball
Men's Teams: baseball, basketball, cross country, golf, indoor track, soccer, swimming, tennis, wrestling

Campus and Community

The 50-acre campus is located in South Orange, New Jersey, a quiet suburban community less than an hour from New York City. The campus lies within walking distance of the village of South Orange, which has shopping, movie theaters, restaurants, and commuter train to NYC. On campus students have a well-designed community of their own with academic, recreational, and residential facilities.

The more than 30 buildings include an old Victorian carriage house, which retains its period architecture even though it was converted into a modern art center; six residence halls offering traditional hall living and suite and apartment accommodations; McNulty Hall, home of the university's sophisticated science facilities; and the Brennan Recreation Center, which houses a 25-meter pool, four-lane running track, multipurpose courts, and a gymnasium with seating for 3,400 fans. The Walsh Library, constructed in 1994, is a 21st-century research center with computerized card catalogue, four electronic multimedia rooms, 10 CD-ROM information search and retrieval stations, and 400 study carrels.

Seton Hall University Academic Offerings

Arts and Sciences: African-American Studies • Anthropology • Art • Asian Studies • Biology • Chemistry • Classical Studies • Communication • Computer Engineering • Computer Science • Criminal Justice • Economics • Engineering • English • French • History • Italian • Liberal Studies • Mathematics • Modern Languages • Music • Philosophy • Physical Therapy • Physics • Political

Science • Psychology • Religious Studies • Social/Behavioral Sciences • Social Work • Sociology • Spanish

Education and Human Services: Developmental Disorders • Elementary Education • Health and Physical Ed. • Nursing • Secondary Ed.

Business: Accounting • Economics • Finance • Management • Management Information Systems • Marketing

Admissions Statement

To be considered for admissions students should have satisfactory completion of a college preparatory program in high school and have attained acceptable scores on the SAT or ACT. Other factors considered in the selection include recommendations from teachers and counselors and extra curricular activities. About 75 percent of Seton Hall students have combined SAT scores of 900 or better.

Southern Arkansas University

Magnolia, Arkansas 71753
(501) 235-4040

Southern Arkansas University enrolls approximately 3,000 students in four undergraduate colleges. As a regional state university, SAU offers degree programs for men and women from many different educational backgrounds. The university has established a climate in which students and faculty work together. The curriculum in each degree program is designed to promote intellectual growth, personal enrichment, and skill development. Students can choose from more than 50 liberal arts and professional majors in preparation for graduate school or a career.

Academics

Degrees Offered: Associate, Bachelor's, Master's

Undergraduate Majors: 50+

Student/Faculty Ratio: 18 to 1

Number of Faculty: 221 full and part time

The four undergraduate divisions at SAU are the School of Business, the School of Education, the School of Liberal and Performing Arts, and the School of Science and Technology. Each division offers an array of courses and programs, so it is easy for students to find an area of study they are interested in.

The School of Business schedules approximately 100 courses each semester, and students can major in traditional business areas like management, marketing, finance, and economics. The Small Business Institute allows students to receive actual field experience and college credit by offering problem solving and management advisory services to community business organizations. Students In Free Enterprise and the Business Student Advisory Council are two other campus programs in which business majors can gain practical skills.

The School of Education has designed a quality academic and professional program which prepares teachers and other educators for work in the public schools. The school is accredited by the National Council for Accreditation of Teacher Education, and the programs in teacher education meet certification requirements for teaching in most states.

The School of Liberal and Performing Arts offers programs in fine and performing arts. The Harold T. Brinson Art Building provides some of the finest facilities for art in the area. Students have access to six major studios, a public art gallery, a student gallery, and a wide range of modern graphics, printmaking, and photographic laboratories. The Dolph Camp Music building has a recital hall, classrooms, and practice rooms. The Margaret Harton Theater, located in the Overstreet Hall, is the center of the Theater and Speech Department. One student commented, "If you come to Southern Arkansas University and want to major in the performing arts, you will not sacrifice craft and opportunity. The facilities here are great, and the opportunities to perform are abundant."

The School of Science and Technology is divided into five departments: Agriculture, Biological Science, Mathematics and Computer Science, Physical Science and Technology, and Nursing. Each department supports several strong programs. The Agriculture department includes a 569-acre laboratory used by the Department of Agriculture and the students at SAU.

A college education at SAU is not just for the bright, talented, well-prepared student. The university is committed to providing scholastic opportunities for students from different educational and cultural backgrounds. In order to do this, SAU has pioneered a university-wide program for students who are underprepared or lack confidence in their ability to do college-level work. The Academic Opportunity Program is a full service component that includes a series of courses, special tutoring, and other personalized assistance designed to meet student's individual academic needs. Learning experiences and courses are structured for students of different learning styles, aptitudes, interests, and backgrounds. Specially trained faculty, counselors, and peer tutors make up the team of instructors who work in the Academic Opportunity Program.

Students and Student Life

2,700 students from 26 states and 15 foreign countries
22% are from out-of-state
25% are students of color
2% are international
900 live on campus

"Diverse" is one way to characterize the students who attend SAU. If you're looking for a university where you can live and learn with people of different cultural backgrounds, this might be the place for you. The university fosters an atmosphere of mutual cooperation and support among students, and encourages participation in the more than 60 student activities. There is a weekly student newspaper, a huge intramural program, and more than 20 department and professional organizations. Other campus clubs include six different recognition and honor societies, seven religious organizations, nine special interest groups, and seven national sororities and six national fraternities.

Athletics: NCAA Division II Gulf South Conference
Women's Teams: basketball, cross country, rodeo, tennis, track, volleyball
Men's Teams: baseball, basketball, cross country, football, golf, rodeo
Coed Teams: rodeo, track

Campus and Community

The 731-acre campus is located in the small town of Magnolia. The university is the center of cultural and recreational activities in the region and has facilities for sports, musical and theatrical performances, and scientific research.

Overstreet Hall fronts the campus and is the entrance to the academic area where most of the classrooms, labs, department buildings, and library are situated. The building that houses the School of Business and Business/Agriculture has a three-story atrium that resembles the entrance to a corporate headquarters. Inside, specially designed rooms feature technologically advanced videographic projection systems that provides access to satellite cable, in addition to conference and seminar rooms. The university even has a Greek amphitheater where outdoor concerts and plays are held.

The three men's residence halls are located at the north end of campus and the two women's residence halls are located at the southeast edge of campus. The university also has apartments for married students.

The north side of campus is where most of the athletic fields, buildings, and stadium are located. There is a great outdoor track, 10 lighted tennis courts, a baseball field complete with pressbox, and Wilkins Stadium, which can seat 6,000 fans. In addition to all this, SAU has a separate Biological Field Station located about 10 miles from campus on Lake Columbia. Ecology laboratories, overnight accommodations, and recreational areas are available to students and faculty.

Southern Arkansas University Academic Offerings

School of Business Administration: Accounting • Business Administration with emphasis in accounting, administrative services, computer information systems, economics, finance, financial planning, management, marketing, international business, information systems, management • Industrial Management

School of Education: Art Ed. • Biological Science Ed. • Business Ed. • Chemistry Ed. • Elementary Ed. • English Ed. • General Science Ed. • Health, Kinesiology, and Recreation • Mathematics Ed. • Physics Ed. • Recreation and Community Service • Social Studies Ed. • Spanish Ed.

School of Liberal and Performing Arts: Art • English • Graphic Design • History • Liberal Arts/Business • Mass Communications: broadcasting • Mass Communications: journalism • Music Ed. • Political Science • Psychology • Sociology • Sociology: social work specialization • Spanish • Studio Art • Theater

School of Science and Technology: Agricultural Business • Agriculture Education • Biological Science • Chemistry • Engineering/Physics • General Science • Industrial Technology • Mathematics • Medical Technology • Nursing

Admissions Statement

Any first-time freshman must meet *one* of the following standards for admission to the University.

1. Graduate from an accredited high school with a class rank in the top half of the graduating class, or
2. Graduate from an accredited high school with an ACT composite score of 19 or higher (combined SAT of 790 or higher).

University of Southern Maine

Gorham, Maine 0438-1088
(207) 780-5670 or (800) 800-4USM

The University of Southern Maine offers an educational environment that includes both urban and rural campus settings, diverse academic majors, and a community of scholars who love to teach, counsel, and advise. Students receive an education that develops specific career skills, prepares them to make appropriate choices, and challenges their sense of discovery. Small classes, coupled with opportunities to study abroad or participate in a cooperative learning experience, expand the traditional educational experiences students receive.

The five undergraduate divisions that make up the university include the College of Art and Sciences, the College of Education and Human Development, the School of Applied Sciences, the School of Business, and the School of Nursing. These divisions offer more than 40 degree programs. For more than 100 years the University of Southern Maine has been the undergraduate school of choice for many New Englanders.

Academics

Degrees Offered: Associate, Bachelor's, Master's

Undergraduate Majors: 40

Student/Faculty Ratio: 15 to 1

Number of Faculty: 536

The University of Southern Maine attracts both traditional and non-traditional students and has degree programs and residential facilities on both its city campus in Portland and its suburban campus in Gorham. The five undergraduate divisions that make up the university offer pre-professional, career-oriented, and liberal arts majors. Areas as diverse as art; hotel, motel, and restaurant management; and industrial technology are available at SMU.

The university has an outstanding music department that even offers a specialization in Jazz Studies, while the School of Applied Science offers degree programs in Applied Technical Leadership and six other areas. The School of Education is initiating a new selective undergraduate teacher certification program in the mathematics and science areas.

Because USM is a member of the Portland Alliance of Colleges and Universities, students can take courses, use facilities, and participate in cultural activities at the Maine College of Art, St. Joseph's College, Southern Maine Technical College, the University of New England, and Westbrook College.

USM offers summer and winter sessions so students who want to accelerate their degree can graduate early. During these two sessions USM offers opportunities to study abroad, participate in research projects, or work one on one with a special professor. As a member of the National Student Exchange, USM students can spend a semester or year at more than 120 universities in the United States. What a great way to check out the job market and meet new friends in a different part of the country! Cooperative Education can also be integrated into all degree programs. In addition to adding a practical, supervised work experience, USM students in this program have the chance to "earn while they learn."

Students and Student Life

7,800 students from 23 states and 31 foreign countries
4% are students of color
1% are international
1,350 live on campus in 7 residential halls: six on the Gorham campus, one on the Portland campus.

The University of Southern Maine is a comprehensive educational institution, one in which co-curricular activities are important and valued. Whether students are beginning college after high school or returning to college after many years, USM has a club, organization, or activity that will interest them. National and local fraternities and sororities contribute to the vitality of the campus, along with performance groups like University Choral, Chamber Orchestra, and the Russell Square Players.

Professional clubs provide forums where students pursuing similar majors can get together and share ideas, plan programs, and meet and work with professionals in the area. SMU has more than twenty professional organizations like the Accounting Society, the Criminology Association and the USM chapter of the American Chemical Society. The Ski Club and Outdoor Club are just two examples of the numerous recreational clubs that provide fun and adventure for the students. There are several honorary societies and special interest groups on campus. The university sponsors a large peer-leadership program in which students can acquire new skills and take on paraprofessional roles on campus as peer advisors, health educators, and student ambassadors.

Athletics: NCAA Division III
Women's Teams: basketball, cross country, field hockey, golf, ice hockey, soccer, softball, tennis, track & field
Men's Teams: baseball, basketball, cross country, soccer, tennis, track & field

Campus and Community

The dual residential campus has opportunities for students to live and experience campus life in the sophisticated city of Portland and the small country village of Gorham. The two campuses are 10 miles apart and linked by a free USM shuttle service. Both campuses have complete classroom facilities, libraries, and residential halls. Students can choose which environment they like best and always have the option of changing the next semester. The southern Maine region includes Portland, the state's largest city and hub of cultural activity. The museums, restored neighborhoods, shops, galleries, and Old Port area are places students can go for a change of pace, and all are accessible from either campus.

University of Southern Maine Academic Offerings

College of Arts and Sciences: Art • Art Ed. • Art History • Associate Degree in Liberal Arts • Biochemistry • Biology • Chemistry/Applied Chemistry • Communication • Criminology • Economics • English • Environmental Science & Policy • French • Geography/Anthropology • Geology • History • Jazz Studies • Mathematics • Media Arts • Music • Music Ed. • Music Performance • Philosophy • Physics • Political Science • Psychology • Self-Designed Major • Social Work • Sociology • Statistics • Theater

School of Applied Science: Applied Technical Education • Applied Technical Leadership • Computer Science • Electrical Engineering • Engineering (U. Maine transfer) • Industrial Technology

School of Business Management: Accounting • Associate Degree: Accounting • Business Adm.

School of Nursing: Associate Degree: Therapeutic Recreation • Nursing • Therapeutic Recreation

Admissions Statement

Admission to the University of Southern Maine is based primarily on the applicant's academic background, the rigor of the high school program and the grades achieved. In addition the University also considers SAT or ACT scores, student essay, recommendations, and individual talents and activities.

Southwest State University

Marshall, Minnesota 56258-3306
(507) 537-6286 or (800) 642-0684

Southwest State University has many of the advantages of a private college at a public school price. A 19 to 1 student faculty ratio and a student enrollment of 2,700 ensures classroom interaction with top-notch faculty. But small classes and good faculty are only the beginning of what SSU has to offer. The campus is modern (the oldest building is only 29 years old) and high tech. All of the facilities on campus are connected by hallways, skyways, and tunnels, so the weather will never interfere with your plans.

The university supports learning experiences that take place off campus. There are study abroad programs with learning opportunities in places like Jamaica, Denmark, and Spain. Students can take courses at any other Minnesota State University, including one in Akita, Japan. Combine all this with the fact that the university offers liberal arts and technical degrees in 43 major areas, and offers 35 minors, five associate and six certificate programs, and you have a pretty good picture of Southwest State University!

Academics

Degrees Offered: Associate, Bachelor's

Undergraduate Majors: 40+

Student/Faculty Ratio: 19 to 1

Number of Faculty: 135 full time

At Southwest State University students can choose from traditional liberal arts majors like history, literature, or political science or more career-oriented majors like restaurant administration or hotel administration. They can complement their studies with a minor in an area as unique as rural studies or as practical as French, German, or Spanish. They can take all of their courses at the campus in Marshall, Minnesota, or they can take some of their classes at any one of the colleges within the State University System. Options like these provide a world of difference in an education!

Many state universities throughout the country offer a solid academic education, but SSU takes it one step further. Here in the core curriculum every student gets a solid academic education that includes areas like communications skills, science, mathematics, humanities, fine arts, social sciences, health, and a course in rural studies. Rural studies acquaints students with their heritage so they can understand and appreciate both the past and contemporary rural life. It is one way all students at SSU can cultivate and revitalize rural values for the sake of future generations.

Another reflection of the quality education offered at Southwest State University is the global studies cluster students can incorporate into any major. A global studies cluster consists of three courses and an accompanying Special Topics Seminar, which is team-taught by three faculty members. The courses are grouped around a central theme, and upon completion of the course work students participate in a voyage to a destination that is closely related to the cluster theme. Previous cluster programs included Water and Life in California, with a trip to Southern California during spring break; Eastern Europe in Transition and a visit to Poland, Russia, and the Czech Republic; and Healing Wounds, involving a trip to Vietnam. The Global Studies program is Southwest State University's way of extending the learning process around the world.

The university offers other study programs that include international learning opportunities. The Common Market Option provides extended study in France, Germany, Denmark, Spain, Taiwan, and England. SSU students can also cross register at any other Minnesota State University. The Minnesota University System has a campus in Akita, Japan where students can experience foreign study at the same tuition cost as SSU!

The university goes beyond the classroom to make sure that students' academic needs are satisfied. The Freshman Advising Center assists new students in their transition to the university. The Learning Resource Center sponsors tutoring programs, supplemental, instruction, and developmental course work. The University Writing Center has faculty and student assistants who can suggest appropriate drafting, revising, and editing changes.

The Writing Lab gives students access to MAC word processing facilities and the Math Lab, which is staffed by paraprofessionals, helps students enrolled in mathematics and computer science courses. One student sums it up by saying, "The faculty, administration, and staff are all concerned about students' success. The university has just about every support service in place if you need it. And we have a good Honors Program for students who want to be challenged beyond the limits of regular classes. It's all here."

Students and Student Life

2,700 students from 27 states and 26 foreign countries
35% from out-of-state
6% are students of color
3% are international
1,200 live on campus

The university sponsors 65 clubs and organization to suit the interests of both residential and commuting students. The campus even has a child care center for student parents. Activities range from intramural sports to concerts, volunteer programs, music groups, student publications, and a campus radio and TV station. A consistent activity that involves almost all the SSU students is community service. There are several organizations, like the Students in Rural Public Service and the Youth Issues Education Project, that focus on service, in addition to a variety of clubs that take on special volunteer projects through out the year.

Athletics: NCAA Division II, Northern Sun Intercollegiate Conference
Women's Teams: basketball, softball, soccer, tennis, volleyball
Men's Teams: baseball, basketball, football, wrestling
Coed Teams: wheelchair basketball

Campus and Community

The 200-acre campus includes 24 academic and residential buildings. Because the college was built during the 1960s, all the structures are modern and reflect a unified planning scheme. All of the major academic buildings are located in one area. The Student Center, residential halls, and commons are grouped together, and the athletic fields and recreational areas are adjacent.

All the academic buildings, the Student Center and Food Service facilities are connected by enclosed tunnels and hallways. Special facilities include the Natural History Museum and greenhouse, the Fine Arts Theater (equipped with professional acoustical and lighting equipment), and a new recreation/athletic facility where 4,000 fans can watch the SSU basketball games. The campus is modern and has a spacious, comfortable feeling. The harmonious structures are laid out in an appealing fashion, and the students enjoy the contemporary style.

The city of Marshall has activities, entertainment, shopping, and employment opportunities for the students at Southwest. There are plenty of areas nearby for hiking, biking, horseback riding, swimming, camping, cross country skiing, and snowmobiling. A recent book lists Marshall among the "100 Best Small Towns in America."

Southwest State University Academic Offerings

Accounting • Agribusiness • Art • Applied Technology/Management • Biology • Business Adm. • Chemistry • Computer Science • Education • Health Ed. • History • Hotel Adm. • Individualized Interdisciplinary • Literature • Literature/ Creative Writing • Marketing • Mathematics • Music • Physical Ed. • Physics • Philosophy • Political Science • Psychology • Radio & TV • Restaurant Adm. • Social Work • Sociology • Speech Communication • Theater Arts • Teacher Certification in early childhood, elementary, and secondary

Admissions Statement

To be admitted to Southwest State University students must complete a college preparatory program in high school and meet *one* of the following requirements:

1. Rank in the upper half of your graduating class.

2. Attain a composite score on the ACT of 21 or above or 900 on the SAT.

Spring Hill College

Mobile, Alabama 36608-1791
(334) 380-3030 or (800) 742-6704

Spring Hill College, established in 1830, was the first Catholic college in the Southeast. Today it is one of 28 Jesuit colleges and universities in the United States and 235 throughout the world. Like most Jesuit colleges, it offers a comprehensive education that focuses on the whole person. At Spring Hill students are encouraged to reach for knowledge beyond the books, lectures, and the boundaries of the classroom. Students are taught by professors who practice what they teach and bring first-hand experience into the classroom. The emphasis is on preparing students for a lifetime of growing and learning instead of just preparing them to become business executives, research scientists, or classroom teachers.

Extracurricular activities extend learning; organizations and activities like campus ministry, intercollegiate sports, sororities, fraternities, and the Ocean Research and Exploration Society help students develop responsibility, self confidence, a sense of justice, and a concern for others—all important qualities for a successful life and career. The college is not just a place where students attend class; it is a community of learners sharing the excitement of achievement in class and throughout the campus.

Academics

Degrees Offered: Bachelor's, Master's

Undergraduate Majors: 30+

Student/Faculty Ratio: 14 to 1

Number of Faculty: 106 full and part time

At Spring Hill College, the curriculum for all majors is built upon a liberal arts foundation. The core is adopted from the traditional Jesuit values-oriented program of studies in which students explore artistic, historical, scientific, philosophical, and religious approaches to reality. Reading, writing, and speaking are integrated into every facet of the curriculum, and theoretical learning is combined with practical experience.

The students refer to the quality that distinguishes this college from other schools as "the Spring Hill experience." It's the small classes with interesting and energetic professors who explore issues not evident in the textbook. It's the exam essay questions that require students to process what they have learned and not just fill in the blanks or determine if a fact is true or false. It's the freshman advisor who notices that one of her first year students is experiencing a little homesickness. Quite simply, it is the individual attention and respect generated by the faculty, administrators, and students that makes Spring Hill a unique college.

Starting at freshman orientation and continuing through graduation, Spring Hill students undergo a four-year experience that includes personal, academic, and career development. Freshman year includes an enhanced program of academic and career assessment, a freshman advising program, and Freshman Seminar, a special course taught by faculty, Student Development Center professionals, and academic administrators. The course is designed to help new students make the transition from high school to college while establishing a bond between students and the college.

During the first two years, the staff of the Career Development Center, the freshman advisors, and the faculty advisors work with students, assisting them to make appropriate course selections and explore the relationship between particular majors and specific and general career paths. In junior year, students have an opportunity to do some "reality testing"; through part-time or summer employment, internships, field work for credit, or volunteer activities, they can gain work experience in their major field and see if in fact it is what they had expected.

In senior year, department advisors help the soon-to-be graduates evaluate and synthesize their college experience, make decisions, and take appropriate action for their next step, whether it is beginning their career or entering graduate or professional schools. At Spring Hill, personal and career development are an integral part of the education process.

Students and Student Life

1,400 students from 31 states and six foreign countries
54% are from out-of-state
15% are students of color
1% are international
600 live on campus

The school was the first college in the state to integrate, and today more than 15 percent of the men and women are students of color. The college is deeply committed to fostering diversity, and continues to attract and support students from diverse cultural, social, and economic backgrounds.

Because extracurricular activities are an important part of the education process, the college sponsors more than 60 clubs and organizations. Student publications include a literary magazine, campus newspaper, the *Global Affairs Journal*, and yearbook. A large and active campus ministry establishes opportunities for student volunteers to work in the community at soup kitchens and shelters or working with inner-city children. Professional organizations like the Accounting Club, American Advertising Federation, and philosophy club bring speakers to campus to discuss and debate current issues. There is an active Greek system on campus and about 30 percent of the student body are members of one of the four sororities or six fraternities.

The college funds a large athletic program for students at every level of competition. Intramural sports provide activity, fun, and camaraderie for less experienced athletes. There are also several club sports including rugby. For the more competitive athlete Spring Hill has a full schedule of intercollegiate sports.

Athletic: NAIA and the Gulf Coast Athletic Conference
Men's and Women's Teams: basketball, cross country, golf, sailing, soccer, tennis
Men's Team: baseball

Campus and Community

Spring Hill College is in Mobile, Alabama, located on the Gulf Coast and close to New Orleans. This seaport metropolitan area has a population of almost 500,000 and provides all the social, cultural, and entertainment activities any college student could want. The Spring Hill campus is located on a 500-acre hill in a residential neighborhood. The beauty and majesty of the campus is imposing. Each of the more than 30 collegiate buildings has been artistically built into the landscape and enhanced by gardens, shrubs, shaded lanes, and walking paths.

Campus architecture includes the ante-bellum Stewartfield house, built in 1845, the site of many college receptions; the modified gothic College Chapel, constructed in 1910; and the new modern Recreation Center, completed in January 1997. Most of the academic buildings were constructed in the 1950s and totally renovated in the 1990s.

Residential facilities include four halls and an apartment complex that together accommodate over 700 men and women. The athletic facilities include extensive practice fields, an 18- hole golf course, and the new Recreation Center.

Spring Hill College Academic Offerings

Accounting • Advertising • Art Business • Art Therapy • Biology • Chemistry • Chemistry Business • Computer Information Systems • English • Early Childhood Ed. • Elementary Ed. • Environmental Science • Finance/Economics • 5-year Public MBA • General Studies • History • International Business • Interdisciplinary Humanities • International Studies • Journalism & Media Writing • Literature • Management • Marine Biology • Marketing • Mathematics • Nursing • Philosophy • Political Science • Professional Writing • Psychology • Public Relations • Radio/Television • Secondary Ed. • Studio Art • Theater • Theology

Admissions Statement

Unconditional admission usually will be granted to applicants who have a general average in specific academic courses of at least C+ (2.5 or 84), rank in the upper-half of their class, present acceptable scores on the SAT 1 or ACT, and receive satisfactory counselor recommendations. The college committee may, at its discretion, grant conditional admission to applicants who do not clearly meet all requirements for unconditional admission but who demonstrate the potential to complete a course of study successfully at Spring Hill College.

Springfield College

Springfield, Massachusetts 01109-3797
(413) 748-3136 or (800) 343-3797

Springfield is a classic small New England College that has a lot to offer. It is the only YMCA-affiliated college in the country and has at its heart an educational philosophy called Humanics, the education of the total person: spirit, mind, and body. Since its establishment in 1885 as a school that trained young men and women for professional careers in the YMCA, the college has gained an international reputation for excellence in the fields of human services, teaching, coaching, psychology, recreation and leisure services, physical therapy, and social work. In the past 100 years, more than 31,000 men and women from over 60 countries around the world have been educated at Springfield College.

Academics

Degrees Offered: Bachelor's, Master's, Doctoral

Undergraduate Majors: 32 majors with more than 50 areas of concentration

Student/Faculty Ratio: 15 to 1

Number of Faculty: 174 full time

"All the academic programs at Springfield College are developed around the theme of HUMANICS—which incorporates the development of spirit, mind, and body in Springfield's curriculum and student activities. Through the Huanics education at the college, students concentrate on becoming well-rounded individuals in service to others through their professional and community endeavors." The College is constantly re-evaluating how it can best serve its students and expanding its degree offerings and academic programs.

A cooperative education program for sophomores, juniors and seniors provides a structured integration of classroom study with paid, career-related positions during the academic year and summers. As a member of the cooperating colleges of Greater Springfield, students can enroll in selected courses and participate in social events at the eight member colleges.

The college also offers international opportunities for students to work or study abroad. They have established an exchange program with Beijing Institute in China and with Richmond College and Regent's Park College in England. Through a supportive atmosphere and substantive services, a faculty that is active and involved, a curriculum that encourages free exchange of ideas, and a campus that maintains some of the finest equipment and facilities to support the 32 major offerings, Springfield College has become a leader in the education of successful people in the helping professions.

Students and Student Life

2,516 students from 37 states and 16 foreign countries
9% are students of color
3% are international
78% live on campus in nine residential halls, including traditional-style halls and townhouse accommodations.

At Springfield College student activities are as important as formal studies, making campus life busy, demanding, satisfying, enjoyable, and rewarding. Students interested in cultural pursuits can participate in dance groups, theater groups, a jazz group, college singers, stage band, and weekly events sponsored by the cultural affairs committee. There are professional clubs and special interest clubs like the equestrian club, physical therapy club, and art club. Religious organizations include Christian Fellowship and Newman Club. The college's newspaper, *The Massasoit*; yearbook, *The Student*; and the college radio station, WSCB-FM, are all run by students.

Many students at Springfield are involved in community service activities and the college reaches out to the Springfield community through organizations like Campus Ministry, Volunteers for Youth, F.R.I.E.N.D.S, and, of course, YMCA. Sports are another popular student activity; more than 90 percent of the student body participates in intramural or club sports while 30 percent of the students belong to a varsity or sub-varsity team.

Athletics: NCAA, Division III
Women's Teams: basketball, cross country, field hockey, gymnastics, lacrosse, soccer, softball, swimming and diving, tennis, track & field, volleyball

Men's Teams: baseball, basketball, cross country, football, golf, gymnastics, lacrosse, soccer, swimming and diving, tennis, track & field, volleyball, wrestling

Campus and Community

The 160-acre campus is divided by Lake Massasoit. Most of the 32 academic and residential buildings are located on Main Campus, with East Campus on the other side of the lake. Main Campus houses the Babson Library, Bemis Science Center, Fuller Arts Center, and the Allied Health Science Center. The multi-million dollar physical education complex, also located here, is equipped with every sport/ recreational apparatus imaginable. The campus also has a beautiful area for recreational pursuits like canoeing, jogging, track, picnicking, cross country skiing, and ice-skating on the lake.

Springfield College Academic Offerings

Art • Art Therapy • Athletic Training • Biology • Business Mgt. • Chemistry/ Biology • Computer & Information Sciences • Education, with certification in early childhood education, elementary education, and secondary education • Emergency Medical Services Mgt. • English • Environmental Science • Gerontology • Health/Fitness • Health Promotion, with concentrations in community health and health studies/health education • Health Services Adm. • History • Human Services Adm. • Mathematics • Medical Technology/ Laboratory Science • Movement and Sports Studies, with a concentration in physical education • Physical Therapy • Physician Assistant • Political Science • Psychology • Recreation Mgt. • Therapeutic Recreation Services • Outdoor/ Environmental Recreation Rehabilitation Services • Sociology • Sports Biology • Sports Mgt.

Admissions Statement

Springfield College actively seeks to enroll students who are motivated to serve others. Our educational philosophy, called HUMANICS, is distinct to Springfield and unlike most other colleges. The Admissions Committee admits young men and women of distinguished academic ability who demonstrate a motivation to follow a career of service to others as evidenced by significant and appropriate co-curricular activities.

Selection for admission is based upon the total preparation of the student. Many factors are considered, including school achievement record; recommendations of secondary school authorities; motivation toward a career in the youth, community, and international service fields; capacity for leadership; performance on the SAT 1 or ACT; and personal references. A personal interview is also required.

St. Ambrose University

Davenport, Iowa 52803-2898
(319) 383-8888 or (800) 383-2627

St. Ambrose University is a mid-sized Catholic university that offers students small classes, modern facilities, and an active campus environment. The university began in 1882, and over the past 100 years the school has grown into a coeducational university offering bachelor's and masters degrees. Educational experiences like internships, cooperative education, and study-abroad programs provide opportunities for students to experience knowledge and not just memorize information. St. Ambrose provides a university education within a Catholic environment that values the individual and provides the support and challenge students needs to fulfill academic goals.

Academics

Degrees Offered: Bachelor's, Master's
Undergraduate Majors: 35
Student/Faculty Ratio: 15 to 1
Number of Faculty: 190 full and part time

One of the most important goals of the university is to "provide the opportunity for systematic exposure to general, professional, and career education in an atmosphere where academic freedom is clearly recognized and cherished." St. Ambrose accomplishes this goal through its diverse course offerings and programs.

Students have several interesting ways to combine theoretical knowledge and experiential learning. One of the most popular ways is through "Co-op." Working with one of the many participating businesses and organizations in the Davenport area, the university lets students work in positions related to their academic majors for a semester or more, while they earn both academic credit and a salary. The cooperative education program is open to all students in good standing after completion of the freshman year.

Another popular work-related experience is the internship. Internships within the College of Human Services and the College of Business, are a required part of the degree programs, and in most cases they are paid internships. Because St. Ambrose has an outstanding reputation in the Davenport area, students have been able to take advantage of some interesting internships at Alcoa, Deere and Company, Davenport Medical Center, Montgomery Elevator, and Hughes Aircraft.

A liberal arts foundation is required in every major, and students complete courses in composition, mathematics, fine arts, natural science, philosophy and theology, social sciences, physical education, and a seminar in library skills. Each semester the university offers over 350 courses in day and evening classes, making it easy for students to design a class schedule that is right for them.

Academic priorities at St. Ambrose University include small classes, knowledge-able professors, interactive course instruction, and experiential learning. The univer-sity has an Academic Support Center staffed by professional and peer tutors. It pro-vides placement testing, tutorial programs, writing and mathematics workshops, and programs on test-taking skills, time management, and problem-solving techniques. The university offers a learning-skills course through the departments of English and Mathematics. In addition the university has a center for students with learning and physical disabilities.

Students and Student Life

1,760 students from 19 states and 9 foreign countries
30% are from out-of-state
7% are students of color
1% are international
900 live on campus

Activities on campus include a Student Government Association that has been in existence for over 75 years. SGA members, along with the College Activities Board, conduct and coordinate all student activities at the university, including student elec-tions and cultural and social events. The university is serious about developing responsible leadership within its students and encourages them to take an active part in the administration of the school. Student representatives sit on all university committees with the exception of tenure. In addition, many St. Ambrose students, faculty, and alumni are active within the Davenport community.

St. Ambrose looks upon collegiate activities as another way in which students learn and because of this philosophy, it offers an extensive extracurricular program. The university publishes a biweekly student newspaper called *The Buz*, and has its own campus radio station (KALA-FM) and cable TV channel (TV-11).

There are more than fifteen professional and academic clubs in addition to numerous fine arts events. Students participate in religious- and service-oriented activities through the Campus Ministry Program. The university has a terrific record within the NAIA, and student support for athletics is high. All of the athletes who compete in collegiate athletics are students first, and the university is proud of the fact that more than 85 percent of their varsity players graduate.

Athletics: NAIA Division II
Men's and Women's Teams: basketball, cross country, golf, softball, tennis,
Men's Teams: baseball, cross country, football, soccer
Women's Teams: softball, volleyball

Campus and Community

The campus of St. Ambrose is located in Davenport, one of the largest municipalities in the area. Davenport is one of the Quad Cities, a metropolitan region made up of Davenport, Rock Island, Bettendorf, and Moline. The area is rich in cultural, historic, and social activity. The Quad Cities are host to the Bix Beiderbecke Jazz Festival, the Mississippi Blues Fest, and the Mozart Festival. The Theater League presents leading Broadway plays, and the Symphony Orchestra is the twelfth oldest in the nation. Students can sail on the river in the spring and summer, or ski and skate in the winter, at area recreational sites. With a population of more than 360,000, the Quad City region is an active community.

St. Ambrose University is located right in the heart of this culturally active region. The campus covers 15 blocks in the city area and houses 13 buildings. Many of the buildings on campus, including the high-tech library, are relatively new, and all older buildings have been renovated. The college is accessible from all major destinations and is literally surrounded by other colleges. In the Quad Cities area there are more than six colleges and universities!

St. Ambrose University Academic Offerings

College of Arts and Sciences: Art • Biology • Chemistry • Computer Science • Economics • Engineering Physics • English • Foreign Languages • History • Interdisciplinary Programs • Management Science • Music • Philosophy • Physics • Political Science • Psychology • Public Administration • Sociology • Speech and Theater • Theology

College of Business: Accounting • Business Adm. • Economics • Environmental Mgt. • Finance • Industrial Engineering • Management Information Systems • Management and Organization • Marketing

College of Human Services: Criminal Justice • Education • Mass Communication • Occupational Therapy • Physical Education

Admissions Statement

Students are eligible for admission to St. Ambrose University as first year students if they meet two of three requirements: a high school cumulative average of 2.50 or above (on a 4.00 scale); a composite score of 20 or above on the ACT or 780 or above on the SAT; and rank in the upper half of their graduating class. Applicants my be admitted on probation if they have a high school cumulative average between 2.00 and 2.49 (on a 4.0 scale) and have an ACT composite score between 16 and 19 or a 700–799 on the SAT.

St. Andrews College

Laurinburg, North Carolina 28352-5598
(800) 763-0198

St. Andrews College was founded in 1958. This relatively new college offers academic majors for students who will take their place in the workforce of the 21st century. The college is affiliated with the Presbyterian Church and is open to students of all backgrounds and beliefs. It has a totally barrier-free campus, academic programs that build up students' strengths, and a community of faculty and administrators who have a vested interest in their students.

Students at St. Andrews College enjoy discussion-oriented classes designed to help them "think, speak, and write with power and self-confidence." Through its strong commitment to teaching, the college provides an exciting environment for learning. All of the degree programs can be individualized to meet student's special interests as they prepare for the future.

At St. Andrews College, students are given many opportunities to develop academically, define their place in a global society, and attain the self-confidence necessary to fill responsible roles in the world. Students attend national conferences with faculty members and present their own research papers. Internships are encouraged in all departments so students can bring their learning to life.

Each year almost 60 percent of the students at St. Andrews College participate in study abroad either as part of the January Winter Term, or in the form of full-term study in locations around the world in countries like Ecuador, Beijing, Japan, Korea, and the Tyrolian Alps. Although it is a small college, St. Andrews provides an enormous amount of academic opportunities.

Academics

Degrees Offered: Bachelor's
Undergraduate Majors: 30+
Student/Faculty Ratio: 15 to 1
Number of Faculty: 57 full and part time

St. Andrews College offers more than 30 majors in individual academic areas; students can also combine two areas into a contract major. Environmental Psychology, English/Journalism, Music Therapy, and Business/Politics are a few examples of contract majors. It is also possible to develop a thematic major like Asian Studies, as St. Andrews offers with nine Chinese languages and cultural courses and study abroad in Beijing. St. Andrews is the only college in the country to offer a Therapeutic Riding Program.

At St. Andrews College, the focus is on student support. Professors are always available for advising, extra help, or just talking through an idea, and it is this individual attention that makes St. Andrews so special. Students receive the guidance and support necessary to fulfill their choices.

The general education core curriculum (SAGE) is a trend-setting program of five courses designed to help students adjust to college-level work and tie together the disciplines of literature, science, philosophy, history, psychology, and religion. The core also sharpens students' ability to analyze and communicate information and lays the foundation for a broad based education.

The college meets the academic needs of a diverse student population. Top students can apply for the General Honors program, which includes honors SAGE classes, a junior year paper, independent study, honors project or thesis, and an oral examination which concludes the honors programs. Students who need additional assistance in meeting the academic demands of the college can obtain tutorial services, academic aids, and even modified testing conditions through Special Academic Services.

Students and Student Life

700 students from 40 states and 23 foreign countries
68% from out-of-state
15% are students of color
5% are international
90% live on campus

At St. Andrews, student life centers around the eight residence halls, which offer computer-equipped rooms and suite mates of all ages and interests. Since more than 90 percent of students live on campus, campus life is almost synonymous with residential life. The college sponsors more than 45 clubs and organizations including *Cairn,* the literary magazine; Caucus on Disabilities; honor societies; pre-professional groups; a Scottish pipe band; and several service clubs.

At St. Andrews College, people get to know each other. As one junior asked, "Where else can you share experiences and make friends with so many different individuals—athletes and poets, pipers and drummers, people who use wheelchairs, Americans from California to the Carolinas, and international students from Zimbabwe, the Czech Republics, and more than a dozen other countries?"

Campus and Community

St. Andrews' 600-acre lakeside campus has won awards for its beautiful and barrier-free architectural design. The causeway over Lake Ansley C. Moore connects the residence halls with the De Tamble Library and other academic buildings. The 200,000 square foot John Blue Science Laboratory is as large as a soccer field! Lautinburg, North Carolina is a city of 17,5000. It is within easy reach of the mountains and beaches of North Carolina and is near charming resort communities and several U.S. Open golf courses.

St. Andrews College Academic Offerings

Allied Health • Art • Asian Studies • Biochemistry • Biology • Business & Economics • Chemical Physics • Chemistry • Communication/Theater • Creative Writing • Education • English • Environmental Science/Biology • Environmental Science/Chemistry • Environmental Science/Physics • History • International Business • Literature • Mathematical Physics • Mathematics • Mathematics/Computer Science • Modern Language • Music • Natural Science • Natural Science • Philosophy • Physical Ed. • Physical Ed./Sport Mgt. • Politics • Psychology • Religious Studies • Sports Medicine

Admission Requirements

St. Andrews accepts both high ability and high-potential students. Admissions is based not only on test scores and high school grades but also on interests, activities, and writing proficiency.

Unity College

Unity, Maine 04988-9502
(207) 948-3131

Unity College is relatively new and very different from most other schools. Established in 1965 on a 200-acre farm in the village of Unity, Maine, the college has become one of the few institutions committed to providing an environmentally oriented education fused with the liberal arts and humanities. With an enrollment of approximately 450 students, the college is noted for the individual concern and support it offers to each student. The curriculum, a combination of the traditional liberal arts with an emphasis on natural-resource management, is academically and physically demanding. It integrates academic preparation and hands-on experience in an environment where faculty, administration, and staff are committed to student success.

Academics

Degrees Offered: Associate, Bachelor's

Undergraduate Majors: 15

Student/Faculty Ratio: 14 to 1

Number of Faculty: 53 full and part time

In order to succeed at Unity College, students are asked to become active participants in the educational process, so if you'd prefer to listen to professors lecture, passively read your text, and never make a comment in class, Unity is not the college for you! Unity students learn by doing, and students learn from one another. At freshman orientation students begin to experience their education by participating in a five-day NOVA outdoor orientation program. NOVA offers a backdrop of shared experiences of living, exploring, and being challenged in a supportive environment.

During the first year, all new students complete a one-credit course called First Year Experience. In addition to helping a student make the transition to college life, the course incorporates a 20-hour community service commitment, workshops, and team-building activities. This integration of hands-on work and academic learning continues throughout the four years.

Some students opt to participate in a cooperative education experience by integrating work experience with academic study. Others will participate in a carefully planned, supervised short-term internship that is directly related to the their academic major. The college works closely with students to find the experiential learning activity that is right for them. The Federal Cooperative Education Program is open to Unity students: It offers 12- to 14-week internships that provide a unique opportunity to earn academic credit, earn a salary, and participate in environmental work done by one of several federal agencies.

The classroom environment at Unity is also very active. Classes are small and students are expected to participate in discussions, projects, and activities. Students who demonstrate academic excellence are asked to take part in the college Mentor Program, a very personal and enriching educational experience. In the Mentor Program, students work closely with a faculty member on special projects such as research, teaching or round-table discussions. Students who may be experiencing academic difficulties are expected to take advantage of all the services offered through the Learning Resource Center. This academic center provides developmental courses, tutorial assistance, study skills instruction, and advisement.

Students and Student Life

450 undergraduate students from 14 states and 5 foreign countries
7% are international
65% live on campus

The students at Unity College enjoy a close-knit community, a rural campus, and a love of the outdoors. They are involved in their student government, make time to contribute service to the community, and enjoy wilderness activities. The student government at Unity is active, highly respected, and an influential voice on campus. Its president is also the student representative on the Board of Trustees and other representatives from student government sit on most college committees.

Students at Unity are primarily interested in outdoor activities. The Unity Forest Fire Crew is recognized by local, state, and federal fire control organizations and functions as both a training and a fire suppression organization. In past years the crew has been sent to Baxter State Park in northern Maine and parts of California for actual firefighting. The Unity Emergency Response Team provides emergency first aid to the campus community. All members hold either First Responder or Emergency Medical Technician certification.

The Outing Club organizes weekend backpacking and canoeing trips, sponsors speakers, and is involved in most outdoor activities in the Maine area.

Publications on campus include *North Wind*, a student literary magazine; *Northern Lights*, a weekly newsletter; and a monthly calendar of events. The college sponsors several typical college organizations like drama club, photography club, and a 50-watt radio station, WRAM-AM.

Athletics: NSCAA, Northeast College Conference and the Maine Association of Intercollegiate Athletics for Women
Women's Teams: cross country, volleyball
Men's Teams: basketball, cross country, soccer

Campus and Community

The 200-acre campus overlooks the village of Unity, Maine. When you come on campus you immediately realize this is no ordinary college. The campus, once a large working farm, has retained much of its outward appearance. Constable Hall, originally the main farmhouse, has been nicely converted into facilities for the Admissions Department and Information Center. In contrast, The Dorothy Webb Quimby Library, constructed in 1976, was designed by Krumbhaar & Holt Architects and provides modern resource facilities. More than half of the students at Unity reside on campus in three traditional residence halls and five smaller modular houses.

The Co-op, a large U-shaped building, houses the art gallery, cafeteria, classrooms, photographic lab facilities, and administrative offices. The largest building on campus is the Activities Center, which provides facilities for sports, lectures, student activities, and the Learning Resource Center. The Environmental Science Building houses classrooms and labs and supplements the research that takes place beyond the classroom in the surrounding woods, lakes, and fields.

The village of Unity is located about 18 miles from Waterville and 40 miles from Bangor, and is surrounded by the natural beauty of northern Maine.

Unity College Academic Offerings

Associate Degrees: Fine Arts • Forest Management Technology • Liberal Studies

Bachelor's Degrees: Community Forestry • Conservation Law Enforcement • Ecology • Environmental Policy • Environmental Sciences, with emphasis in aquaculture • Fisheries • Forestry • Outdoor Recreation with emphasis in administration • Park Management • Recreation Leadership • Self-Designed Majors • Social Sciences, with emphasis in environmental education • Urban Adm. • Wildlife

Admissions Statement

Admission to Unity College is based upon a student's academic record, recommendations, extracurricular and co-curricular achievements, work experience, and special talents.

Utica College of Syracuse

Utica, New York 13502-4892
(315) 792-3006 or (800) 782-8884

Utica College is one of five academic divisions of Syracuse University. It is part of the university, but a college of its own, located on a 185-acre campus, 50 miles from Syracuse in the scenic and historic city of Utica. At the college, students can pursue a bachelor of arts or bachelor of science degree in 40 major and 20 minor areas of study. In addition to a four-year program of study, the college also offers a comprehensive three-year plan, which gives students a head start on a graduate degree or career, and cuts down on the cost of a college education.

The college also offers other practical choices for students. Through a cross-registration program, students can take courses at Hamilton College and Syracuse University. Utica College also offers study-abroad opportunities in countries including Italy, China, Finland, Poland, and Israel. Students can incorporate an exciting internship into any degree program they choose. The 2,500 men and women who attend Utica College enjoy the autonomy of their own campus and faculty, but still have all the benefits of being part of Syracuse University.

Academics

Degrees Offered: Bachelor's

Undergraduate Majors: 40

Student/Faculty Ratio: 15 to 1

Number of Faculty: 110 full time

Utica College is a young university established in 1946 to meet the educational needs of returning veterans of World War II. From its beginning, the college established an informal and personal atmosphere where students were treated as adults with all the rights and responsibilities associated with being an adult. This includes representation in the governance of all college affairs: academic, social, cultural, administrative, and regulatory. Today, Utica students continue to meet the challenge of full participation in campus government and continue to share responsible for all aspects of the college. Perhaps that's why the college has a broad view of education that stretches beyond what is learned within the classroom.

At Utica students can validate their previous learning in several ways: they can earn a maximum of 30 college credits through Advanced Placement courses, accredited correspondence courses, and relevant life experience.

Through an extensive international and study-abroad program, Utica students become involved in service and employment learning opportunities in China, Japan, and Finland. The college participates in a faculty and student exchange through the American-Council of Teachers of Russia. Other experiential and international learning programs offered at Utica include the Washington Semester Foreign Policy, the United Nations Semester Programs, and the London Theater Tour.

The Cooperative Educational program is another way Utica students can apply classroom learning in a real-world environment and receive college credit. Students may alternate periods of work and school throughout the calendar year, or follow the parallel model, where they work and take courses during the same semester. Most work assignments are 12 to 14 weeks in duration and are managed by a site supervisor who directs and evaluates the students' activities on the job.

Classes are small at Utica, with usually no more than 20 students per class. This fosters mentoring associations between students and their professors. The core curriculum consists of 45 credits in liberal arts courses and includes a writing portfolio that contains a collection of writing assignments from six different academic courses taken at intervals through out the students' four years in college.

Students and Student Life

2,600 students from 26 states and 13 foreign countries
30% are from out-of-state
15% are students of color
2% are international
850 live on campus

The student body is diverse and represents men and women from many socio-economic backgrounds and ethnic groups. The 1,600 full and 1,000 part time students who share the campus enjoy a close community atmosphere. Utica College was one of the first institutions in the nation with full student participation in campus government. Today, the College Council continues to be the chief governance forum of the college, and students, faculty, and professional staff make decisions together on issues concerning the entire college community.

More than 800 students live on campus, and the college sponsors more than 60 clubs and organizations where students can develop their talents and interests. The two most important student organizations are the Student Senate, the voice of the student body, and the Student Programming Board, which plans and implements a wide variety of social and cultural activities.

Utica has more than 20 academic and career-related clubs in which students can expand and enrich their knowledge, working with others who share similar career interests. These clubs include organizations like the Psychological Society of Utica College, the Student Contractors Association, and the Economic Crime Investigation Association.

The eight cultural organizations include the Jewish Student Union, the Students of African-American Descent Alliance, and the International Students Association. The college also sponsors two service organizations, five honorary fraternities and societies, seven political/social organizations, seven recreational clubs, and four major media organizations (including a weekly newspaper, literary magazine, and radio station). There are several national fraternities and sororities which have chapters at Utica College.

Athletics: NCAA Division III, Eastern College Athletic Conference
Women's Teams: basketball, soccer, softball, swimming, tennis
Men's Teams: baseball, basketball, soccer, swimming, tennis
Coed Team: golf

Campus and Community

The 185-acre campus is located in the greater Utica-Rome metropolitan area, which has a population of more than 250,000. The area is rich in history and culture and includes Revolutionary War battlefields, colonial-era houses, Fort Stanwix, and modern features like the Baseball Hall of Fame and the Utica Zoo.

The campus is located on the edge of the city in a residential area, beautifully laid out with trees and spacious lawns. The four residence halls are all modern and located at one end of campus, with lots of space to toss a frisbee or play touch football. The view from most of the college buildings is of the surrounding Adirondack foothills, yet students can be in the heart of the business or shopping areas in less than 10 minutes!

The Utica campus is composed of 12 academic buildings that reflect the youthfulness of the college and the presence of technology in education. Hubbard Hall, one of the main classroom buildings, is air-conditioned and houses specially equipped construction-management classrooms and laboratory facilities. Gordon Science Center, a full-service science facility, includes modern laboratories for biology, microbiology, embryology, physics, chemistry, geology, and physical and occupational therapy.

The Gannett Memorial Library is the focal point for learning, teaching, and research on the Utica campus. The library delivers personalized references, and students and faculty alike receive professional client-centered consultation. The librarians work one-on-one with students to teach the techniques required to access local, national, and international information resources. The library also houses the Edith Barrett Art Gallery and exhibits the works of regional, national, and international artists.

The social and recreational center of the campus is the Strebel Student Center where the dining hall, bookstore, student offices, and student activities are housed. The massive Clark Athletic Center is large enough to accommodate three basketball courts and the largest swimming pool in the Northeast, as well as a mini-gym, dance area, Nautilus room, and bleacher seating for 2,200 people.

Utica College of Syracuse Academic Offerings

Accounting • Actuarial Science • Biology • Business Administration, with concentrations in computer science, finance management, human resource management, international business management, marketing management, operations management, resource management • Business-Economics • Chemistry • Computer Science, with concentrations in business applications, scientific applications • Construction Mgt. • Criminal Justice • Criminal Justice/ Economic Crime Investigation, with concentrations in computer security, finance investigation • Economics • Education (PreK-6) • English • Fine Arts • Gerontology • History • Human Studies • International Studies, with concentrations in area studies, international business management, language, world literature and civilization • Journalism Studies • Mathematics • Nursing • Occupational Therapy • Philosophy • Physical Therapy • Physics • Political Science, with concentrations in campaign management, international business management, public administration, social sciences • Psychology • Public Relations • Secondary Education, with certification in biology, business administration, chemistry, computer science, economics, English, history, mathematics, physics, political science, sociology, social studies • Social Studies • Sociology/Anthropology • Speech Communications and Dramatic Arts, with concentrations in film studies, radio/TV, speech communications, theatre • Therapeutic Recreation

Admissions Statement

Admissions decisions are based on a comprehensive evaluation of past academic performance including courses of study, GPA, rank in class, extra-curricular involvement, personal characteristics, and the applicant's potential for academic and personal success at the college.

Wayne State College

Wayne, Nebraska 68787
(402) 375-7234 or (800) 228-9972

Wayne State College provides an ideal social, cultural, and academic environment in which to pursue your college degree. Forty major programs, more than 200 experienced faculty members, and 1,500 courses set the stage for the type of education you will get at Wayne State. To ensure success in academic pursuits, the college emphasizes classroom learning as its number-one priority, and offers a variety of classroom experiences including lecture halls, classes, and seminars.

Professors motivate students to explore their academic potential by taking advantage of the research facilities on campus, including the Dale Planetarium, 10 computer labs, modern science and research areas, state of the art physiology diagnostic equipment, and world access via the library's network. The combination of priority classroom teaching and sophisticated technology prepares Wayne State graduates for today's competitive job market.

Academics

Degrees Offered: Bachelor's, Master's
Undergraduate Majors: 60+
Student/Faculty Ratio: 21 to 1
Number of Faculty: 228 full and part time

Wayne State College offers both graduate and undergraduate degrees in a variety of liberal arts, technical and professional fields. While the college originally began in the early 1900s as an institution to prepare teachers, today Wayne State graduates are prepared for careers in such diverse areas as industrial technology, law enforcement, computer information systems, speech communication, and public relations.

Wayne State offers eight academic divisions that include applied science, fine arts, humanities, mathematics and science, and social sciences. Students have 40 majors, 40 minors, and close to 30 pre-professional programs to choose from!

But that's not all Wayne State has to offer. No matter what academic programs students choose, the college has resources that complement their education, support their goals, and prepare them for success. The Learning Center offers credit courses that build proficiency in beginning algebra, critical thinking, writing with a computer, and vocabulary development. The center, which is staffed by professionals and peers, gives students individualized and group assistance. The Early Alert Program is specifically designed to identify students who are experiencing difficulties in class while there is still time to intervene. The Peer Tutoring Program at Wayne State is nationally certified, and all students, no matter what their GPAs, can receive tutorial assistance.

On the other side of the spectrum, academically talented students get special opportunities to stretch their imagination and challenge their abilities. The Honors Program is open to qualified students who want a rigorous academic program. Learning opportunities include honors courses, independent study, honors colloquium, and a senior project and presentation. Students work closely with faculty from their academic division and are designated Neihardt Scholars at graduation.

Students and Student Life

3,500 students from 36 states and 10 foreign countries
20% are from out-of-state
5% are students of color
1,500 live on campus

There are two national sororities and two national fraternities on campus, 36 organized intramural sports, five to seven major theatrical productions each year, and seven musical performing groups. The campus houses both an FM radio station, which is on the air daily, and a TV station, which broadcasts several nights a week on the local cable station. The Black and Gold Series brings renowned speakers, musicians, and other interesting performers to campus. There are six religion clubs, 12 professional clubs, and a weekly newspaper. The Recreation Center, which is large enough to contain a running track and three full-size basketball courts, also has facilities for swimming, weight training, dancing, tennis, and racquetball.

Athletics: NCAA Division II
Women's Teams: basketball, cross country, golf, soccer, softball, track, volleyball
Men's Teams: baseball, basketball, cross country, football, golf, soccer, track

Campus and Community

The 128-acre campus contains 22 academic and residential buildings. It is a beautiful campus that combines traditional architecture and modern design. Wayne State has been designated a Nebraska State Arboretum because of the variety and number of trees and shrubs located on campus.

The most recognized landmark on campus is the Willow Bowl, an outdoor amphitheater where commencement exercises take place. Over half of all buildings on campus have been erected within the past 30 years, and all the older structures have undergone significant renovations, making the entire campus ready for the technology of the 21st century. The campus is nicely laid out, with the majority of the academic and residential buildings located on the south side of Lindahl Drive. Sports and athletic facilities, including Memorial Stadium, are located in the north area of campus.

The town of Wayne, Nebraska has about 5,000 residents. It's a safe, friendly place where students can shop, see a movie, or work. When students want a more urban atmosphere, Omaha and Sioux Falls, South Dakota are both about a two-hour drive.

Wayne State College Academic Offerings

Accounting • Agri-business • Art(*) • Biology(*) • Broadcast Communication • Business Adm.(*) • Chemistry(*) • Chemical Sciences • Computer Science(*) • Computer Info. Systems • Counseling • Criminal Science • Early Child-hood(*)• Economics • English(*) • Fashion Merchandising • Finance • Food Service Mgt. • French(*) • Geo-Studies(*) • German(*) • Graphic Design • Health Sciences(*) • History(*) • Home Economics(*) • Human Service • Industrial Management • Industrial Technology(*) • Interdisciplinary Studies • International Business • International Studies • Interior Design • Life Sci-ences(*) • Literature • Management • Marketing • Mass Communication • Medical Technology • Mortuary Science • Office Adm. • Respiratory Therapy • Journalism • Applied Music: history, composition, theory • Music Merchandis-ing • Political Science • Political Systems • Psychology(*) • Public Adm. • Public Relations • Recreation • Social Sciences(*) • Sociology(*) • Spanish(*) • Special Education(*) • Speech Communication(*) • Sports Management • Technology • Theater(*) • Wellness • Writing

(*) Teacher certification in these areas

Admissions Statement

Wayne State College is an open-admissions institution. It is recommended that students complete a college prep program in high school that includes four years of English, three years of mathematics and social studies, two years of science, and additional credits in foreign languages, fine arts, and computer literacy.

Wesley College

Dover, Delaware 19901
(302) 736-2400 or
(800) 932-1113 in-state
(800) WESLEY-U out-of-state

Wesley College's history and traditions reach back to 1873, when the Methodist Episcopal Church opened the Wilmington Conference Academy for men. Within seven years, the school admitted women, and during the next 30 years the school flourished. Even then, its emphasis was on educating the whole person. Over the past 115 years, Wesley College has developed into a premier institution where students acquire knowledge, and skills, along with the moral and ethical attitude necessary to achieve their personal goals and contribute to their community.

The curriculum at Wesley College is a blend of liberal arts and pre-professional programs that include internships and study abroad. Classroom and academic buildings offer students an institutional environment conducive to learning. The 12-acre campus and the 30 college organizations provide facilities and activities where students can gain self-confidence and develop into the leaders of tomorrow.

Academics

Degrees Offered: Associate, Bachelor's
Undergraduate Majors: 15
Student/Faculty Ratio: 16 to 1
Number of Faculty: 106 full and part time

Wesley offers a blend of liberal arts and career-oriented programs, taught by faculty members who are professional teachers and active, recognized leaders within their fields. In class, students quickly realize that some of the most important lessons they learn come directly from their professor's own experience and expertise, and not from class notes and textbooks. One student comments that among the best things about Wesley is "the close associations that are formed among students and professors. The people who teach here are concerned about their students above and beyond what they learn in class."

The three most popular majors at Wesley College are business, education, and health sciences, and almost half of all students are enrolled in a major within these three disciplines. As a liberal arts college, Wesley requires that students take 50 credits in a college wide core curriculum that insures competency in areas including literature, natural science, physical education, humanities, social sciences, and fine arts.

The college balances this general education with experiential learning through internships, study-abroad, and "Winterin" programs in England and France, along with other projects where classroom experience is integrated with the world of work. More than 70 percent of Wesley students complete a fieldwork component within their major. The focus on experiential learning not only provides professional relationships which can help students clarify their career goals, it also provides an edge when it comes to landing that first job.

Students and Student Life

1,300 students from 15 states and 7 foreign countries
Less than 10% from out-of-state
14% are students of color

4% are international

650 live on campus

Campus life includes performing arts, sports, community service, sororities, and fraternities. There are six national sororities and fraternities on campus and about half of all students are members. The Henry Belin duPont College Center, located almost in the middle of campus, is the center of activities for both residential and commuting students.

Students can join professional clubs related to their academic major, write for *The Whetstone* (the college newspaper), participate in many community service projects sponsored by the Student Volunteer Service Office, or relax and enjoy the nearby ocean with the Sailing Club.

The five residence halls have a governing board that establishes and monitors the hall rules, and a staff of resident advisors who provide hall programming. Varsity sports are very popular and are supported by students, alumni and community residents.

Athletics: The Wolverines are members of the Eastern Collegiate Athletic Conference and the NCAA Division III.

Women's Teams: basketball, field hockey, soccer, softball, tennis

Men's Teams: baseball, basketball, football, golf, lacrosse, soccer, tennis

Campus and Community

The 12-acre campus is located in a residential neighborhood of historic Dover, Delaware. Students can easily walk to shops and eateries in town. On campus, the students are surrounded by 14 first-rate academic and residential facilities. All of the classroom buildings are air-conditioned and the laboratories are well equipped. The new, modern, and expansive athletic facilities are located four blocks from main campus. Included in this 12-acre outdoor area are practice and playing fields for soccer, football, lacrosse, baseball, field hockey, and softball.

Dover is the capital city of the nation's first state. It is close to Philadelphia, Baltimore, Washington DC, and New York City, for those who are looking for the city lights. But it is also close to winter ski resorts and beautiful Atlantic beaches. The college is located in an ideal area, and within an hours' drive, students can visit one of 15 different colleges.

Wesley College Academic Offerings

Accounting • Biology • Communications • Education • English • History • Liberal Studies • Management • Marketing • Medical Technology • Nursing (RN) • Paralegal Studies • Physical Education (professional and K-12) • Political Science • Psychology

Admissions Statement

Many factors are considered in the selection of a Wesley College student. The applicant's secondary school record and the curriculum taken in high school as it relates to the applicant's educational objectives are most important.

University of West Alabama

Livingston, Alabama 35470
(205) 652-9661 or
(800) 621-7742 in-state
(800) 621-8044 out-of-state

The heart of any college is its academic offerings, and at the University of West Alabama, these offerings include associate, bachelor's, and master's degree programs in liberal and professional studies; 650 course offerings each semester; and a rigorous core curriculum that prepares students for their field of concentration and strengthens their analytical and creative abilities. More than 20 majors are available and each is enhanced by faculty and facilities that bring education to life.

The campus is home to its own greenhouse, fossil collection, lake and ecological study area, and the Hunt Technology Complex. There is an Honors Program for superior students, and academic assistance, tutoring, and workshops for students who need additional guidance. At the University of West Alabama, the emphasis is on a quality education.

Academics

Degrees Offered: Bachelor's, Master's

Undergraduate Majors: 20

Student/Faculty Ratio: 18 to 1

Number of Faculty: 100+ full time

The University of West Alabama is composed of five distinct undergraduate divisions: the College of Liberal Arts, the College of Education, the College of Business and Commerce, the College of Natural Sciences and Mathematics, and the Division of Nursing. Together, they provide a strong career or graduate-school preparation, and offer more than 20 majors and 40 minor areas of study.

The College of Liberal Arts includes the departments of Fine Arts, History and Social Sciences, and Languages and Literature. Its course offerings include majors and minors in 30 areas, and all of the subjects that make up the university's general education requirements.

The College of Business and Commerce combines theoretical concepts and practical applications to create a business curriculum that focuses on accounting and finance, computer science, general business, quantitative analysis, and technology. Students can choose from associate and bachelor's degree programs and incorporate minors in both liberal arts and business areas.

The College of Education is the cornerstone of the university. What is now the University of West Alabama was originally called Livingston University. It was established before the Civil War as a private academy preparing women to teach school. Today, the Julia Tutwiler College of Education is a strong and vital part of the university and offers a variety of nationally recognized programs for students interested in careers as teachers.

The College of Natural Sciences and Mathematics is part of a unique association of 24 colleges and universities called the Alabama Marine Environmental Science Consortium that share marine laboratories at the MESCA center on the Gulf Coast at Dauphin Island, Alabama. Other natural science facilities located on the West Alabama campus include greenhouses, a wild flower garden, nature trails, and an ecological study area on the campus lake.

The Division of Nursing specializes in providing an associate degree program, accredited by the National League for Nursing, that prepares students to become registered nurses. Students have the opportunity to receive individualized instruction, experience a variety of health care settings, and still be part of a university environment.

While each college at the University of West Alabama is a separate division, they all provide an environment where students can grow in knowledge and self-discovery; work with dedicated professors who are accomplished scholars, researchers, artists, and writers; and experience a blend of life-enriching experiences in and out of class.

Students and Student Life

2,000 students from 27 states and 14 foreign countries
30% are from out-of-state
33% are students of color
1% are international
1,000 students live on campus

The university has created an exciting balance of living, learning and leadership opportunities within its more than 30 clubs and organizations. The 2,000 men and women enrolled at West Alabama enjoy extracurricular opportunities that broaden their social and cultural perspective, provide healthy outlets for their energy, and establish an atmosphere of community on campus.

The Tiger Tail Productions is the activities programming division of the student government. It brings a film series and special events to campus year round, and sponsors student union activities . Weekends and weekdays, students can participate in or enjoy watching plays, recitals, art exhibits, band concerts, choral programs, and sports events.

A large intramural program engages most of the students in organized recreational sports like bowling, badminton, basketball, and table tennis. Religious organizations also make up an important element of campus life and provide opportunities for students of all faiths to join with others in community service projects, lectures, and fellowship. The university has several fraternity and sorority chapters on campus, and about 20 percent of the students are members of the six national fraternities and five national sororities.

Athletics: NCAA and the Gulf South Conference
Women's Teams: basketball, rodeo, softball, tennis, volleyball
Men's Teams: baseball, basketball, football, rodeo, tennis

Campus and Community

The campus of the University of West Alabama is made up of more than 600 acres of beautiful landscape that includes a 54-acre lake, seven residence halls and apartments, the football stadium (Tiger Field), and eight academic buildings. The campus is self-contained, much like a small town, and provides academic, recreational, and spiritual facilities for all the students. The George C. Wallace Student Union has recreational facilities including an Olympic swimming pool, racquetball courts, and weight room. The seven residence halls offer dormitory, suite-, and apartment-style accommodations. There is even a faculty apartment complex on campus.

The campus is located in the town of Livingston, Alabama, a small town in Sumter County which is accessible by air, train and bus. The Sumter area provides a host of outdoor recreational activities including camping, fishing, hunting, and hiking. The mild climate is ideal for outdoor exploration. Located just an hour away are Stillman College, the University of Alabama, and Judson College. Students can easily visit these neighboring schools.

University of West Alabama Academic Offerings

College of Business and Commerce: Accounting • Business Adm. • Computer Information Science • Industrial Technology • Management

College of Education: Athletic Training • Early Childhood • Elementary • Nursery-12 • Physical Ed. • High School Teacher Education programs in biology, chemistry, English, history, language arts, mathematics, science, social sciences • Teacher Education programs in music, physical education, special education

College of Liberal Arts: English • History • Music • Psychology • Sociology

College of Natural Sciences and Mathematics: Biology • Chemistry • Environmental Sciences • Marine Biology • Mathematics • Mathematics/Computer Science • Medical Technology

Division of Nursing: Associate Degree in Nursing

Admissions Statement

To be considered for admissions to the University of West Alabama, students must be high school graduates with a "C" average or have a GED, have completed college preparatory courses in high school, and attain acceptable scores on either the ACT or SAT 1.

West Liberty State College

West Liberty, West Virginia 26074
(304) 336-8076

West Liberty State College is the oldest institution of higher learning in West Virginia. The college takes pride in its 160-year heritage while maintaining three of its founding principals. The first is, "Faculty are the heart of the institution," and the 130 professors who teach at the college today continue to encourage student participation and make the classroom an active learning environment. Outside the classroom, faculty are available to assist students to reach beyond the text books to master academic skills.

The second principal focuses on the campus, which "should be a quiet and restful place." The campus of West Liberty State College is an expansive, serene environment that provides areas conducive to study, relaxation, investigation, research, and recreation. The neighboring community of West Liberty provides a safe yet active place for students to go, and the surrounding areas are filled with history and Indian folklore from the frontier era.

The third principal is that "student activities are an essential component of the learning process." There are more than 60 student-run clubs and organizations that provide personal, social, and academic opportunities where students can develop their individual interests, skills, and abilities. These include national and local fraternities and sororities; seven men's and women's athletic teams; intramural club sports; and plays, concerts, and dance performances.

Academics

Degrees Offered: Associate, Bachelor's
Undergraduate Majors: 40+
Student/Faculty Ratio: 18 to 1
Number of Faculty: 130 full time

West Liberty State College offers more than 40 academic majors within the School of Business, School of Education, School of Liberal Arts, and School of Natural Science, Health Professions and Mathematics. Through a well-designed curriculum, the college combines a solid liberal arts base with interesting, career-oriented majors.

The versatility infused into the major offerings assures graduates that they will be well prepared for careers in the 21st century. The School of Business Administration is a member of the prestigious American Assembly of Collegiate Schools of Business, and provides a quality education in 11 areas of business including special programs in travel and tourism, one of the fastest-growing industries in the world. The School of Natural Science is the only one in the country to offer a major in Energy Management, designed to educate students who will pursue careers with large energy related industries.

For a small state college, West Liberty has broad course offerings, yet it is very student centered. Students are taught by professors who, in addition to being master teachers, are also professionally recognized within their area of specialization. In the classroom, they establish an atmosphere where close, interactive teaching and learning can take place. It is not surprising that one student comments, "West Liberty is not your typical state college. It's more like a private college, with small classes and a lot of special academic programs. I think the education here is terrific, it's affordable, and it's comprehensive."

Students and Student Life

2,350 students from 17 states and 11 foreign countries
32% from out-of-state
53% are students of color

1% are international

1,350 students live on campus

The college sponsors more than 60 campus organizations, so students have ample opportunity to participate in activities that foster social and cultural growth. The atmosphere on campus is friendly and relaxed, and there's always something going on.

The more than 20 professional organizations, like the fashion marketing club, dental hygiene association, and the art education association, bring speakers to campus and arrange trips and events where students can integrate their knowledge with practical applications.

The college offers several good opportunities for students in the arts. The Hilltop Players produce at least four major shows a year, and there are more than six musical and choral groups that perform both on and off campus.

There are two national and three local sororities and fraternities, and about 10 percent of the students at West Liberty are members. The college sponsors a large intramural program that includes residence and fraternity/sorority teams who compete in sports like bowling, ping-pong, basketball, and racquetball.

Athletics: West Liberty State College is a member of the NCAA and NAIA and the West Virginia Intercollegiate Athletic Council.

Women's Teams: basketball, softball, tennis, volleyball

Men's Teams: baseball, basketball, cross country, football, golf, tennis, wrestling

Campus and Community

The beautiful 290-acre campus easily accommodates the more than 20 academic and residential buildings that make up the college. The seven residence halls located throughout the campus provide exceptional living/learning facilities. Krise Hall is just one example. It accommodates 312 students in carpeted, air-conditioned suites with semiprivate baths. There is limited housing for married students, and the college has 50 duplex apartments, and houses on campus for faculty.

Main Hall is a four-story structure located just beyond the entrance to the college. It houses several administrative offices and also serves as the major classroom area. The Paul N. Elbin Library collection contains more than 200,000 print volumes, nearly 800 periodical and newspaper subscriptions, CD-ROM databases, and numerous titles in media or microfilm formats. The library has Internet connections, and the Media Center accesses satellite programming and accommodates teleconferencing and SATNET courses.

The Bartell Fieldhouse, one of several new buildings on campus, is the center of athletic activity, both intramural and interscholastic. It is an architectural showpiece, designed with only one of its three stories visible from ground level. Facilities include a main arena the size of three basketball courts, an indoor track, gymnasium, locker facilities, and offices. College Hall is one of the main performance buildings and features a 500-seat auditorium, voice studios, and a 42-rank, three-manual Moeller pipe organ. Located right next-door is the Hall of Fine Arts, which houses the departments of music, art, oral communication, and theater arts.

The rural campus is located on the Ohio River, just nine miles from Wheeling, West Virginia and only four miles from Oglebay Park, one of the nations richest areas for recreational facilities and outdoor opportunities. Wheeling is known as "America's safest city," and students have easy access to shopping, entertainment, and social activities. West Liberty State College has the best of both worlds. It is located in a serene and safe area close to unlimited recreational opportunities and the conveniences of a small city. In addition, it is only 47 miles from Pittsburgh, Pennsylvania and all the cultural, educational, and sports activities a large city has to offer.

West Liberty State College Academic Offerings

School of Business Administration: Accounting • Administrative Mathematics • Administrative Science • Banking and Finance • Computer Information Systems • Economics • Fashion Marketing • General Business • Management • Marketing • Travel and Tourism Mgt.

School of Education and Human Resources: Criminal Justice • Health Ed. • Physical Ed. • Professional Education programs in early childhood and middle childhood (K-8), early ed. (pre-K -K), middle childhood (5-8), adolescent ed. (K-12, 5-12, 9-12), special ed. (K-12, 5-12) • Psychology • Safety Ed. • Science of Exercise • Social Work

School of Liberal Arts: Art • Art Ed. K-12 • English • English-Language Arts 5-12(*) • Graphic Design • History • Journalism • Music Ed. K-12(*) • Political Science • Public Relations • Radio & TV • Social Sciences 5-12(*) • Sociology • Spanish 5-12(*) • Theater

School of Natural Science, Health Professions, and Mathematics: Biology • Biology Ed. 9-12(*) • Chemistry • Chemistry Ed. 9-12(*) • Dental Hygiene • Energy Mgt. • General Science 5-12(*) • Math Ed. 5-12(*) • Mathematics • Medical Technology • Nursing
(*) Teacher Education Programs

Admissions Statement

To be eligible for admission, applicants must have a high school diploma or GED, and an overall GPA of at least 2.0, or a composite score of at least 17 on the ACT or a combined score of 810 on the SAT 1.

Western New England College
Springfield, Massachusetts 01119
(413) 782-1321 or (800) 325-1122

The major characteristics of a Western New England undergraduate education are the exciting academic programs, the interactive teaching styles used by the professionals on the faculty, and the individual attention, strong support, and overall concern students receive.

As an independent private college with an enrollment of about 1,900 full-time undergraduates, WNEC provides all the tools necessary for academic success. Degree programs balance theory with practical application. A writing center, math center, and peer advising and college-success skills programs facilitate the learning process. Internships, study-abroad, and leadership programs provide academic and personal challenges. A full co-curricular program with more than 40 student organizations keeps students active and involved.

Academics

Degrees Offered: Associate, Bachelor's, Master's, Law

Undergraduate Majors: 26

Student/Faculty Ratio: 18 to 1

Number of Faculty: 250 full and part time

Western New England College is composed of the School of Arts and Sciences, School of Business, School of Engineering, and the Law School. Together they have academic offerings similar to those found at small to midsize universities.

Students majoring in one of the 14 programs in the School of Arts and Sciences can build several career options into their degree program. They can pursue a minor from the schools of Business or Engineering, prepare for a teaching career by completing the Teacher Education Program, or they may want to design their own degree program.

The School of Business offers eight majors that correlate with specific areas in the business field. A strong business core of 30 credits is taken by all majors in the school, in addition to 30 credits in their specific area. A WNEC degree from the School of Business includes knowledge of specific business applications, managerial decision-making skills, an understanding of ethics and human relations, and the historical and contemporary economic, social, political, and cultural environment of our international society. It is a foundation for careers in all areas of business.

The School of Engineering offers the broad liberal arts background and professional engineering courses needed by the modern professional engineer. The curriculum is based on mathematics and science coupled with the engineering science common to all branches of the profession. Each program offered in the School of Engineering prepares graduates to enter practice as professional engineers or to continue in graduate study.

Students and Student Life

1,950 students from 21 states and 22 foreign countries
7% are students of color
2% are international
1,300 live on campus

Western New England College has an activity for just about everyone! With more than 40 clubs and organizations to choose from, even students with diverse interests will find a place to develop leadership skills, make friends, and have fun. There are recreational clubs like the bowling, martial arts, and outing clubs; special focus clubs like the International Student Association and United and Mutually Equal; nine professional societies (including Alpha Kappa Psi, one of the oldest professional associations for students pursuing business-related careers) and the Society of Women Engineers.

Students can become involved in community service projects through Campus Ministry and the Springfield School Volunteer Program. *The Cupola* college yearbook, *The Review of Art and Literature* magazine, and the bimonthly *Westerner* newspaper are perfect activities for students who love to write. WNEK, which broadcasts throughout the Greater Springfield community, provides news, music, public affairs, and sports programming. The college also supports a national fraternity and sorority system with several chapters on campus.

Athletics: NCAA Division III, Eastern College Athletic Conference
Women's Teams: basketball, bowling, cross country, field hockey, soccer, softball
Men's Teams: baseball, basketball, bowling, football, golf, ice hockey, lacrosse, soccer, tennis, wrestling

Campus and Community

Western New England's attractive and spacious 131-acre campus, located three miles from downtown Springfield, provides a traditional student-centered environment and community atmosphere. The traditional red-brick and white-columned buildings are linked by walkways that cut through beautiful grounds. The oldest of the 19 collegiate buildings was erected in the late 1950s, and construction on the newest building, the modern Healthful Living Center, was completed in 1993.

Most of the academic buildings are in Center Campus and have comfortable classrooms and modern laboratory facilities. The D'Amour Library, built in 1983, has online search capabilities and lots of quiet areas for study. The residential facilities are based on the concept of progressive responsibility. First-year students are normally assigned to one of three traditional residence halls that form the Quad. Sophomores and juniors have the opportunity to live in traditional residence halls or suite-style accommodations in the Plymouth Complex. Seniors can choose ranch-style apartments in the Gateway Village area of campus.

Springfield, a large New England city, is only a short bus ride away and provides all the amenities of a big city plus five other colleges.

Western New England College Academic Offerings

Arts and Sciences: Biology • Chemistry • Communication • Computer Science • Criminal Justice • Economics • Economics/Quantitative • English • Government • History • Mathematical Sciences • Psychology • Social Work • Sociology
Business: Accounting • Computer Information Systems • Finance • General Business • Management • Marketing • Quantitative Methods • Technical Mgt.
Engineering: Bioengineering • Electrical • Industrial • Mechanical

Admissions Statement

Students must graduate from an approved secondary school or have a GED.

Western State College of Colorado

Gunnison, Colorado 81231
(303) 943-2119 or (800) 876-5309

Western State College is perched 7,700 feet above sea level in scenic Gunnison, Colorado. The school is framed by unmatched beauty and is surrounded by alpine tundra, irrigated farm land, and mountain lakes and rivers. The 3,300 square miles of untamed nature provides a classroom beyond the campus. Field research opportunities that include excavation of prehistoric campsites, volcano cavities, and reconstruction of dinosaur remains are among the unique experiential learning projects offered at the college. The vast wilderness plays host to several extracurricular clubs as well, including Wilderness Pursuits, the Whitewater Club, and the fully accredited Mountain Search-and-Rescue Team.

The integration of this outdoor approach to learning is only one component of the educational philosophy at Western. The core curriculum is a rigorous 30-credit program that provides a foundation for all majors and introduces students to lifelong learning. Class sizes are small, usually under 25 students. Features like this make Western State College a favorite choice for many students.

Academics

Degrees Offered: Bachelor's

Undergraduate Majors: 20+

Student/Faculty Ratio: 20 to 1

Number of Faculty: 138 full and part time

Innovation is a major characteristic of the educational environment at Western State College. The school calendar, course clusters, curriculum, and campus activities are all designed to be innovative and student focused. The Western Scholars Year is unlike any other college calendar. While most other schools have either two 16-week semesters or three 12-week quarters, Western's school year is divided into four terms that alternate in lengths of 12- and 8-week sessions. This design creates winter and summer 8-week terms for intensive interdisciplinary courses (course clusters) that can be taken beyond the confines of the campus. Each academic year, students can choose two 12-week and one 8-week terms, or attend all four terms and graduate in three and a half years.

Western offers several exciting and interesting courses during Winter Term that cross over several areas of study and include extended research trips. In a recent winter term, students enrolled in the Baja Culture and Natural History cluster. During campus study they focused on the marine biology, ecology, art, literature, language, and culture of the Southwest. They also spent three weeks on a research field trip to the Baja Peninsula of California. The college also has built into the school term Western Wednesdays. Each Wednesday is set aside for alternative campus involvement that may include cooperative learning projects, co-curricular activities, field trips, special presentations, or simply uninterrupted study time.

Experiential learning is an important part of a Western education: The surrounding area is the classroom where students can investigate ecological changes in the region and measure the environmental effect upon local natural resources. Qualified students work beside professors on experiments using electronic microscopy, nuclear magnetic resonance, and other types of spectrophotometry.

Performing arts students can work on major theatrical productions on campus and at Gunnison's community theater. In any year the college schedules more than 50 appearances for its numerous music and voice groups, and runs its own TV and radio station. Western students can also participate in the National Student Exchange, a consortium of over 100 colleges and universities that facilitate student exchanges for one semester or an academic year. They can also take a general studies program that incorporates four years of sequential courses that builds competencies in academic skills and provide a basis for future learning.

Students and Student Life

2,450 students from 50 states and 12 foreign countries
35% are from out-of-state
7% are students of color
1% are international
1,400 live on campus

Western State College has a national reputation and attracts students from almost every state in the country. The college values diversity, and encourages students to enjoy a broad-based cultural experience through campus-sponsored clubs such as the Black Student Alliance, Non-Trad Student Organization, Amigos, Hui-O-Ka-Aino, and the Native American Alliance, all of which provide opportunities for students to celebrate and share their cultural heritage with others.

Many Western students are involved in outdoor recreation and service projects. Three popular clubs on campus are the Mountain Search and Rescue Team, the Rodeo Club, and Wilderness Pursuits. The college also sponsors a large intramural sports program in which more than 80 percent of the students participate. In addition, students can participate in 15 club sports, including men's and women's lacrosse, rugby and soccer, and a full roster of intercollegiate athletics. Mountaineer athletic teams have won respect at both the regional and national levels.

Campus programming includes concerts, plays, lectures, art exhibits, coffee houses and dances. Peak Productions, the college theatrical group, produces six full-length shows and several one-act productions each year. In addition to the campus newspaper, students publish an electronic magazine distributed worldwide through the Internet, and manage and operate KWSB-FM radio station and WSC-TV.

Athletics: Division II member of the NCAA, Rocky Mountain Athletic Conference
Women's Teams: basketball, cross country, track & field, volleyball
Men's Teams: basketball, cross country, football, track & field, wrestling
The men's and women's downhill and cross-country ski teams compete at the Division I level.

Campus and Community

Western State College has 40 buildings on 130 acres of landscaped area and is adjacent to another 250 acres of undeveloped land. The campus is large and spacious, with plenty of grass and treed areas nicely dispersed among the academic and residential buildings.

The 15 residential facilities provide a variety of living options for the 1,400 men and women who live on campus. There are two all-male halls, one all-female hall, five coed halls, six apartment complexes for upperclass students, and two apartment buildings for married and non-traditional students.

The Savage Library is both the physical and intellectual center of the college. In addition to its own resources, students have access to other libraries in and out of state via electronic networking. The new Wellness and Fitness Center features a two story complex with free weights, circuit training, a cardiovascular area and areas for martial arts, yoga and aerobics. The two theaters on campus, a formal auditorium with traditional proscenium arch and a smaller mini theater for more intimate productions, provide stage facilities for student productions. The Quigley Art Gallery has exhibit areas for student and faculty work in addition to the outdoor sculpture that graces the campus.

The college is located in the small town of Gunnison, Colorado, with a population of about 8,000 people. Surrounded by the central Rocky Mountains, the Upper Gunnison River valley area has many opportunity for recreation and study. The town supports a large ranching economy, yet is within easy reach of the booming Crested Butte ski areas. The huge resource of public land, mountain forests and stream make it mecca for outdoor adventure.

Western State College of Colorado Academic Offerings

Accounting • English • French • Spanish • Art: graphic design, studio art, history, theory • Biology: botany, environmental biology/ecology, molecular, zoology • Business Administration: global environment, entrepreneurship, management, marketing • Chemistry: computer science, professional studies • Communication & Theatre: community journalism, mass media, information specialist, theater, organizational communications • Economics: public policy • Education with state licensure in elementary and secondary geology: anthropology, geophysics • History: American studies • Kinesiology: health promotion/wellness, K-12 certification • Mathematics: computer science • Music: music education • Physics: computer science, geophysics • Political Science: public policy • Psychology: biopsychology, clinical, counseling, school psychology, law enforcement, personnel management • Recreation: contractual track, outdoor leadership, instruction, ski and resort mgt. • Sociology: criminal justice, social services • Technology: environmental technology, technology and society

Admissions Statement

To be considered for admission to Western State College students should be: a graduate from an accredited high school; have completed four years of English, three years of mathematics, two years of natural science and social science; have a GPA of 2.5 or higher; and/or rank in the upper two-thirds of their graduating class, score 20 or higher on the ACT or 950 on the SAT 1.

Wheeling Jesuit College

Wheeling, West Virginia 26003-6295
(304) 243-2359 or (800) 624-6992

Founded in 1954, Wheeling Jesuit College is an independent, Catholic liberal arts college directed by the Society of Jesus. The youngest of America's 28 Jesuit Colleges, it has been coeducational from the beginning. The focus of the college is to develop men and women who think clearly and act wisely with courage, competence, and compassion. The college accomplishes this goal through challenging and relevant academics, the integration of technology in the learning environment, and presenting opportunities both in and out of the classroom where men and women can develop their individual gifts and talents, and serve others. The Jesuit spirit, with its passion for excellence and service in all areas of endeavor, is evident in every aspect of college life.

Academics

Degrees Offered: Bachelor's, Master's
Undergraduate Majors: 30
Student/ Faculty Ratio: 13 to 1
Number of Faculty: 90 full and part time

At Wheeling Jesuit College, students, faculty, and administrators challenge and enable each other to excel. It's a school where consideration of values and ethics is a part of every academic discussion and every college activity. It is a friendly, active college community that is person-centered with small classes, individual attention, and interactive learning modes. The academic majors combine interdisciplinary study, a core liberal arts foundation, understanding and integration of new technology, and proficiency in a specialized area.

Students at Wheeling Jesuit College are encouraged to reach beyond the classroom and even the campus in their pursuit of knowledge. In support of new and innovative initiatives, Wheeling has developed the National Technology Transfer Center and The Center for Educational Technologies in conjunction with NASA.

Located on campus, the centers offer students the opportunity to explore the management, use, and control of technology in the 21st century. At the National Technology Transfer Center, students and faculty are developing ways to make the research of over 100,000 scientists and 700 federal laboratories available to business and industry. The Center for Educational Technologies brings students and faculty together to explore the "Classroom of the Future" and develop ways future teachers will educate children. The center has its own space shuttle simulator and other high-tech resources.

The Wellness Program is another example of innovation. As a requirement for graduation, Wheeling students design their own plan for personal growth that incorporates eight specific areas of knowledge focusing on the development of self. They include career development, emotional, cultural/intellectual, physical, risk prevention, sexual, social concerns, and spirituality. The college offers workshops, activities, retreats, community service projects, and lectures that focus on these eight aspects, but it's up to each student to design and participate in his or her program.

The Wheeling curriculum allows academically talented and academically challenged students to engage in meaningful educational encounters. The Stephen J. Laut Honors program spans four years and includes learning experiences that integrate interdisciplinary, multimedia, and project-oriented honors seminars, with cultural events and resources that take place in the Wheeling-Pittsburgh area. The program gives talented and motivated students a learning community where they can explore intellectual pursuits with fellow scholars, develop leadership skills, and prepare for graduate or professional schools.

The college also has resources for students who may not have had a solid pre-college background. The ARC (Academic Resource Center) has created remediation, reinforcement and enrichment programs in reading comprehension, writing, and mathematics. Personal instruction and computer software are available and students can receive assistance in developing academic papers, study habits, and test-taking skills. The center is staffed by both professional staff and peer tutors.

Students and Student Life

1,500 students from 25 states and 14 foreign countries
48% are from out-of-state
5% are students of color
4% are international

At Wheeling Jesuit College, more than 65 percent of the students live on campus. There are six residence halls and students are offered a variety of living arrangements. Each hall elects its own government, which provides programming and hall rules.

More than 30 campus organizations and more than 350 student activities provide opportunities for involvement and leadership. The student government is a strong and important component of campus life; through it, students participate fully in formulating the policies of the college. Board members serve on college-wide committees, are directly involved in the governance of the college, and plan and control the entire student activities budget. As one student comments, "We have a real voice in the running of the college. We are encouraged to be active, we learn how to be responsible, and we are serious about making this college *our* college."

Wheeling is affiliated with the Catholic Church, but the college in no way imposes any religious view or conviction on students. It is clear that "the Jesuit example of faith calls upon students to examine the importance of belief in their own lives, whatever their individual faith or religion, and provides a supportive, value-centered environment in which to do so." More than one third of the students at Wheeling are non-Catholic.

The Appalachian Experience Club, Students in Union, and Campus Ministry are three of the largest and most active social outreach organizations, and more than 95 percent of students at Wheeling participate in some type of social outreach activity. There is a literary magazine, student newspaper, and a weekly entertainment publication that students produce. Club sports and intramurals are available, along with professional honor societies and academic clubs.

Athletics: West Virginia Intercollegiate Athletic Conference and holds dual membership in the NAIA and NCAA Division II
Women's Teams: basketball, cross country, soccer, swimming, track & field, volleyball
Men's Teams: basketball, cross country, golf, soccer, swimming, track & field

Campus and Community

Wheeling Jesuit has recently completed a 40 million dollar expansion and renovation program. All 15 academic and residential buildings are modern and provide first class facilities. The Bishop Hodges Library can be accessed via computer from both classrooms and dorm rooms, and provides state of the art research, educational, and communications technology. The McDonough Health and Recreation Center offers two gymnasiums, racquetball courts, swimming pool, jogging track and fitness center.

The 65-acre hilltop campus is an ideal environment for learning. Wheeling, West Virginia is known as one of the country's most livable and safe small cities. With a population of around 50,000 people, the city has its own symphony orchestra, pro hockey team, and country/western music concert hall. The area surrounding the city is a haven for outdoor recreation. Camping, hiking, fishing, boating, and winter sports are all close by. The college is also just an hour's drive from Pittsburgh and all the amenities of big city life.

Wheeling Jesuit College Academic Offerings

Accounting • Biology • Chemistry • Computer Science • Criminal Justice • English Literature • Environmental Science & Policy • Foreign Languages • General Science • History • Independent Majors • Industrial Engineering • Innovation & Technology • International Business • International Studies • Management • Marketing • Mathematics • Nuclear Medicine Technology • Nursing • Philosophy • Physics • Political and Economic Philosophy • Political Science • Professional Writing • Psychology • Respiratory Therapy • Teacher Preparation • Theology/Religious Studies

Admissions Statement

Applicants to Wheeling Jesuit College are evaluated on the basis of their high school performance, their scores on the ACT or SAT, and recommendations from high school counselors or teachers. To be considered for admission a student should have: a high school diploma or GED, 15 units of high school academic courses, rank in the upper half of the high school class, and submit the official results of SAT or ACT scores.

Western Carolina University

Cullowhee, North Carolina 28723
(704) 227-7317

Nestled between the Great Smoky Mountains and the Blue Ridge is Western Carolina University. This midsize university is situated on 260 rural acres in Cullowhee, North Carolina. It is one of the 16 campuses of the University of North Carolina, and with a student body of about 6,000, it can offer a more personalized education than some of its sister schools.

The university has the advantages of a rural campus with fabulous recreational opportunities, a safe location, and a slower pace of life, while having access to the more cosmopolitan city of Asheville, a popular resort area that plays host to artists, nationally known musical performers, and thousands of tourists. It is a university where students can realize their potential while developing lifelong friendships.

Academics

Degrees Offered: Bachelor's, Master's
Undergraduate Majors: 90
Student/Faculty Ratio: 17 to 1
Number of Faculty: 499 full and part time

While Western Carolina University possesses all of the academic characteristics of a large research institution—including noted professors, outstanding research facilities, and diverse offerings—this university also places a major emphasis upon teaching undergraduates, providing a learning environment with interactive classes, and recognizing and supporting different learning styles and backgrounds. It has adopted a general education program that gives students a foundation in subjects like mathematics, computers, leisure and fitness, physical science, and human history and culture.

Small classes are the norm, enabling professors and students to ask questions and discuss issues. The university states that 78 percent of the classes offered have less than 30 students enrolled, and that 62 percent of classes actually have less than 20 students enrolled! This intimate teaching/learning setting is not usually found at other universities.

The four undergraduate divisions of Western Carolina University include, the College of Applied Sciences, the College of Arts and Sciences, the College of Business, and the College of Education and Psychology. While each one has its own academic focus, students can complete a major from one college and a minor from another.

The College of Applied Sciences offers professional programs in criminal justice, health sciences, human environmental sciences, industrial and engineering technology, military science, and nursing. The College of Arts and Sciences provides a varied curriculum in the fine arts, humanities, and sciences. In the College of Business, teaching, learning, research, and service in the business areas are conducted in an environment of professional and academic integrity, mutual respect, and ethical behavior. The College of Education and Psychology has a 100-year history of preparing professional personnel for the schools and colleges throughout the state and nation. Its curriculum meets the guidelines established by the National Council for Accreditation of Teacher Education (NCATE).

Students and Student Life

5,700 students from 36 states and 24 foreign countries
Less than 10% are from out-of-state
8% are students of color
1% are international
2,890 students live on campus

Western Carolina University enrolls approximately 5,700 men and women in undergraduate degree programs and an additional 1,000 students in graduate programs. The university celebrates Mountain Heritage Day, an outdoor festival that draws 35,000 people, and Homecoming, which includes events for students and alumni. It sponsors guest speakers and artists from all over the world, and more than 100 campus clubs and organizations.

There is a strong Greek participation on campus; about 20 percent of the students belong to the 23 sororities and fraternities (including six that are historically African-American) that have chapters on campus. Greek Life on campus includes social activities and college and community service projects. Weekday evenings and weekends feature performances by ballet companies, major musical groups, comedy talent, theater productions, art exhibits, and concerts.

Campus clubs and organizations include special interest clubs like the Organization of Ebony Students, numerous performance groups like Last Minute Productions, chorus, jazz ensemble, and a weekly student newspaper. There is a large intramural sports program that includes 30 teams and sports like archery, table tennis, softball, and bowling.

Athletics: NCAA Division I, football is Division I AA.
Women's Teams: basketball, golf, indoor and outdoor track, tennis, volleyball
Men's Teams: baseball, basketball, football, golf, indoor and outdoor track, tennis

Campus and Community

The 260-acre campus is located in Cullowhee, North Carolina, just a short distance from the Great Smoky Mountains and national park. The campus mirrors the surrounding beauty of the area, and the buildings seem to nestle into the gorgeous countryside.

Hunter Library, the largest in western North Carolina, houses more than a half million volumes and is equipped with online computer search facilities. The 11 residence halls accommodate about 3,000 students and offer a variety of living styles. Recreational and sports facilities include lighted tennis courts, a golf driving range, jogging trails, indoor swimming pool, racquetball courts and weight room, and are located in three buildings: the Reid Health and Physical Education Building, Breese Gymnasium, and the Hinds University Center.

There is a bus that runs from the University Center to area shopping malls, movies, and restaurants in Cullowhee and the town of Sylva. Within a half-hour of campus, students can find just about any outdoor recreational activities they are interested in, including hiking, swimming, camping, and mountain climbing. Ashville is only about an hour away and nearby colleges include Gardner Webb University and Belmont Abbey College.

Western Carolina University Academic Offerings

Accounting • Anthropology • Art • Art Ed. (K-12) • Biology • Biology Ed. (9-12) • Business Ad. & Law • Business Ed. (9-12) • Chemistry • Child Dev. & Family Relations • Clinical Lab. Sciences • Communications • Cloth, Textiles & Merchandising • Communication Disorders • Computer Information Systems • Computer Science • Criminal Justice • Economics • Elementary Ed. • Emergency Medical • English • Electronic Engineering Technology • English Education (9-12) • Environmental Finance • French • French Ed.(9-12) • Health Care • Home Economics • Geography • Geography Planning • Geology • German • German Ed. (9-12) • Health Information • Health Services • History • Hospitality Mgt. • Industrial Chemistry • Industrial Distribution • Interior Design • Management • Marketing • Mathematics • Math Ed (9-12) • Manufacturing Engineering Technology • Middle Grades Education • Music • Music Ed (K-12) • Natural Resource Mgt. • Nursing • Nutrition & Dietetics • Office Adm. • Parks & Recreation Mgt. • Philosophy • Physical Ed. (K-12) • Physics • Political Science • Psychology • Recreation Therapy • Science Ed. (9-12) • Secondary & Special Subject • Social Science • Social Science Ed. • Social Work • Sociology • Spanish • Spanish Ed. (K-12) • Special Ed. (K-12) • Special Studies • Teaching • Theater

Admissions Statement

Students who rank in the top 50% of their class or who have minimum "C" average in a college preparatory curriculum and whose SAT score is equal to or higher than 350 on each part of the test or whose ACT composite score is 19 or higher, are normally admitted and placed into the regular freshman course sequence.

West Virginia Wesleyan College

Buckhannon, West Virginia 26201
(304) 473-8510 or (800) 722-9933.

Academic excellence, marketable degrees, leadership opportunities, and one of the most picturesque campuses in the region set West Virginia Wesleyan apart from other liberal arts colleges. The interdisciplinary curriculum combines personal attention in the classroom with exciting internships. Professors, coaches, and resident assistants are readily available to work with students. Located in the foothills of West Virginia, the 80-acre campus offers the perfect setting to foster intellectual inquisitiveness and fellowship among students.

Academics

Degrees Offered: Bachelor's, Master's

Undergraduate Majors: 40+

Student/Faculty Ratio: 15 to 1

Number of Faculty: 136 full and part time

Wesleyan has built its reputation on preparing confident and capable men and women for over a century. The curriculum is structured around a liberal arts base that encourages broad learning across all areas of knowledge and 40 majors that instill a depth of understanding in a chosen academic field. Characteristics of a Wesleyan education include an intellectual and professional faculty, outstanding computer and research equipment, modern student centered facilities, and small interactive classes.

The college calendar runs on a 4-1-4 system. The focus in January term is an intensive concentration within a single area. Students can participate in internships, independent study, and study abroad programs, or enroll in one of several special courses offered on campus. In a typical January Term more than 40 different credit opportunities are available both on and off campus.

The college demonstrates its commitment to students' individual academic needs through the Organization of Honors Students. Qualified men and women can be invited into the honors program as first semester freshmen or during subsequent semesters throughout their four years at Wesleyan. The college has developed honors courses in English, humanities, divinity, history, and other disciplines that are intended to challenge academically bright students to think, understand, appreciate and apply their knowledge in today's society.

Students who find the academic atmosphere at college more challenging than they are prepared for can receive assistance through The Learning Center. The center has nine developmental courses that can be taken for credit and several workshops which can improve students' reading, writing, listening and study skills and improve the performance in specific academic areas.

No matter what students major in they can be sure that Wesleyan will provide them with an outstanding education. The proof of Wesleyan's quality education can be seen in the fact that 50 percent of Wesleyan's graduates from 1969-1978, (generally those who are now 35-40 years old) are currently earning in excess of $50,000 a year.

Students and Student Life

1,450 students from 33 states and 22 foreign countries
55% are from out-of-state
10% are students of color
3% are international
1,300 live on campus

Wesleyan's United Methodist tradition, community spirit, and campus activities bring the men and women together to form an active, vibrant student body. While the college is affiliated with the United Methodist Church, students of all religions attend the college.

More than 85 percent of the students live on campus, and social activities are scheduled throughout the day and evening. Music and theatrical programs, a campus newspaper, intramural sports, volunteer services, and religious organizations are only a few of the ways students spend their time. Wesleyan's Jazz Ensemble and Concert Chorale tour throughout the country each year and recently the Jazz Ensemble traveled to Hungary, Romania, and Russia to perform. The theater department presents four major productions each year, so aspiring thespians have ample opportunity to put on the grease paint. The college has five national fraternities and four national sororities. About 25 percent of all students belong to the Greek system.

Athletics: The Bobcats compete in NCAA Division II athletics.
Women's Teams: basketball, cross country, soccer, softball, swimming, tennis, track & field, volleyball
Men's Teams: baseball, basketball, cross country, football, golf, soccer, swimming, tennis, track & field

Campus and Community

The beautiful 80-acre campus reflects the feeling that this is a school where excellence is encouraged, developed, and appreciated. All of the buildings are modern and reflect Wesleyan's student centered focus. The eight residential facilities provide housing for more than 1,000 students in a variety of accommodations including hall style, suites, and apartments. Meal service is provided in the new Frenchsee Dining Center. The Hall of Science, Haymond Hall Learning Center and Annie Merner Pfeifer Library provide state-of-the-art academic facilities. The John D. Rockefeller IV Physical Education Center, four athletic fields, six tennis courts, and McWhorter-Goodwin Track offer both athletic and recreational activities.

West Virginia Wesleyan is in Buckhannon, very close to the center of the state. "The Mountain State," as West Virginia is called, is home to four-season recreational opportunities. There are snow-covered mountains to ski; long, adventurous rivers to whitewater raft; fascinating caves to discover; and camping and backpacking trails that will bring you to beautiful vistas. The Buckhannon area is surrounded by beautiful scenery. A commercial airport, major shopping mall, and the cultural activities and social opportunities offered in Clarksburg are all within a 45-minute drive. Elkins, another small college town is less than 20 minutes away, and Pittsburgh is two hours to the north.

West Virginia Wesleyan College Academic Offerings

Accounting • Biology • Business Adm. • Chemistry • Computer Science • Christian Ed. & Church Leadership • Computer Information Science • Dramatic Arts • Economics • Engineering Physics • Environmental Science • Finance • History • Human Ecology • Individualized Major • International Studies • Management • Marketing • Mathematics • Music (Applied and Theory) • Nursing • Nutrition/Dietetics • Philosophy • Philosophy and Religion • Physics • Political Science • Psychology • Public Relations • Religion • Social Science • Sociology • Speech Communication • Speech Communication & Dramatic Arts • Sports Medicine

Art: Art Education • Art History • Ceramics • Graphic Design • Painting and Drawing

Education: Combined Elementary/Secondary Ed. • Elementary • Endorsements in Athletic Training, Learning Disabilities • Secondary

English: Literature • Teaching • Writing

Physical Education: Fitness Management • Health Promotion

Admissions Statement

Students are accepted on the basis of ability, interests, academic preparation, character, and promise, as indicated by their own statements on the application, as well as by high school records, recommendations, and test results.

Guide to College Costs

College costs include tuition, fees, room, and board per year.

$	$5,000-$10,000
$$	$10,001-$15,000
$$$	$15,001-$20,000
$$$$	$20,001-$25,000
$$$$$	$25,001 and over

College/University	State	Costs
Abilene Christian University	TX	$$$
Adams State College	CO	$$
American International College	MA	$$$
Ashland College	OH	$$$$
Assumption College	MA	$$$$
Belmont Abbey College	NC	$$$
Bemidji State University	MN	$$
Benedictine College	KS	$$$
Black Hills State University	SD	$ in-state
		$$ out-of-state
Bradford College	MA	$$$$$
Bryant College	RI	$$$$$
Canisius College	NY	$$$$
Castleton State College	VT	$$ in-state
		$$$ out-of-state
Catawba College	NC	$$$
Cazenovia College	NY	$$$$
Central Methodist College	MO	$$$
Chadron State University	NE	$ in-state
		$$ out-of-state
Chowan College	NC	$$$
Colby Sawyer College	NH	$$$$$
Curry College	MA	$$$$$
Daemen College	NY	$$$
Dakota State University	SD	$ in-state
		$$ out-of-state
Davis & Elkins College	WV	$$$
Delaware Valley College	PA	$$$$

College/University	State	Costs
Delta State University	MS	$ in-state
		$$ out-of-state
Dickinson State University	ND	$ in-state
		$$ out-of-state
Eastern New Mexico State University	NM	$ in-state
		$$ out-of-state
Eastern Oregon State University	OR	$$
Emporia State University	KS	$ in-state
		$$ out-of-state
Endicott College	MA	$$$$
Ferrum College	VA	$$$
University of Findley	OH	$$$$
Florida Southern University	FL	$$$
Fort Lewis State University	CO	$$
Franklin Pierce College	NH	$$$$
Frostburg State University	MD	$$ in-state
		$$$ out-of-state
Georgia College	GA	$ in-state
		$$ out-of-state
Green Mountain College	VT	$$$$
University of Hartford	CT	$$$$$
Hawaii Pacific University	HI	$$$
Henderson State University	AR	$ in-state
		$$ out-of-state
High Point College	NC	$$$
Iona College	NY	$$$$
Johnson State College	VT	$$ in-state
		$$$ out-of-state
Keene State College	NH	$$ in-state
		$$$ out-of-state
Lake Superior State University	MI	$$ in-state
		$$$ out-of-state
Lewis University	IL	$$$$
LIU—Southampton College	NY	$$$$
Lyndon State College	VT	$$ in-state
		$$$ out-of-state
Lynn University	FL	$$$$$
MacMurry College	TX	$$$

College/University	State	Costs
Mansfield University	PA	$$ in-state $$$ out-of-state
Marian College of Fond du Lac	WI	$$$
Mayville State University	ND	$ in-state $$ out-of-state
McMurry University	TX	$$$
Menlo College	CA	$$$$$
Missouri Valley College	MO	$$$
Monmouth University	NJ	$$$$
Morehead State University	KY	$ in-state $$ out-of-state
Mount Marty College	SD	$$$
New England College	NH	$$$$
New Hampshire College	NH	$$$$
University of New Haven	CT	$$$$
Nichols College	MA	$$$$
North Adams State College	MA	$$ in-state $$$ out-of-state
Northern State University	SD	$ in-state $$ out-of-state
Northwest Missouri State College	MO	$$
Olivet College	MI	$$$$
Pacific Lutheran College	WA	$$$$
Peru State College	NE	$ in-state $$ out-of-state
Plymouth State College	NH	$$ in-state $$$ out-of-state
Rider University	NJ	$$$$
Rocky Mountain College	MT	$$$
Roger Williams University	RI	$$$$$
Sacred Heart University	CT	$$$$
St. Ambrose College	IA	$$$$
St. Andrews College	NC	$$$$
Saint Joseph's College	IN	$$$$
Saint Joseph's College	ME	$$$$
Saint Leo College	FL	$$$
Saint Mary's University of Minnesota	MN	$$$

College/University	State	Costs
Salve Regina University	RI	$$$$$
College of Santa Fe	NM	$$$$
Seton Hall University	NJ	$$$$
Southern Arkansas University	AR	$
University of Southern Maine	ME	$$ in-state
		$$$ out-of-state
Southwest State University	MN	$ in-state
		$$ out-of-state
Spring Hill College	AL	$$$$
Springfield College	MA	$$$$
Unity College	ME	$$$
Utica College of Syracuse	NY	$$$$
Wayne State University	NE	$ in-state
		$$ out-of-state
Wesley College	DE	$$$
University of West Alabama	AL	$
West Liberty State College	WV	$ in-state
		$$ out-of-state
West Virginia Wesleyan	WV	$$$$
Western Carolina University	NC	$ in-state
		$$ out-of-state
Western New England College	MA	$$$$
Western State College	CO	$$
Wheeling Jesuit College	WV	$$$$